CW01560738

BOWIE AND BIG-KNIFE FIGHTING SYSTEM

TEXT AND DRAWINGS BY DWIGHT C. McLEMORE

BOWIE AND BIG-KNIFE FIGHTING SYSTEM

Paladin Press • Boulder, Colorado

Also by Dwight C. McLemore:

Advanced Bowie Techniques
Fighting Sword
Fighting Tomahawk

Bowie and Big-Knife Fighting System
by Dwight C. McLemore

Copyright © 2003 by Dwight C. McLemore

ISBN 13: 978-1-58160-389-7
Printed in the United States of America

Published by Paladin Press, a division of
Paladin Enterprises, Inc.
Gunbarrel Tech Center
7077 Winchester Circle
Boulder, Colorado 80301 USA
+1.303.443.7250

Direct inquiries and/or orders to the above address.

PALADIN, PALADIN PRESS, and the "horse head" design
are trademarks belonging to Paladin Enterprises and
registered in United States Patent and Trademark Office.

All rights reserved. Except for use in a review, no
portion of this book may be reproduced, stored in or
introduced into a retrieval system, or transmitted in any
form without the express written permission of the publisher.
The scanning, uploading, and distribution of this book by the
Internet or any other means without the permission of the
publisher is illegal and punishable by law. Please respect the
author's rights and do not participate in any form of electronic
piracy of copyrighted material.

Neither the author nor the publisher assumes
any responsibility for the use or misuse of
information contained in this book.

Visit our website at www.paladin-press.com

WARNING

The information and techniques included in this text could result in serious injury or death. The author, publisher, and distributor of this book disclaim any liability from damage or injuries of any type that a reader may incur from the use of such information.

Additionally, it is the reader's responsibility to research and comply with all local, state, and federal laws and regulations pertaining to the possession, carry, and use of edged weapons. This text is *for academic study only*.

James Bowie
1796–1836

Figure 1. "He rides forever out on the frontier, where reality and fact become one with myth and legend."

TABLE OF CONTENTS

Introduction: The Migration of Fighting Methods to the American Continent 1

Section One: Grips, Holds, Stances, Guards, and Presenting 17
 Grips 19
 Holding the Weapon 23
 Fighting Stances 24
 Guards 38
 "Presenting the Blade" 41

Section Two: The Thrust 43
 Fundamentals of the Thrust 49
 "Giving Point" (Point of Impact) 50
 Straight Thrust 52
 Punta Mandritta 54
 Punta Reversa 57
 Reverse-Step Thrust 60
 Matador Thrust 61
 Punta Lunga (Lunge) 62
 Primary Targets for the Thrust 64
 Knife-Fighting Concept A: Target Areas 65
 Knife-Fighting Concept B: Timetable for Death 72

Section Three: The Cut 75

Cutting Techniques 77
Application of the Cut 89
Knife Fighting Concept C: Window of Combat 89
Knife Fighting Concept D: Angles of Attack 94
    Eight Angles of Attack 96
    Angles of Attack to the Hand 105
    Twelve Angles of Attack 109
Knife Fighting Concept E: Parry Against Angles of Attack 121
    Parrying with the Edge, Flat, and Heel of the Blade 122
    The Parry as a Single-Flow Drill 123
Knife Fighting Concept F: Disruption Attack (Taking the Hand) 141
    Twelve-Angle Drill versus Eight-Angle Disruption Attacks to the Hand 142

Section Four: The Forever Principles 167
Anatomy of a Knife Fight 170
Inside the Area of Engagement 171
Ranges of Combat 172
Movement 173
    Into the Engagement Area 173
    Inside the Engagement Area 173
    Distance 184
    Angles (Angling) 185
    The Spanish Circle 191
    Seeing 198
    Height or Elevation 199

Section Five: A Portfolio of Techniques, Drills, and Training Notes 201
Side Parry 204
Solo Set 1 (Side Parry, *Punta Mandritta*, Curl to Midline Back Cut or Side Parry to
    High-Line Back Cut) 211
Solo Set 2 (Inside Parry to the Left, Attack with Angle 3,
    Cross-Body Chamber to *Punta Reversa*) 217

Selected Bibliography 221

NOTE ON THE ILLUSTRATIONS

The techniques, guards, and stances in this book are pen and ink illustrations that were drawn from photographs depicting actual action. Techniques are shown sequentially either from left to right or vice versa, as depicted by the arrows.

Although an attempt was made to reproduce movement as close to reality as possible, there was room for interpretation, and some artistic license was taken to better capture the movement.

PREFACE

My study of the big fighting knives of the past began while I was a child in northeastern Louisiana. From Monroe to Marksville, from Boeuf River to Crowville, the area near my childhood home ran deep in the lore of Jim Bowie: his fighting prowess, his land deals, and above all the haunting memory a deadly knife. I still remember seeing the movie *The Iron Mistress* and much later, after convincing the local librarian that I was old enough, reading the novel by Paul Wellman.

> He considered the knife. This metal thing had been a headland in his life, too, made
> him the kind of man he was. Bowie and his knife—the iron mistress, always faithful
> to him—to go down together at last. His fist closed on the haft lovingly.

As with many, I was caught up in the legend, taking many sources, such as R.W. Thorpe's *Bowie Knife* (1949), completely as fact. Lately, with William Davis' *Three Roads to the Alamo* (1998), I was introduced to a more factual account of James "Jim" Bowie, the man.

Looking back over my years of studying about Jim Bowie, I can honestly say that the man and the knife have been with me for a long time.

I want to make clear right now that the material in this text cannot be historically documented as authentic "Bowie Knife Techniques" developed by Jim Bowie. Actually, there is really no hard evidence that "Big Jim" ever fought another knife fight after the historic sandbar duel. By the same token, there is no evidence that all the knife-fighting stories about Bowie, many of which sprang up after his death at the Alamo, are not based on truth and maybe ... just maybe ... Bowie actually participated in all those fights credited to him.

The study of the Bowie knife has been a journey for me that has covered fighting techniques back through time and cultures. When I read the newspaper accounts of the 1800s, I found Spaniards fighting Frenchmen, Frenchmen fighting Englishmen, and all being credited with using Bowie knives. Any knife design was a termed a "Bowie," and the method of fighting using these knives was referred to as the "Bowie system" regardless of the country of origin. This is part of the mystery of the Bowie knife.

The use of big knives in combat was with us long before the time of Jim Bowie. In this text you will find a group of assorted techniques that have been used consistently throughout history, from the gladiatorial arenas of ancient Rome to the Dueling Oaks of New Orleans, regardless of culture or fighting style. They represent the common knife-fighting fundamentals that flowed into the vast cultural "melting pot" that we call America.

This book is also a notebook of personal thoughts and comments on some of the interesting information I stumbled across in my journey. It contains a compilation of observations and views that were passed on to me by some good knife players. I ask for no agreement on my observations and conclusions, only the sincere hope that you enjoy working with the Bowie knife as much as I have.

Dwight C. McLemore
March 2003

INTRODUCTION:
THE MIGRATION OF FIGHTING
METHODS TO THE AMERICAN
CONTINENT

If we could move back through time and travel the major waterways that opened up so much of the United States to colonization, we might have a picture of where some of the so-called Bowie fighting systems came from.

A look at the period between 1526 and 1650 on this continent would show basically European immigrants who had brought their weapons and fighting methods with them. There were soldiers and civilians using swords as well as daggers. From the 1650s though the 1780s you would see fighting techniques begin to be modified based on the latest technical improvements in firearms that took place on the European continent. The single-shot limitation and potential for misfire created a need for backup blades that could be brought into play if the firearm failed: sabers, cutlasses, tomahawks, and bayonets made their appearance.

If we could see some of the brawls and duels that took place in or near the major river cities of the 1800s, we would witness a melting pot of fighting techniques. Anyone observing these fights probably took mental notes and added to his own arsenal of skills. Some historians feel that many of the Bowie knife techniques we see today come from the New Orleans dueling teachers, many of whom witnessed fights among members of the diverse cultures that poured into that frontier port in the 1840s. Maybe that's true. We do know that the core of the fighting system was European and definitely of Western martial arts at its best.

My research into the New Orleans dueling schools of the 1800s has yet to produce a formal program of instruction for the Bowie knife, although I am still working on this.

HISTORY OF THE BOWIE KNIFE

On September 16, 1827, on a sandbar of the Mississippi River, just below the town of Vidalia, Louisiana, a duel between Dr. Thomas Maddox and Samuel Wells turned into a brawl that quickly involved the observers. The most historically accurate account of this fight is in *Mr. Bowie with a Knife: A History of the Sandbar Fight* by J.R. Edmondson (1999). Bowie—after being knocked almost to his knees by a thrown pistol, shot through a lung and in the thigh, and then stabbed in the breast and hand—drew a foot-long butcher knife with which he killed one of his attackers and drove the rest from the field.

Sometime before the Sandbar Fight Jim Bowie's older brother, Rezin Bowie, had given him a knife because the folding knife Jim had used in a previous altercation with one Norris Wright had failed him. Jim Bowie killed Wright at the sandbar duel with the knife Rezin had given him. Of that knife Rezin Bowie wrote: "The first Bowie knife was made by myself in the parish of Avoyelles."

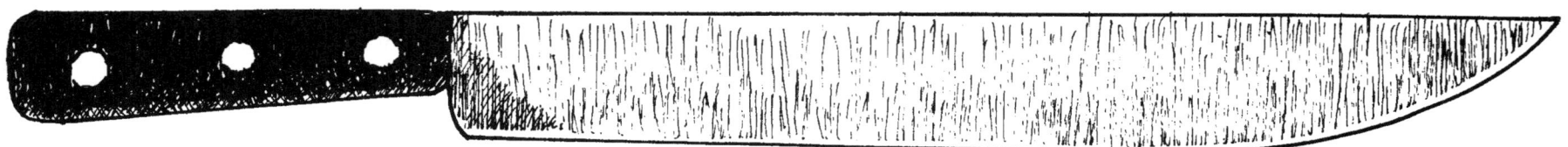

Figure 2.

Rezin's granddaughter described the knife: " This instrument was never intended for ought but a hunting knife, was made of an old file in the plantation blacksmith shop … the maker was a hired white man, named Jesse Clift."

One source states that the origin of the design for Rezin's knife was the Spanish dirk, but in all probability it was based on the more broad-bladed Spanish hunting knife from the 16th and 17th centuries that caught his attention and more closely resembles the design. Figure 3 shows another knife that may be similar to the knife Bowie used in the Sandbar Fight and that now resides in the Mississippi State Historical Museum. This knife is awesomely simplistic and functional and appears to be a "working knife" rather than one intended for presentation. Inscribed on the sheath is the inscription "Presented to Jesse Perkins by R.P. Bowie—1831."

History tends to support the idea that Rezin Bowie was the knife designer of the family. (At least he was known for having had several knives made to be given away as presentation weapons during his life.) The absence of ornamentation on this weapon could indicate that this may have been the personal knife of Rezin himself. It just might be the knife (or at least one similar to the one) Rezin lent to his brother before the Sandbar Fight.

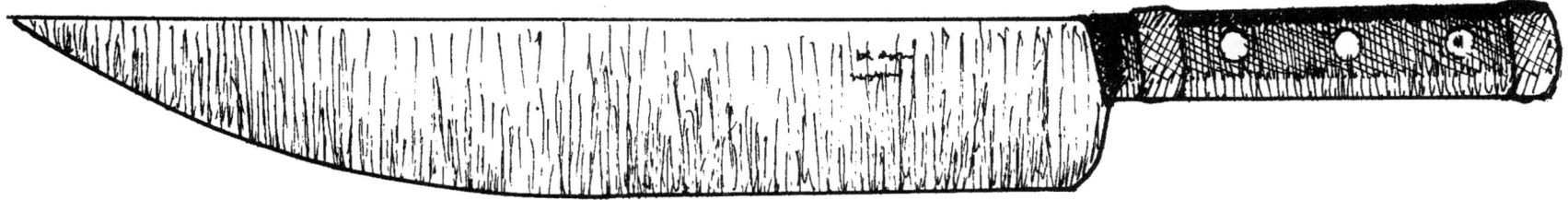

Figure 3.

Jim Bowie reportedly lost the knife during a hunting trip, although an identical one has turned up, purported to have been given to the actor Edwin Forrest by Bowie. The facts supporting this, however, are scant.

The first recorded use of the term "Bowie knife" was in 1834 by the the Englishman George W. Featherstonhaugh, as he commented on the big knives he saw in Arkansas: "These formidable instruments, with their sheaths mounted in silver, are the pride of an Arkansas blood, and got their name of Bowie knives from a conspicuous person of this fiery climate."

Displayed today in the Alamo chapel is a knife titled as the Searles/Fowler Bowie. The inscriptions on this knife indicate that it was made by Daniel Searles of Baton Rouge sometime prior to or in the year 1836. Another inscription reads "R.P. Bowie to H.W. Fowler U.S.D." Documents show that Rezin gave this knife to Fowler between 1836 and 1841. The design of this knife bears a strong resemblance to the blade Rezin gave Jim before the Sandbar Fight. After looking at this and the previous knives, we can conclude that Rezin preferred the flat-back design and that the original Bowie was of that shape. One slight difference is that the Searles/Fowler Bowie has a back edge.

Figure 4.

A dubious claim exists that this knife may have actually belonged to Jim Bowie. This is based on a handwritten note on the back of a photograph of the knife, which refers to a Dr. Crim, whose collection the knife was in at the time the photograph was taken. The note states that an Indian woman who was nurse to Jim Bowie at the Alamo took the weapon to Rezin after the battle. Again this appears to be fanciful thinking.

Rezin took Jim's death at the Alamo very badly, and it is hard to believe that Rezin would give away any knife belonging to his beloved little brother.

The knife shown in Figure 5 has also been presented as the actual knife Jim Bowie took with him to the Alamo. It is supposedly the weapon Bowie commissioned from the legendary Arkansas blacksmith, Jim Black. The owner of the knife, the Bart Moore family, asserts that an elderly Mexican gave the weapon to Mr. Moore's grandfather as payment for a debt. Jim F. Moore stated that the Mexican had found the weapon next to one of the funeral pyres after participating in the storming of the Alamo.

The knife is in very poor condition. It has an 8 1/4-inch blade with clipped point. In the middle of the right side of the blade is crudely scratched "J. Bowie." On the left side near the guard are the initials "J.B." inside what appears to be an acorn design, possibly the initials of knifemaker Jim Black.

Figure 5.

Many historians doubt that this knife ever belonged to Jim Bowie, and there is no historical documentation to support a claim of ownership. Handling a replica of this knife, however, I came away with the impression that it was definitely a no-nonsense fighting weapon. Its balance is good, but it feels like the blade is a bit too short . The point may well have been reground from a broken tip. Is this Jim Bowie's knife . Who knows? But it sure meets all the specifications.

Another part of Bowie knife literature indicates that Jim may have commissioned the making of another knife between 1830 and 1836. Some historians believe he did this because his fame from the Sandbar Fight was attracting an element of men eager to make their reputations by defeating the great Jim Bowie. And Jim Black claimed to have made the weapon for Bowie. The design is what we commonly think of today when we hear the term Bowie knife. Author Raymond Thorpe described the design of the weapon as being like that depicted in Figure 6.

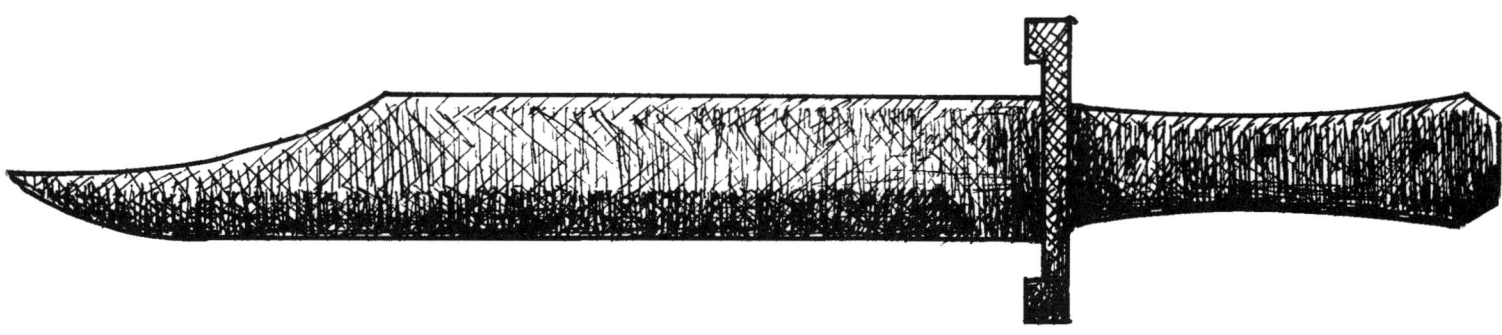

Figure 6.

Again, as with so many of the Bowie knife designs, there is no historical proof other than Black's own testimony to support this story.

After the Sandbar Fight, the Bowie knife took on a life of its own. Everyone wanted one, from experienced frontiersmen to riverboat gamblers. The Bowie became the weapon of choice to back up the single-shot rifles and pistols of the day. It did not take the merchants and profiteers long to realize that "Bowie" would sell knives. Tiffany's of New York, Will & Finck of San Francisco, and Kitteredge Company of Cincinnati began to sell knives of all descriptions as Bowie knives. The same was true for cutlers in Germany, Spain, and England. Many of these weapons, though now considered collectable, offer little insight into exactly what the "original Bowie knife" looked like.

The bottom line is simply that no one really knows for sure what Bowie's original knife looked like, and it is doubtful that anyone ever will.

In reality Jim Bowie probably owned many knives, and his brother Rezin may have been a collector/designer.

Some Personal Opinions About Jim Bowie's Knife

After considerable research into the myths and historical documentation surrounding Jim Bowie and the design of his knife, I believe the following.

1. The knife used during the Sandbar Fight was probably lost by Jim during a hunting trip or returned to Rezin. I think that weapon held no special meaning for Jim Bowie and that it was one of many he would own.
2. Sometime between 1830 and 1836, Jim Bowie went to Washington, Arkansas, and had a knife of his own design made for him by Jim Black. This was the weapon he carried with him to the Alamo. This knife closely resembles the Thorpe Bowie currently made by Randall Knives. The Moore Bowie discussed earlier may well be this design.

HISTORY OF JIM BOWIE, THE KNIFE FIGHTER

Two points are very well documented about Jim Bowie's life:

1. After Jim's death at the Alamo, Rezin Bowie made the statement that the only time his brother was involved in a duel was at the Vidalia sandbar (August 24, 1838).
2. Jim and Rezin's involvement with land swindling, slave running, and mercenary work likely exposed both to the danger of knife fights.

Based on Rezin's words, one might reasonably argue that what he meant was that Jim never fought a *duel* in the true since of that word, and that Rezin did not include all the fights both he and his brother got into. When you consider the shady aspects of how Jim and Rezin made their fortunes, there were lots of opportunities for involvement in knife fights.

Almost all historical documentation of Jim Bowie's personality indicates that although he was slow to anger, he was not one to back down easily or go out of his way to avoid a fight. Bowie historian William Davis once made the following comment about Bowie's personality: "If Bowie had not been sick at the Alamo, Santa Anna might still be trying to get over the walls …[Bowie] could be one mean Son of a Bitch."

Figure 7.

Almost all accounts of Bowie as a knife fighter come from two original newspaper stories that appeared long after the fall of the Alamo. These stories are certainly nothing more than fabrications designed to sell newspapers. However, if historical reliability could be based on the number of times a particular story is retold, then the following incidents might well give a faint indication that Bowie was indeed a very proficient knife fighter.

1. 1827—the Vidalia Sandbar Fight
2. 1832–1835—knife fight with a gambler on the deck of a steamboat
3. Unknown date (published in *San Francisco Chronicle* February 28, 1881)—knife fight with a slave owner over the owner's beating of a slave
4. Unknown date—knife fight against five attackers outside a tavern
5. Unknown date—knife fight with a Spaniard while Bowie sat astride a log with his pants nailed down
6. Unknown date—knife fight with gambler Jack Sturdivant in a circle with Bowie's wrists strapped together

I suppose the bottom line on Jim Bowie the knife fighter is that simply no reliable historical record exists. The following are what I have come to believe.

1. Although the ethic of the South during Bowie's life would have glorified any traditional duels he may have had, I don't think spontaneous knife fights would have been looked upon that favorably. Usually the only attention would come from the newspapers and "penny novels"—both of which often involved writers interested in painting any picture to make a buck. This is why the information about Jim Bowie's knife fighting skill is so unreliable.
2. I think that Jim and Rezin were both trained in a classical knife/saber fighting style of the 18th century, which featured techniques that were very similar to the backsword techniques of the 1600s. Some weak sources indicate that the brothers were taught these skills by their father, Rezin Sr., who had fought in the Revolutionary War and bore a scarred hand from a British saber. After the Sandbar Fight, Jim's reputation attracted many challengers. He had to know how to use a knife.

HISTORY OF BOWIE KNIFE TECHNIQUES

The techniques Jim Bowie supposedly used in his fights are not obscured by the same fog of legend as the man himself. In fact Bowie's successful fighting skills may have been based on the solid principles that evolved from such Renaissance swordsmen as Camillo Agrippa, Joseph Swetnam, and

George Silver. You can find various parallels between the techniques used by Bowie and the Renaissance swordsmen throughout the writings of both periods.

Most of the Bowie knife-fighting systems you see today come from the training manuals of Lt. Col. Anthony Joseph Drexel Biddle and his book, *Do or Die* (1937). As an instructor for the U.S. Marine Corps, Lieutenant Colonel Biddle was a classicist in the true sense of the word. He viewed knife fighting through the eye of a duelist. His background in the saber, broadsword, épée, and dagger was extensive, having studied with such experts as Maj. W.J. Hermann, an early American fencing champion; J.H. Hawkins, a sword instructor of the Royal Horse Guards; M. Thomas, a broadsword champion; Jean-Marie Surget, an international sword champion; and J. Martinez Castell, a fencing master in New York.

Biddle felt that classic swordsmanship would provide a solid base for improving knife fighting techniques. William Cassidy's *The Complete Book of Knife Fighting* (1975) more or less sums up Biddle's contribution: **"**He was a gentleman instructing other gentlemen in the ritual of knife fighting. As such, many of the methods he advocated come down to us as nothing more than quaint reminders of an earlier (and perhaps better) age of conflict."

Biddle's contribution to myths surrounding the Bowie fighting system came from the following statement in his own book "The following course of instruction teaches the use of the knife as prescribed by the late Colonel Jim Bowie, U.S.A. . . . The following course of instruction is after the teachings of the Bowie Knife as prescribed by the Colonel himself: He was a celebrated sword duelist."

Many of today's knife experts have wondered why the normally factual, historically accurate Biddle made such an unsupported statement. Did he have access to documents that supported this assertion? Was he just trying to portray the Bowie knife as a uniquely American system? No one knows—Biddle took those answers with him to his grave.

Regardless of Biddle's reasoning, he did touch upon a link that tied the Bowie family to knife and sword fighting. As previously mentioned, Jim and Rezin's father had fought in the Revolutionary War, and it is quite possible that he had some training with the broadsword and saber. Many Scotsmen recently immigrated had brought their martial traditions to this country. Did the father pass on sword and dagger skills to his sons? If so, what were those skills based on? The broadsword and the saber. What were the techniques? Probably very similar to what Biddle advocated.

Trying to track down the Bowie knife-fighting system has taken me down many interesting paths. While reviewing some Bowie articles by COMTEC's Jim Keating and the great knife maker Bill Bagwell, I found repeated references to Bowie knife training in the New Orleans fencing schools before and after the Civil War. This led me to the discovery of Master Don Jose Llulla, who did indeed teach and fight with the Bowie knife. Like Biddle, this Spanish master (who died in 1883) had a background in the broadsword, saber, and rapier and dagger. Llulla taught duelling methods.

I also found that many historical fighting manuals of the Renaissance described in detail techniques now attributed to the Bowie knife system. One example is the back-cut technique, which is often described as unique to the Bowie. However, Swetnam's 1617 text describes how this technique is performed with the backsword.

Based on my research, the following are my personal beliefs about the Bowie knife-fighting system.

- Jim Bowie never developed a unique fighting system for his knife. Rather, he used the system handed down to him from his Scottish family. This system was probably quite similar to the Highlands broadsword, backsword, and smallsword methods addressed in Henry Angelo's and Donald McBane's 18th-century manuals (if Jim Bowie was ever trained at all).
- Bowie techniques have a historical basis in backsword, saber, and broadsword techniques. There are some ties to Spanish *navaja* and cutlass. It all depends on the culture and training of the man using the knife.
- Bowie techniques are not uniquely American, but rather a synthesis of techniques brought from Europe.

BOWIE AND BIG-KNIFE-FIGHTING TECHNIQUES

The weapon used throughout this text and shown in Figure 8 is a Bowie design that appeared shortly before the American Civil War. This popular knife was used throughout the South and Southwest in the 1800s.

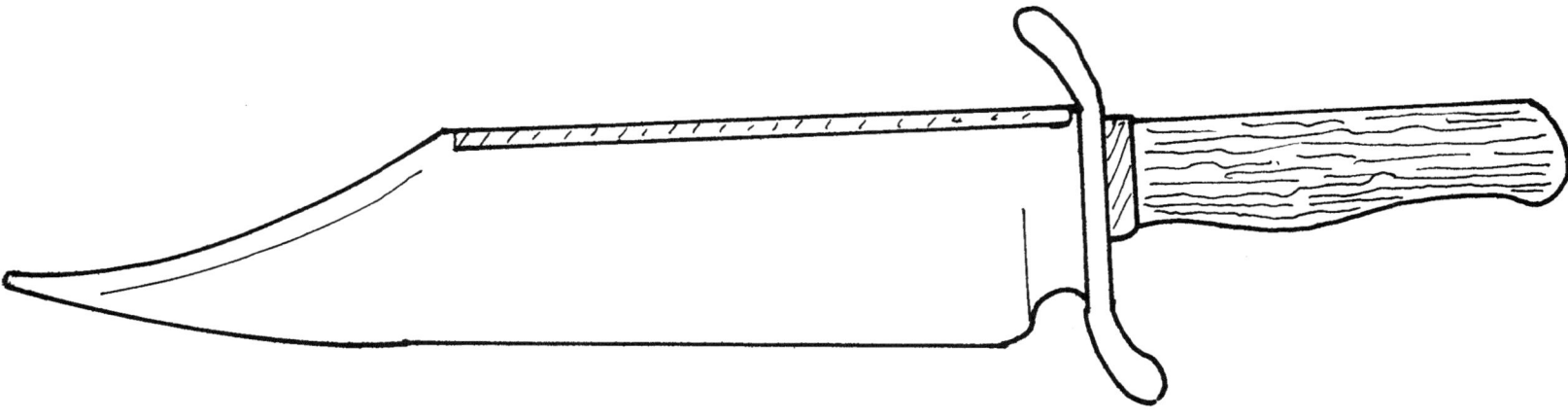

Figure 8.

It has a simple wooden handle with an **S**-shaped brass guard that protects a 13-inch blade. The heel of the blade has a conspicuous brass strip running its entire length. Some knife experts say that this strip was designed to catch the opponent's edge in the soft brass during a fight. In all probability, the strip served to protect the heel of the blade and give it additional strength for a multitude of tasks besides knife fighting. This is a sturdy, multipurpose knife and a capable tool for defense and outdoor use.

When one hears the term *Bowie knife*, the massive clipped point and sharpened back edge seen on this weapon come to mind. Contrary to popular belief, the clipped point and the back edge are not native to the American continent. Even the most cursory review of historical weapons will reveal examples used throughout Europe, Asia, and the Middle East. The design for the Bowie has been around a long time.

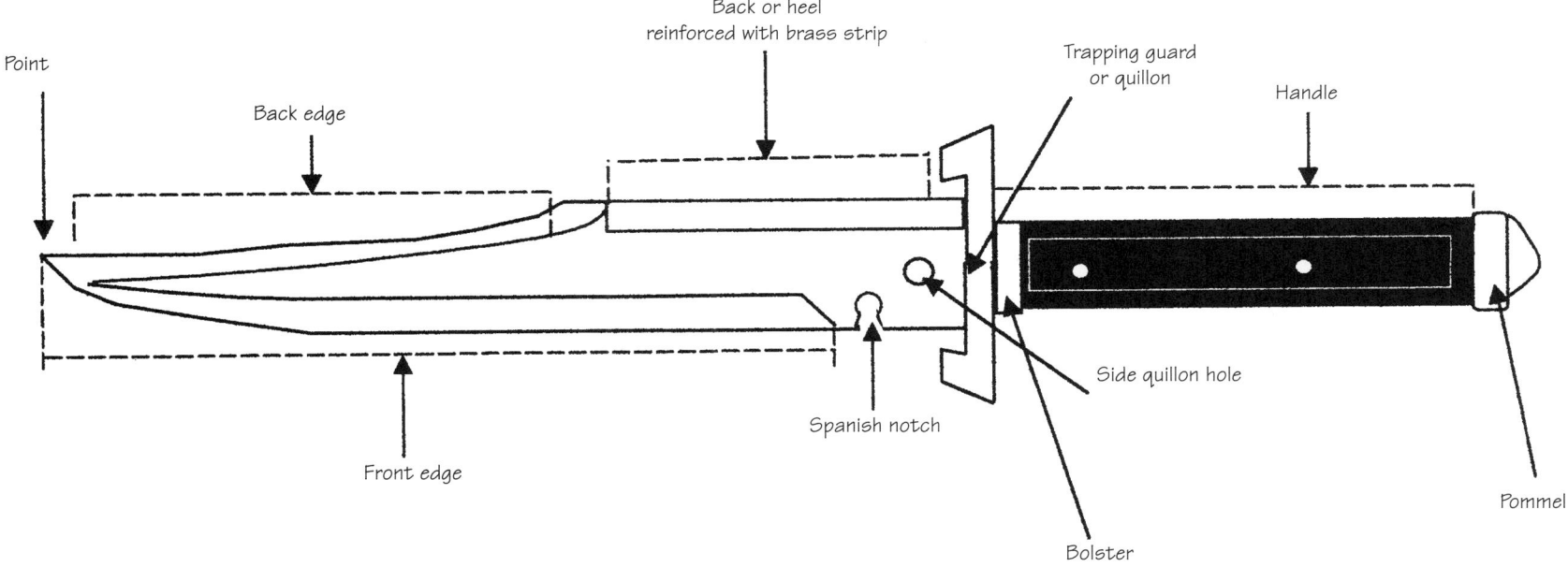

Point

Back edge

Back or heel reinforced with brass strip

Trapping guard or quillon

Handle

Side quillon hole

Spanish notch

Front edge

Bolster

Pommel

Figure 9.

Training Weapons

The ultimate goal of any knife training is to acquire the skill to perform all the individual drills and exercises with a fully functional steel blade. Two-man partner drills should never be performed with functional live-steel blades. First, no matter what the skill level of the training partners, the risk of injury from a mistake is extreme and could even result in death. Second, the edge of a good knife usually ends up being ruined. It is important to note the words *acquire the skill* in the first sentence—this is essential in preventing injury to anyone in training.

Patience is the key. Start out by training with wooden weapons, progress to blunted aluminum blades, and then move on to blunted steel blades.

There are many commercially available wooden training weapons on the market today that repli-

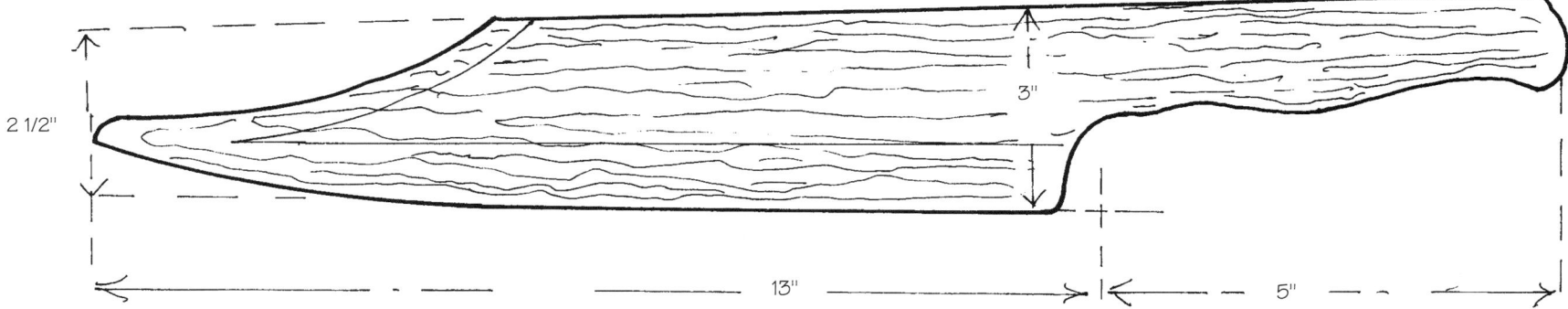

Figure 10.

cate the weight and balance of their steel counterparts. If one is not readily available to you, you can construct your own from red oak, which is reasonably easy to carve and finish, and holds up well to the abuse of blocking or parrying. The design in Figure 10 is taken from that of the historical Bowie in Figure 8. It is simple and can easily be constructed using a keyhole saw, rasp, small block plainer, and three grades of sand paper (coarse, medium, and fine). It was selected as the Bowie trainer because of its remarkable balance and feel for what the historical Bowie of the 1800s was like. Today, as then, it is a reasonably inexpensive weapon that is available from a variety of commercial firms.

Basic Bowie and Big-Knife Training

One of the constants of knife training is that it takes time! The skills, timing, and techniques must be honed regularly and consistently. One must acquire a level of mastery before progressing to the next level. While many teachers use the term *dedication* when addressing training, we probably need to think in terms of what we desire to learn and how much time can reasonably be devoted to doing it. Everyone's schedule is different. Some people devote 12 hours a week, while others can only manage three. That is reality. Each student must develop his own formula for training success to fit his schedule.

This book is divided into five sections for basic Bowie and big knife training. Ready? Let's start training.

SECTION ONE: GRIPS, HOLDS, STANCES, GUARDS, AND PRESENTING

GRIPS

When talking about the grip, we deal with how the weapon is held and manipulated in the hand. For our purposes, three grips are considered when training with the Bowie: saber, universal, and foil.

Saber

The first and most popular grip used with the big fighting knives is the saber grip. Unlike with some Asian fighting styles where the handle is held low with the point slightly raised, the Bowie is usually held with the wrist locked and the blade kept in line with or parallel to the forearm. In Figure 11 note the position of the thumb resting on the top of the handle and against the guard.

Figure 11. The saber grip.

Figure 12. The universal grip.

Universal

The universal grip is a modification of the saber grip. With the universal grip, the fingers are curled around the handle in the same manner, but the thumb is positioned to the side of the handle and pressure is exerted between it and the second finger. This popular grip is often preferred because it takes pressure off the thumb and allows a greater variety of forward and backhand thrusts and slashes.

Foil

The foil grip originated with the left-hand parrying daggers of the Renaissance. The theory behind this grip rests with the belief that the left hand did not possess the same degree of coordination as the right. It was discovered that when the thumb was pointed at an object, anything held in that hand was also pointed in the same direction. Foil grips enhanced the accuracy of a left-hand thrust or parry. The foil grip is functional, but the thumb is not protected by the guard. Some Bowie practitioners feel that this grip facilitates better application of the back-cut technique.

Personal Preference

All too frequently debate arises over which grip is superior, when in reality the key factor is not so much the grip as the shape of the handle as it fits in the user's hand. Bowies and daggers come with a variety of handle shapes and sizes, as do hands. Experimenting with a variety of grips and handles is the best way to find which is best suited to you. The universal grip with a coffin-handled Bowie is a good place to start.

Figure 13. The foil grip.

Some Handle Designs to Consider

The "business end" of the Bowie is the blade. Just as there is debate about which grip is better, there is also debate about which blade design is more efficient. Just as important as the blade is the shape of the handle. Depending on the size of the hand and the strength of the grip, the handle shape is the key factor in determining the range of motion and efficiency of the blade. The fundamental factors are ease of manipulation and retention during cutting or thrusting. The Bowie blade was designed to perform both actions with equal dexterity. During the Bowie knife craze of the 1840s these basic handle designs became very popular because they met the use criteria: oval-shape, coffin-handle, enhanced grip, and sloping pommel.

Figure 14. An example of the oval-shape handle on the controversial Bart Moore Bowie of the 1830s. This handle design, with its swell at the center, facilitates the use of the universal grip that allows the thumb a free range of movement from the side of the handle to behind the top guard.

21

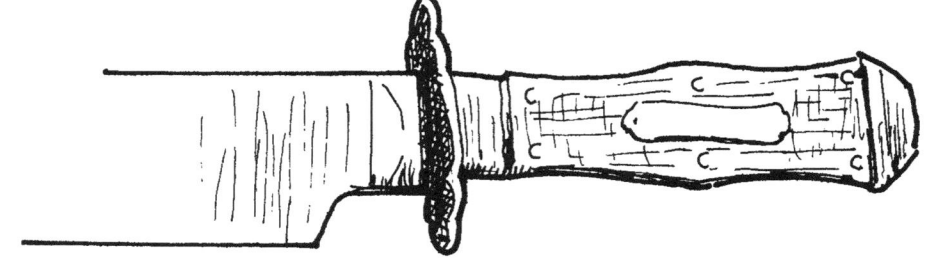

Figure 15. An example of the coffin handle made in Sheffield, England, around 1830 and sold in the shop of Samuel Bell. Most coffin-shape handles work well with the saber grip.

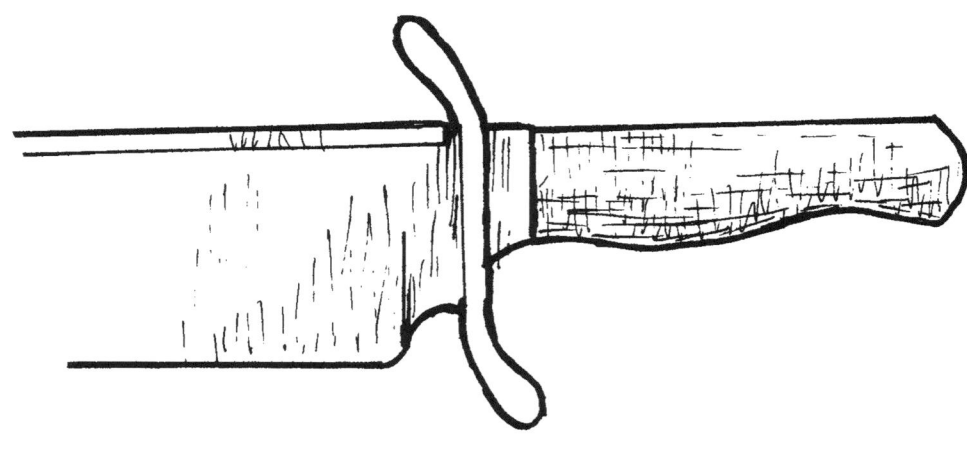

Figure 16. This 1840s Bowie design has an enhanced grip, which is suitable for saber, foil, and universal grips.

Figure 17. This Civil War–period Bowie has an antler grip with sloping pommel. This style has excellent retention capabilities.

HOLDING THE WEAPON

How firm a grip should you have on the weapon? Although the answer to this can be as vague as that of which grip to use, there is one solid rule of thumb from an old Japanese swordsman: "Hold your weapon as you would an egg—light to keep from crushing it and firm enough to prevent [your] dropping it."

Throughout history you'll read such phrases such as, "The grip must be supple and flexible, not rigid or fixed," or "The hand and handle must be so as to become one with the weapon."

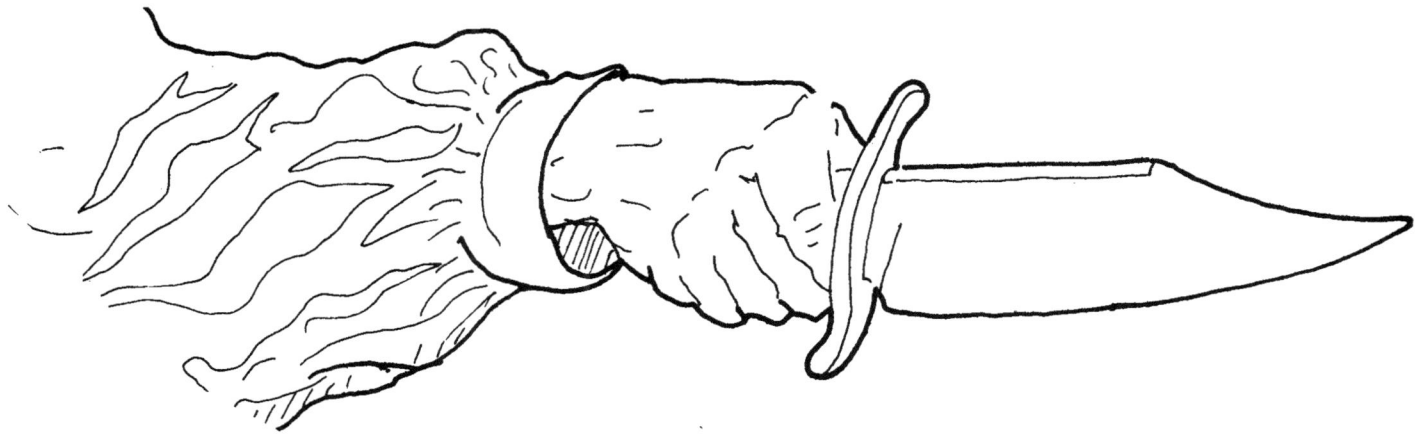

Figure 18.

FIGHTING STANCES

What fighting stance did Jim Bowie use? Answer: we have no idea. This was never documented historically, and anything you hear or see today that claims to be the authentic stance is nothing more than conjecture.

What was the common fighting stance during the period of the Bowie knife craze (1830–1840s)? Answer: that depends on what culture the knife fighter came from and the training he had received from his relatives or instructors.

Actually, when we discuss the use of Bowies and other big knives there are several stances that could be used. These stances came down to us from Renaissance times, evolving through the various fighting systems to become what we see today. If one is looking to history for the "authentic Bowie knife technique," then one has a lot of material to cover. If the user hailed from the Andalusia region of Spain, the use of the Bowie might reflect the stances and style demonstrated in the 1849 *Manual del Baratero*. If the user was an Englishman with deep martial roots, the use of the backsword covered in Joseph Swetnam's 1617 treatise might well represent how he employed his big fighting knife on the American frontier.

Today some people claim that the "Bowie fighting system" evolved from the European saber methods taught at the same time. Historically speaking, there is some indication that members of the Bowie family were familiar with these saber techniques. The only historical fact we have here is that up until the late 1800s saber techniques were passed down to young knife users of the period in various "boy's texts." Therefore it seems highly probable that these were easily adapted to the popular Bowie knives of the time.

From the training perspective, the important fact to note is that fighting stances evolved for a variety of reasons. Using "authentic" stances is not nearly as important as knowing the advantages and disadvantages of each stance when you're facing an opponent. With that in mind, the following are some of the stances that could have been common during the period when the Bowie knife was popular. Work with all of them.

Italian Stance

One of the very early knife-fighting stances can be seen in Achille Marozzo's 16th-century text, *Opera Novo* (1536, 1568). Renaissance fighters used a dagger similar in size to the Bowie, but its double-edge tapered to a keen point made it more like what some historians have called the "Arkansas toothpick."

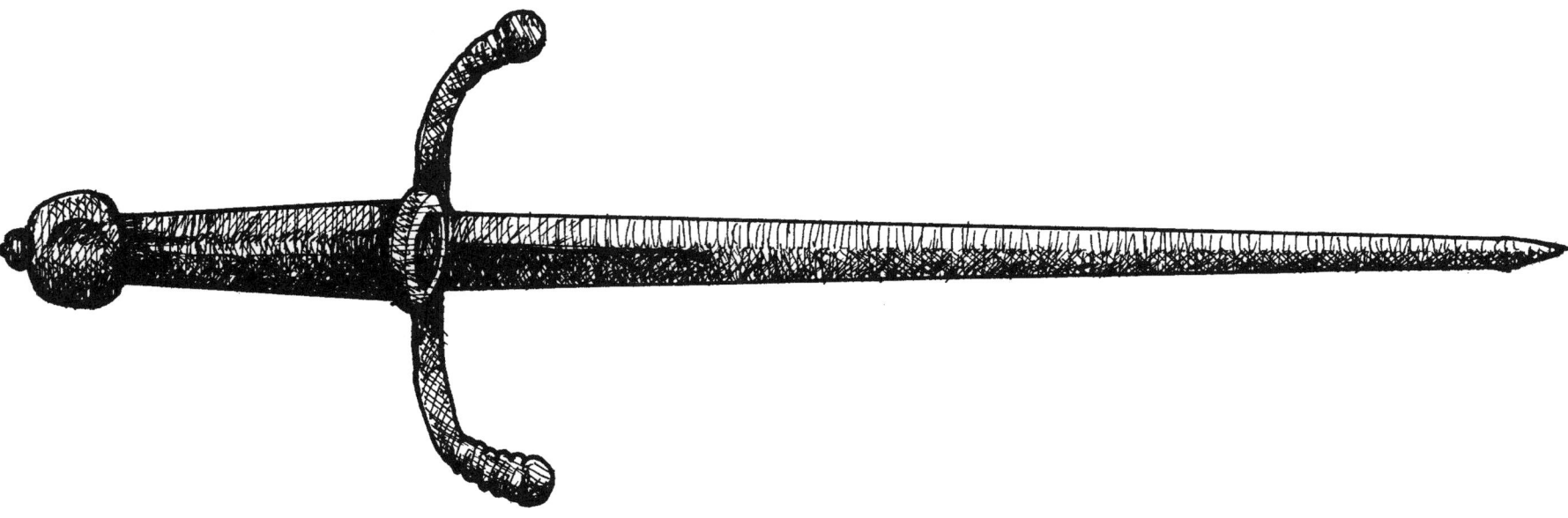

The news accounts of the 1840s often reported this kind of weapon being used in some of the Bowie knife duels. In Figure 20, note that the empty hand is tucked behind the back to protect it from becoming a target. The weapon hand is extended to facilitate thrusting techniques through a simple rotation and shift of the hips. The head and torso have the slight forward lean often seen in some rapier-and-dagger styles of the period. The wide, deep stance of the legs is used to enhance movement through passing (one leg passes the other during offensive or defensive movement). The disadvantages of the forward lean are that it exposes the head and that the empty hand tucked to the rear cannot readily be employed to pass or deflect an opponent's attack.

Figure 19. One of the left-handed *main-gauche* daggers of the Renaissance.

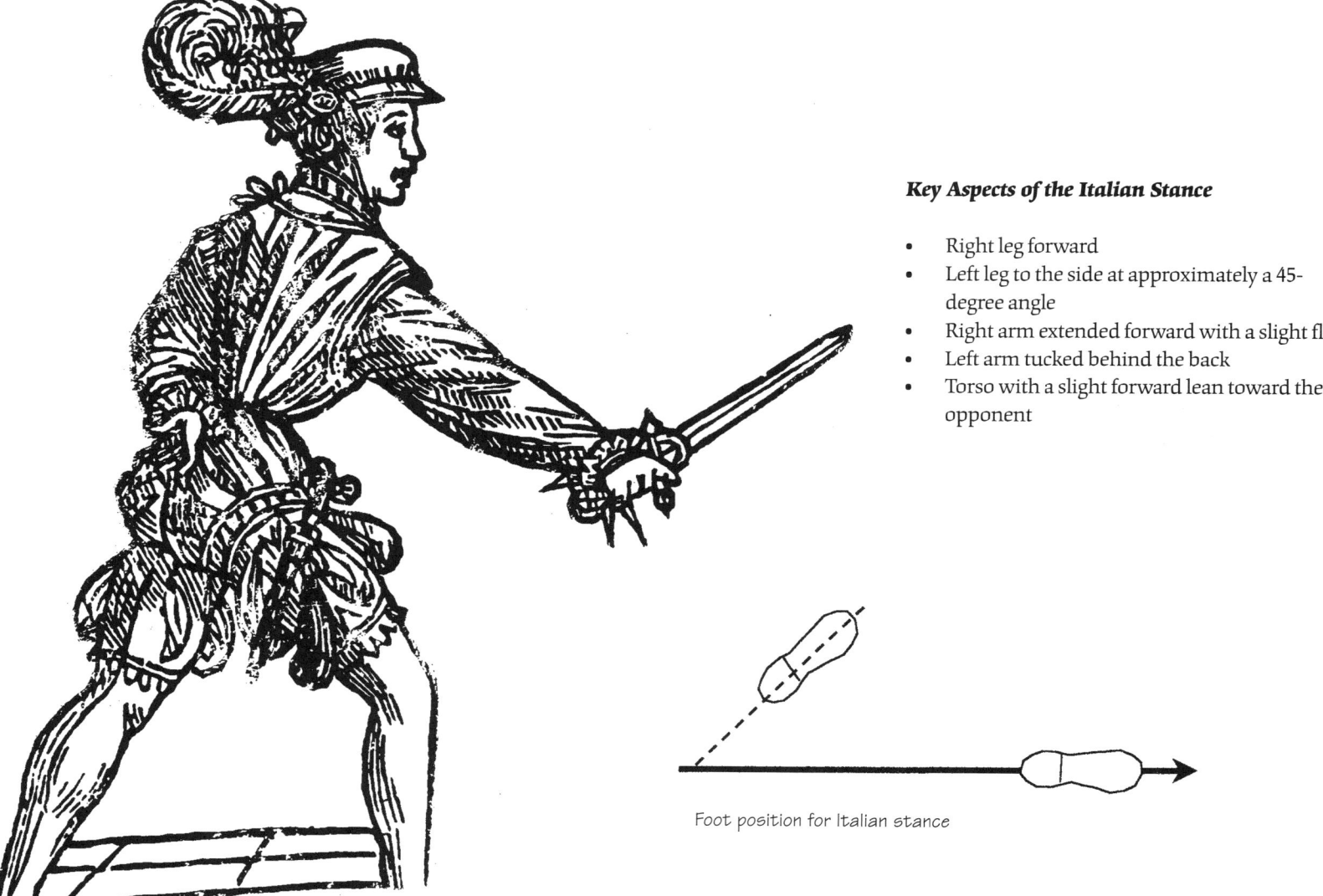

Key Aspects of the Italian Stance

- Right leg forward
- Left leg to the side at approximately a 45-degree angle
- Right arm extended forward with a slight flex
- Left arm tucked behind the back
- Torso with a slight forward lean toward the opponent

Foot position for Italian stance

Figure 20. The Italian stance as depicted in Achille Marozzo's 16th-century *Opera Nova*.

The Spanish Stance

Another early fighting stance that should be examined was *la destreza*, or the Spanish system for rapier fighting. This stance was used to attack and defend within an imaginary circle that moved with the fighter on the ground. While Marozzo's Italian stance was the hub for a series of fighting techniques, *la destreza* permitted the creation of techniques based on body shifting and movement within the circle.

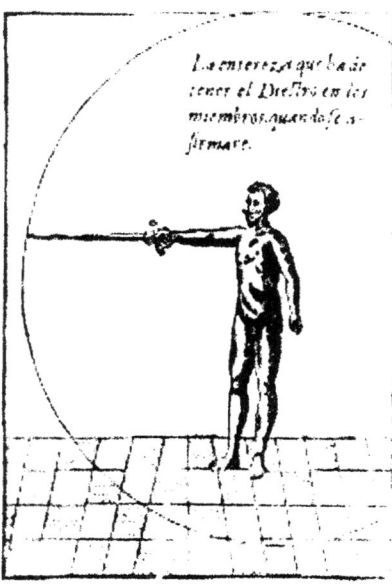

The applications here for Bowie knife fighting rest with this type of movement within the circle rather than any benefits associated with this upright stance. (I will discuss this later when movement is addressed.) This stance permits rapid body movement around the narrow circle of the stance and is useful in avoiding thrusting techniques from longer weapons. An immediate counterattack along the same line of that of an opponent's attack is also facilitated. While the extended arm is effective for immediate thrusts, the hand and arm are exposed to attack. The upright posture invites closing techniques to the torso.

Figure 21. The guard position from Narvaez's text.

Key Aspects of the Spanish Stance

- Right leg forward facing the opponent
- Left leg slightly behind at approximately 45 degrees
- Right arm extended with a slight flex
- Left arm may be forward to protect the torso or may hang straight at the side
- Posture completely upright with the chin tucked in and the head slightly down

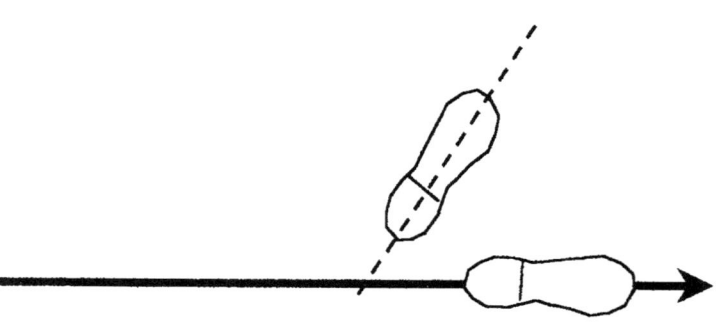

Figure 22. The Spanish stance.

Saber Stance

The saber stance has a long historical evolution. It is clearly seen in the military training of the 1700s and 1800s for both Highland broadsword and cavalry saber. Modern sport saber fencing gives a limited view of how this stance was used. *Hungarian and Highland Broadswords* (1799) by Henry Angelo reflects some to the classic saber stances and guards that may well have been adapted to the Bowie knife. Biddle alludes to this stance in *Do or Die*. The great John Styers' seminal manual, *Cold Steel*, demonstrates how this stance can be modified for saber grip knife fighting. The advantages of this stance are that only the side of the torso is presented to the opponent and it protects the upper and lower leg quite well. The position of the free hand to the rear, however, makes it difficult to use for traps, passes, or the seizing of the opponent's weapon arm.

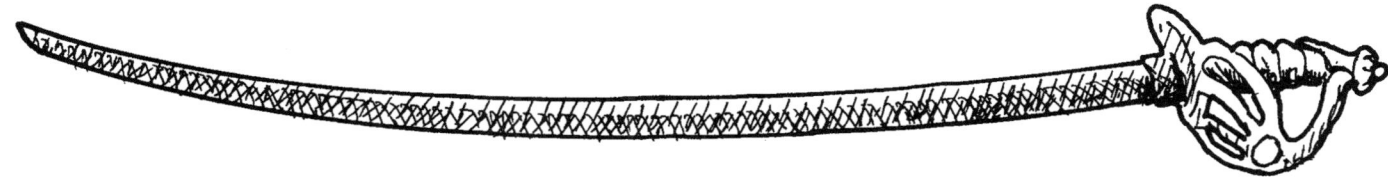

Figure 23.

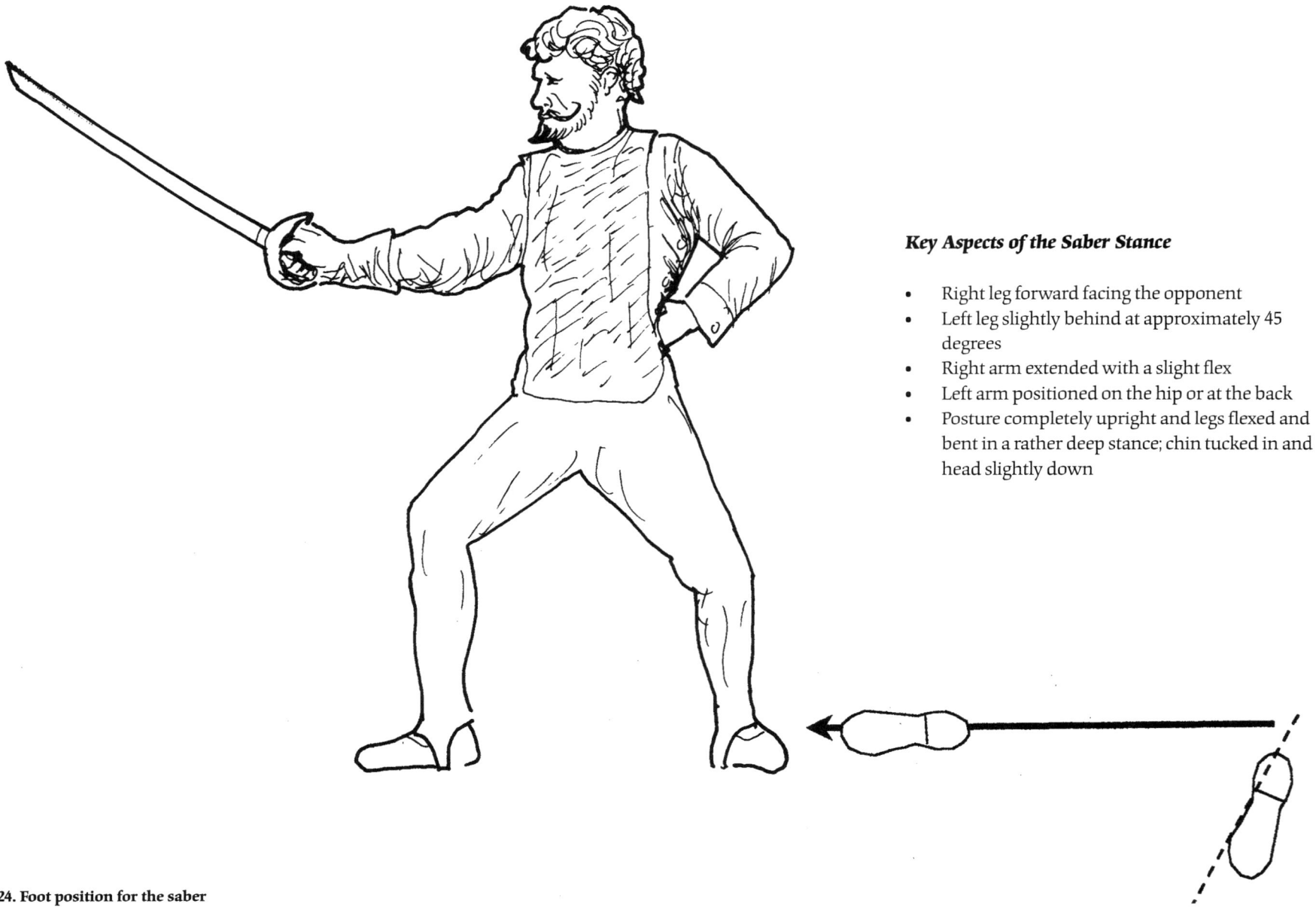

Key Aspects of the Saber Stance

- Right leg forward facing the opponent
- Left leg slightly behind at approximately 45 degrees
- Right arm extended with a slight flex
- Left arm positioned on the hip or at the back
- Posture completely upright and legs flexed and bent in a rather deep stance; chin tucked in and head slightly down

Figure 24. Foot position for the saber stance.

Biddle Stance

Historically known as the classicist of knife fighters, Biddle designed a knife fighting system prior to World War II that was based on the old sword methods. Figure 26 illustrates his "on guard" position.

Biddle contended that this particular stance was effective in delivering cuts to the hand and lateral shifting to avoid an attack. He saw the knife as being used somewhat like the Renaissance rapier, primarily with small slashes to the hand of an opponent, followed by thrusts to the body and throat. Biddle did not teach much on the use of the left hand, but rather felt it should be kept to the side or thrown back to improve balance. His stance reflects this.

Figure 25. The Biddle stance.

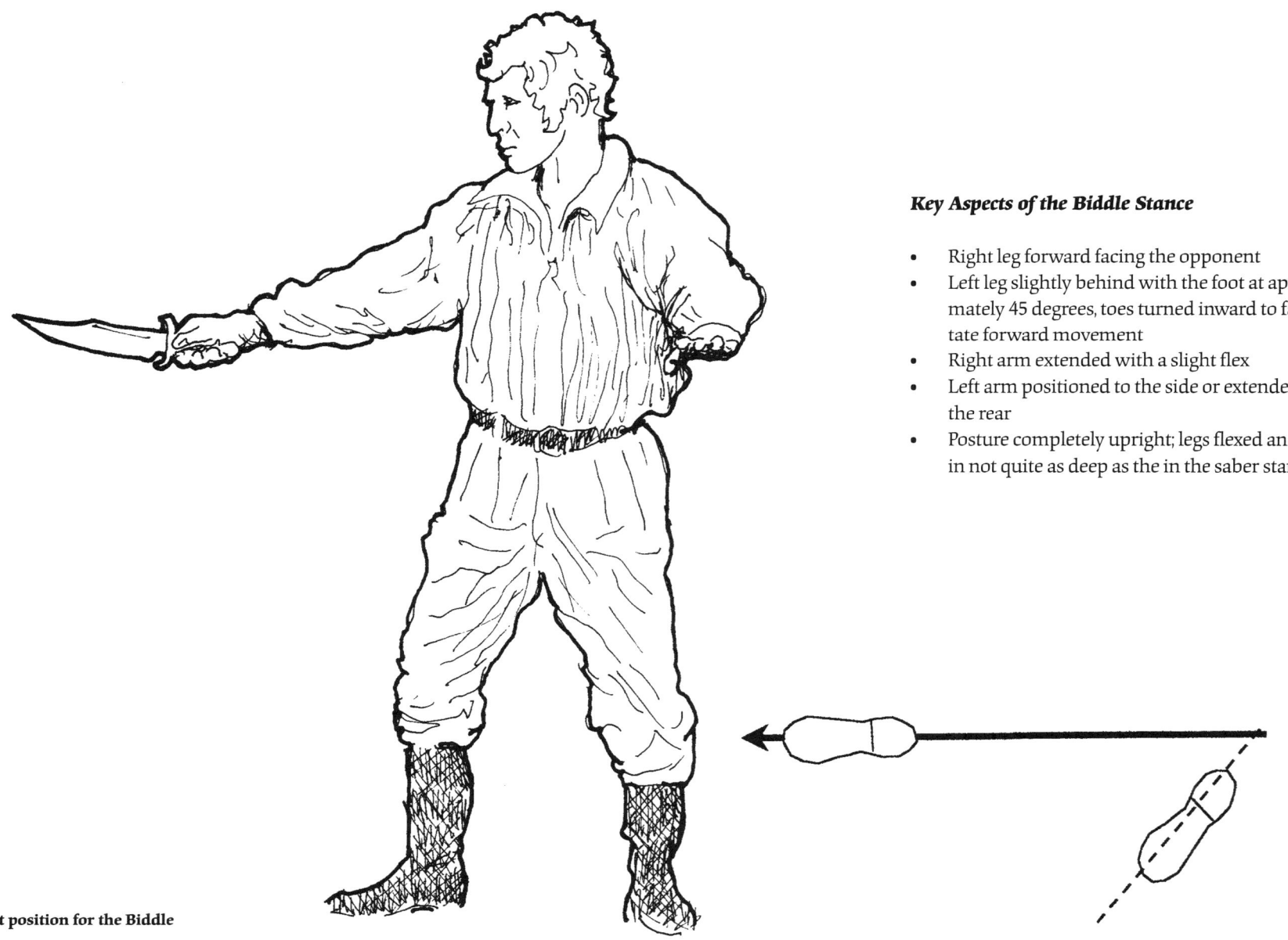

Key Aspects of the Biddle Stance

- Right leg forward facing the opponent
- Left leg slightly behind with the foot at approximately 45 degrees, toes turned inward to facilitate forward movement
- Right arm extended with a slight flex
- Left arm positioned to the side or extended to the rear
- Posture completely upright; legs flexed and bent in not quite as deep as the in the saber stance

Figure 26. Foot position for the Biddle stance.

Styers Stance

One of Biddle's star pupils was the great military trainer John Styers, whose *Cold Steel* is a classic in modern knife fighting. Styers called his stance "the perfect guard position." In this stance the feet are in a modified saber stance, achieved by stepping out 90 degrees to the left and rear of the lead foot (pointing toward the opponent). The lead foot is almost flat on the floor, with the rear one positioned slightly on the ball of the foot.

Here for the first time we see that the arms are chambered (withdrawn) back against the body to present less of a target from attacks to the hand. This chambering technique makes it difficult for an opponent to "sense" (touch) the blade prior to launching an attack. The advantage of the Styers stance comes from the ease with which frontal thrusts can be launched. Its disadvantages rest with the deep crouch and the flex of the knees, which make it a bit slower for lateral movement. It is ideally suited for fighting close and inside the window of combat of the opponent's torso. This was a popular stance with the military during the 1950s and 1960s.

Figure 27. Changing from the saber stance (left) to the Styers stance.

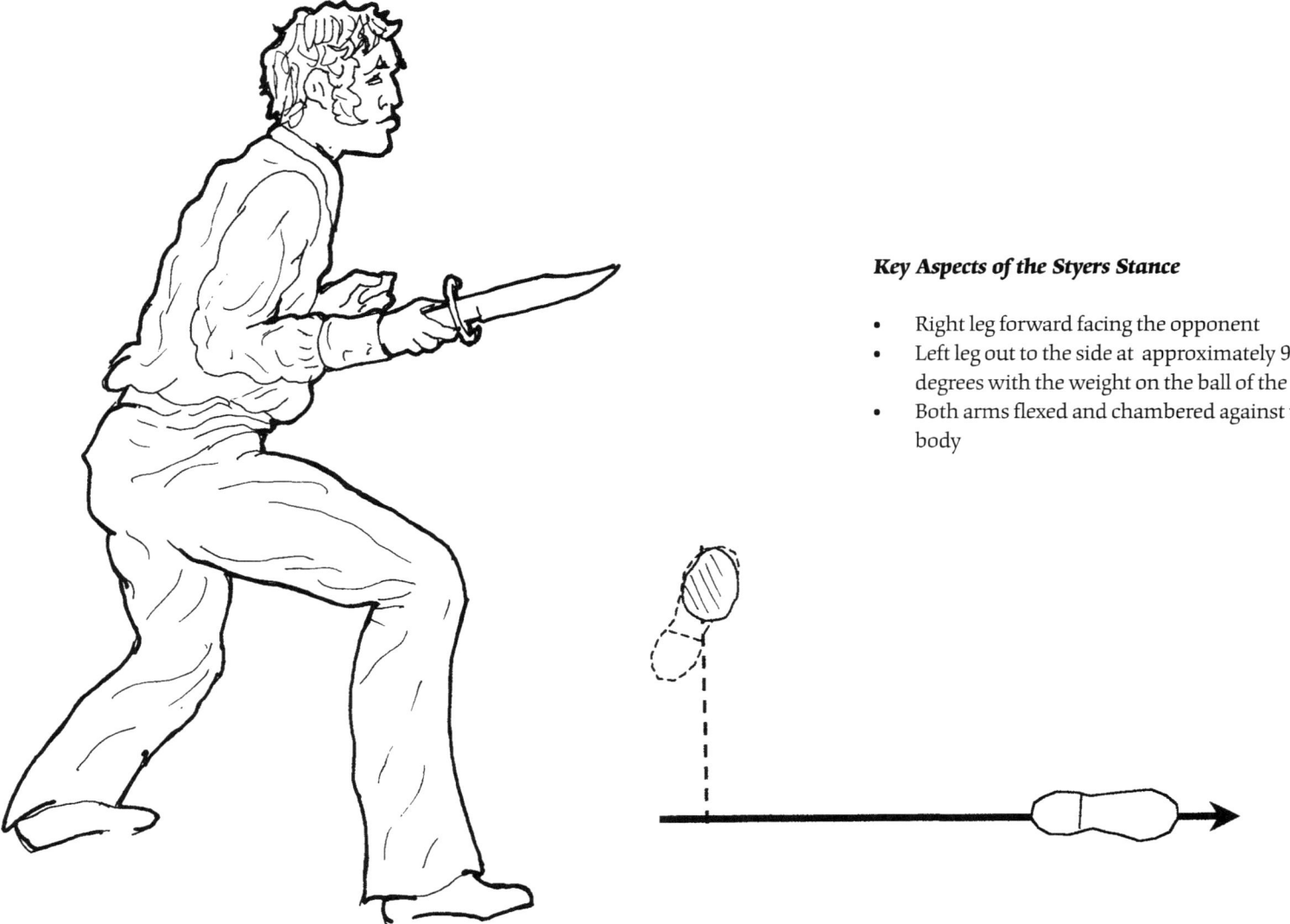

Key Aspects of the Styers Stance

- Right leg forward facing the opponent
- Left leg out to the side at approximately 90 degrees with the weight on the ball of the foot
- Both arms flexed and chambered against the body

Figure 28. Foot position for the Styers stance.

Stances—Strong Side or Weak Side Forward

As you studied the most significant stances both from the practical and historical perspective, you probably noticed that these are all what has been termed "the strong-side-forward" positions, where the weapon-bearing arm is forward. No discussion of knife fighting can conclude without addressing this and the "weak-side-forward" aspects of a stance, in which the empty hand is forward. Figure 29 depicts both approaches.

Figure 29. Strong-side-forward (left) and weak-side-forward approaches.

The weak-side-forward approach is used with those styles that favor a blade less than 6 inches in length, where little blade-to-blade contact occurs, with the action being in the close-quarter-combat window. You might say that "range" determines whether to use the weak-side-forward stance or not. The Sevillian *navaja* techniques depicted in the 1849 *Manual del baratero—Arte de manejar la navaja* demonstrate this approach. For the purposes of this book, we are working with a weapon that has 12 to 13 inches of steel that can be put between us and our opponent.

The size of these knives allows blade-to-blade parrying that is not possible for the shorter weapon.

In this type of engagement the weak-side-forward position really exposes the hand to attack. For big-knife fighting it is probably best to think of the weak-side-forward approach as a transitional move during an engagement rather than a place to start.

Three Key Principles of the Stance

There are three principles to keep in mind when selecting the stance that is right for you:

1. Ensure that you can quickly move side to side and forward to rear with ease. Mobility is the key.

2. You must be able to maintain your center of gravity (CG). People of shorter stature find their CG to be best with the wider stances, while taller individuals are more comfortable in a more upright stance and with the feet closer together. This is a matter of personal choice and subject to the unique physical abilities of the individual and his training. Bottom line? Practice with several stances to determine what works for you.

3. Remember that any stance is just a starting point from which to initiate an attack or a defense. Fighters return to the stance periodically when there is a lull in the fight, but knife fights are fights of movement where the opponents pass through many guards and stances during an engagement.

Figure 30. This stance has evolved for me after a few years of training and sparring with the big Bowie. It is sort of a modification of Styers' stance except that it is more upright, with a narrow center of gravity to accommodate my bad knee and to give me quicker lateral movement than the wider version does.

GUARDS

Along with the stance there are a series of arm positions, commonly referred to as guards, that have been used historically. The ones depicted here may be used with either strong- or weak-side forward, and, as with the stances, they are not firmly fixed positions but rather just starting points. These guards may be used with the arms either extended or chambered.

Figure 31. This is the basic stance with the commonly used center or middle guard. The figure on the right depicts the middle guard with the blade presented edge out.

High or Hanging Guard

This is another guard that has a reasonably long history. Although it was used primarily with the backsword, cut-and-thrust sword, and rapier, it does have applications for big-knife fighting.

Scottish sword master Sir William Hope in his 1707 text, *The New, Short and Easy Method of Fencing*, discusses this guard extensively and uses it as the cornerstone for a simplified method for teaching small sword, spadroon, broadsword, and backsword:

> In standing to this Guard, which in effect, is but an Improving of the ordinary Hanging Guard; a Man is to keep his Feet at a pretty good distance from one another, for his more firm standing; His Right Knee a little more bent than the Left; Is to show as little of his Left side to his Adversary as possible, without constraining and weakening too much his Posture; Is to present his Sword with his Hand as high as his Head, and in second, with the Nails of the hand almost quite down; His Sword's Point must slop[e] toward the middle part of his Adversary['s] advanced Thigh, but sometimes higher or lower, as occasion requires: and either without or within it, according as his Adversary presents his Sword; and this for the better securing of himself upon one side: For 'tis a general Rule in Fencing and punctually to be observed never to present one's Sword, without perfectly Covering, or Securing as we call it, one side of the Body.

Figure 32.

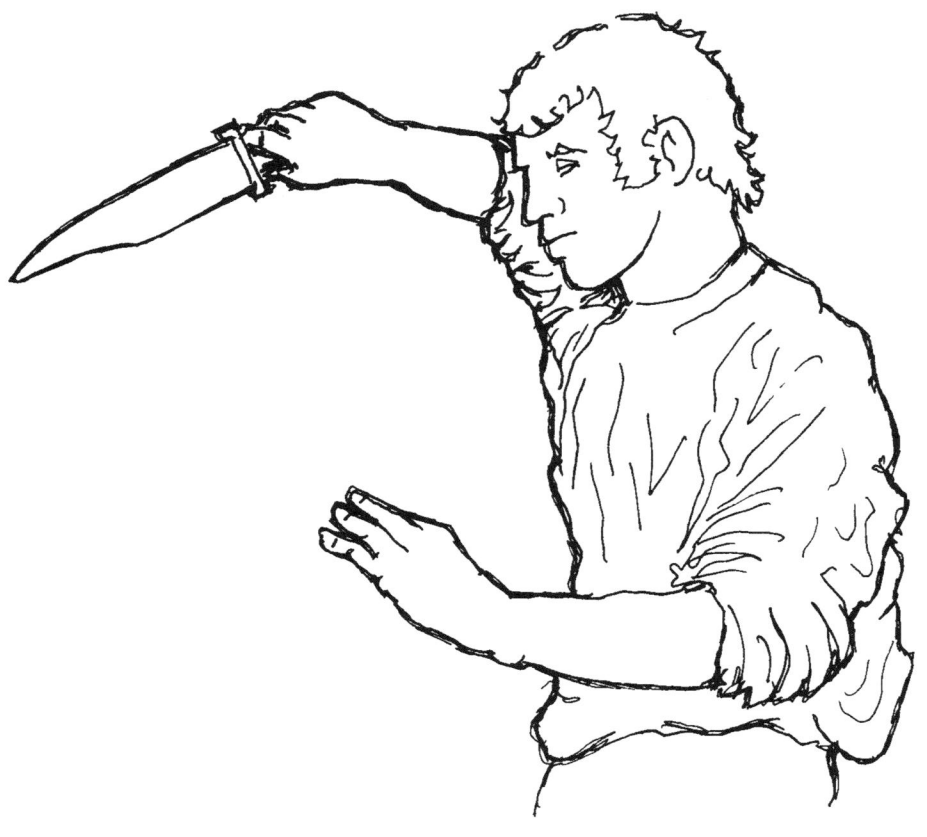

Figure 33. Hope's high, or hanging, guard application to the Bowie or big knife.

Figure 34. The low guard for the Bowie or big knife.

"PRESENTING THE BLADE"

The stance, the guards, and the concept of "presenting the blade" are all tied together in that moment of the initial engagement of a knife fight. The stance is the start point, the initial foot position. The guard is more concerned with the position of the arms in relation to the stance. When one presents the blade, the key elements are the wrist and the angle of the blade presented by specific turns of the wrist. This concept is closely tied to the technique called *parrying*, which will be covered later.

There are two fundamental positions for presenting the blade: edge down and edge up.

Edge Down

The standard knife-fighting presentation of edge down is very efficient because it presents the largest edge surface to the opponent. Thrust, cuts, chops, and snipes can be performed with equal dexterity from almost any angle.

Edge Up

While the edge-down presentation is more suited to the attack, one might say that the edge-up presentation is more suited to the defense. By presenting the thicker heel of the blade to the opponent, a stronger parry can be achieved without fear of damaging the edge of the blade. One of the unique aspects of the Bowie knife is its very functional back edge and reinforced heel. Some experts say that the strip of brass along the heel of some versions was for catching the opponent's blade. In all probability this strip was there to strengthen the heel to allow for a heavier parry without damaging the blade.

Edge up

Edge down

Figure 35. Two methods for presenting the blade.

SECTION TWO: THE THRUST

The debate over which is the most effective knife-fighting technique, the thrust or the cut, will probably never be concluded. The Roman army found the thrust so effective it adopted the *gladius hispaniensis*, or *gladius*, for the thrusting task. The narrow point swelling to a wide double-edged blade produced wide, deep, terrible wounds.

This same shape also could produce effective cuts or chops, potentially capable of taking off an opponent's limbs. The history of weapons is replete with examples of blades that were specialized for either the cut or thrust; however, it also shows that the truly effective ones were those that could accomplish both tasks equally well. The legionary's drill of thrust, thrust, chop, thrust, step, batter, and shove demonstrates this. In the gladiatorial arena the *gladius* performed a wider function, relying as much on the weapon's cutting capability as the thrust. The world of the gladiator was that of single combat at both close and medium range and at times against multiple opponents. The gladius of the legions was normally 16 to 20 inches in length, while the mosaics, wall paintings, and period sculpture reflect the gladiator's using a blade of about 13 to 18 inches.

While there is no historical trace to tie the Bowie knife to the gladius, a simple comparison of the design of the blades (narrow, tapering point and wide, double-edged blade) shows a clear functional relationship that suited both weapons to cut-and-thrust capability at both close- and medium-range combat. So with the Bowie we have a weapon that can be thrust. Let's examine this a bit more.

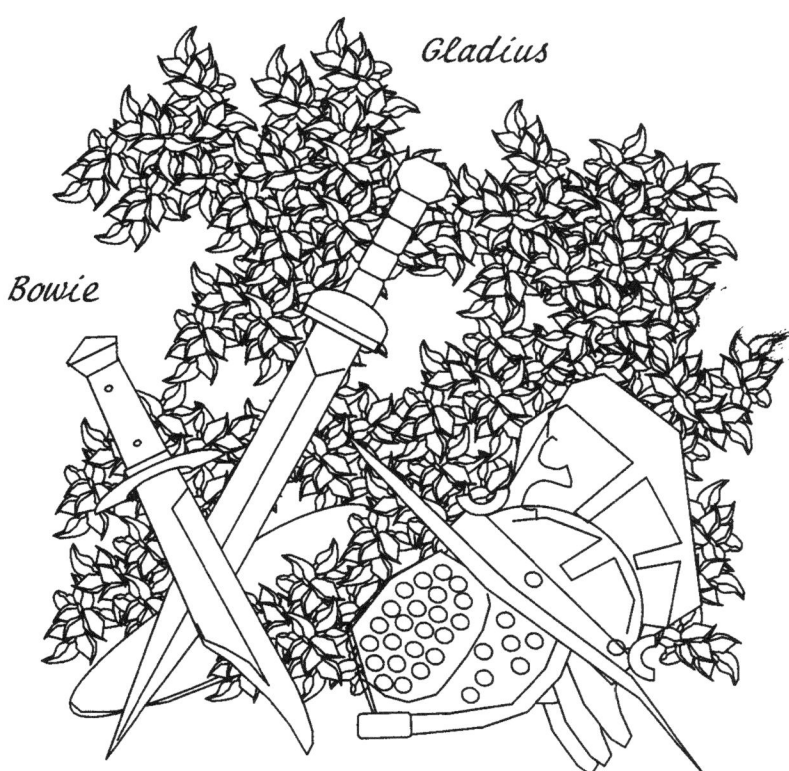

Figure 36.

From the standpoint of speed and rapid engagement from a guarded position, the Richard Burton in his 1884 text, *The History of the Sword*, contends that the thrust is superior to the cut. This is a solid fact; however, from the aspect of lethality, much depends on the width of the blade. Australian swordsman, historian, and emergency medical technician Bill McConnell, in his fine paper "The Cut and Thrust of Blade Combat," effectively addresses this issue.

> I am always amused when I hear remarks about the superiority of the thrust over the cut in sword combat. Although it is true that a thrust will more often result in a mortal wound, death is rarely swift. Most penetrating wounds from a slim blade will not kill quickly, and the most likely result is a dying opponent who will insist on taking their nemesis with them, since the already dying have nothing to lose. Damned inconvenient to say the least. Most exponents of civilian weapon combat were overly fond of the thrust attack. De Grassi mentions in his arguments the fact that Romans used thrust to great effect. This is of course true, but a quick examination of the gladius and *pugio* (dagger) shows that these thrusting weapons are gifted with broad dimension ... being stabbed in the stomach with a *pugio* would be rather like being disemboweled with a small shovel. Of course, we can wonder if the Italian 5-finger dagger (*cinqueda*) of the Renaissance period wasn't a rediscovery of this fact.

McConnell addresses the fact that

> human beings are by design very durable with many redundant systems that can prove surprisingly resilient. ... To kill or disable an opponent with an edged weapon you have a choice between damaging the mechanicals or the hydraulics.

> To damage the mechanicals you need to cut nerves, ligaments, muscles, and tendons; break bones and joints. ... The hydraulics are damaged by making holes in the largest blood vessels or a large number of smaller ones. ... Where the cut is better for mechanical damage, the thrust is indeed better for upsetting the hydrodynamics of the opponent.

In terms of the ability to deliver an effective thrust, a visual comparison of the gladius with the Bowie reveals a weapon that can deliver very lethal thrusts capable of producing massive wounds that upset the hydrodynamics of an opponent.

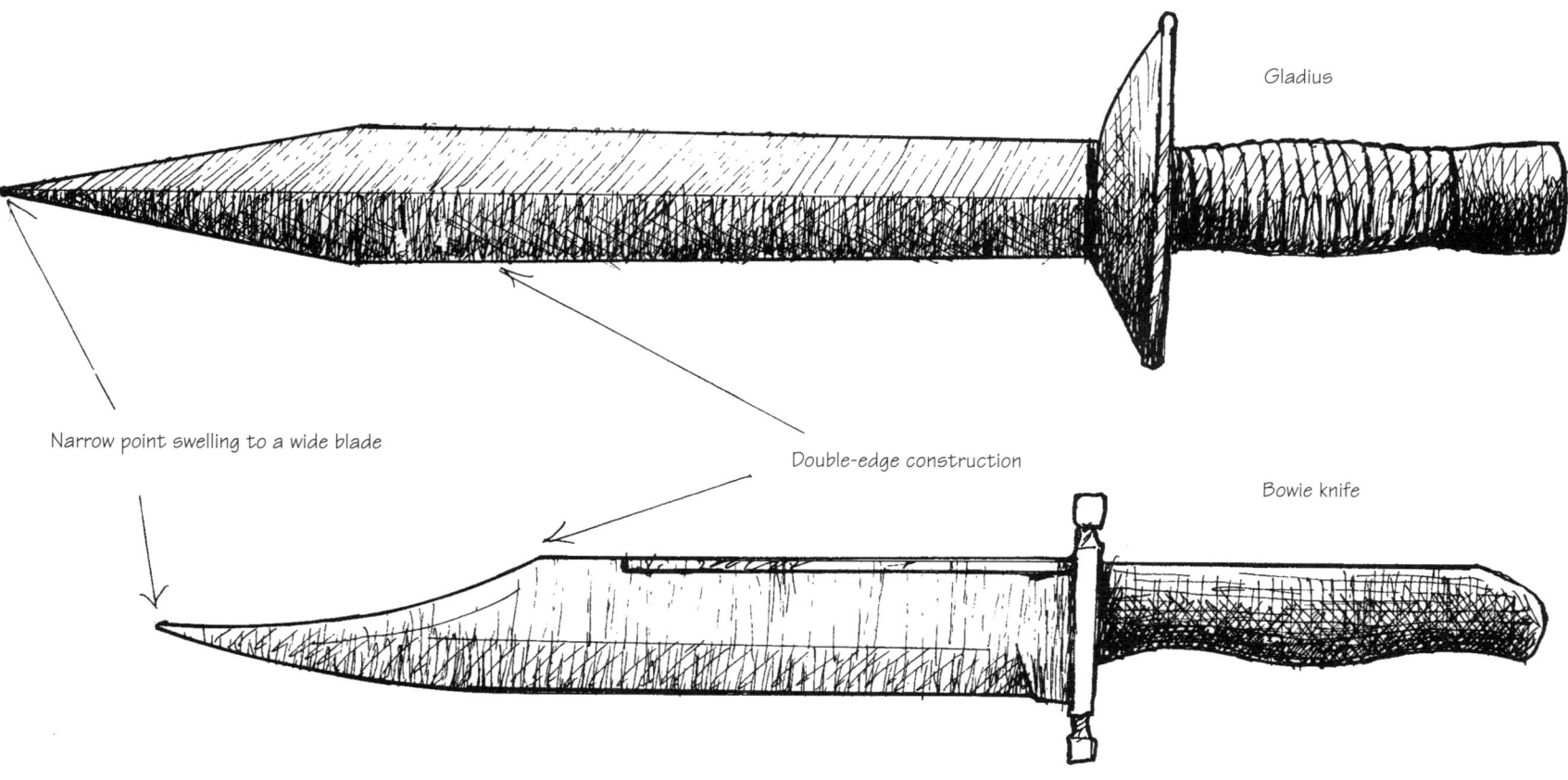

Gladius

Narrow point swelling to a wide blade

Double-edge construction

Bowie knife

Figure 37.

A further historical examination of the thrusting effectiveness of the drop-point shape of the Bowie blade is found in Burton's book. He addressed the difficulty in thrusting with a curved saber and describes the use of a circular-thrust technique to compensate for the curve of the saber blade. Burton cautioned that this circular movement of the entire arm often left the attacker exposed and also that it could not be performed with the straight thrust or lunge. Burton discussed how the French Colonel Marey, in an 1841 work, recommended the adoption of the Turkish *yataghan* blade design to enhance the ability of both the saber and bayonet to perform cut and thrust equally. The similarities between the *yataghan* and the Bowie are evident in Figures 38 and 39.

Figure 38. Yataghan short sword.

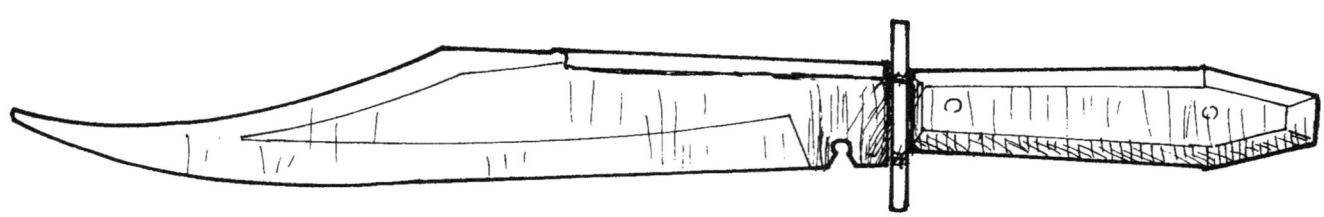

Figure 39. Coffin-handle Bowie.

FUNDAMENTALS OF THE THRUST

At this point, what we have with the Bowie knife is a big, broad-bladed, narrow-pointed weapon that will produce massive wounds rapidly and efficiently when thrusting techniques are used. Let's examine some of the basics of the thrust.

Arm Position

From the aspect of arm position, the thrust can be performed with arm extended and flexed (Figure 40) or with the arm in the chambered position (Figure 41).

Movement

From the aspect of movement, the thrust can be performed by body shifting, advancing step, passing step, and the lunge (more on this after I finish describing the mechanics of the thrust).

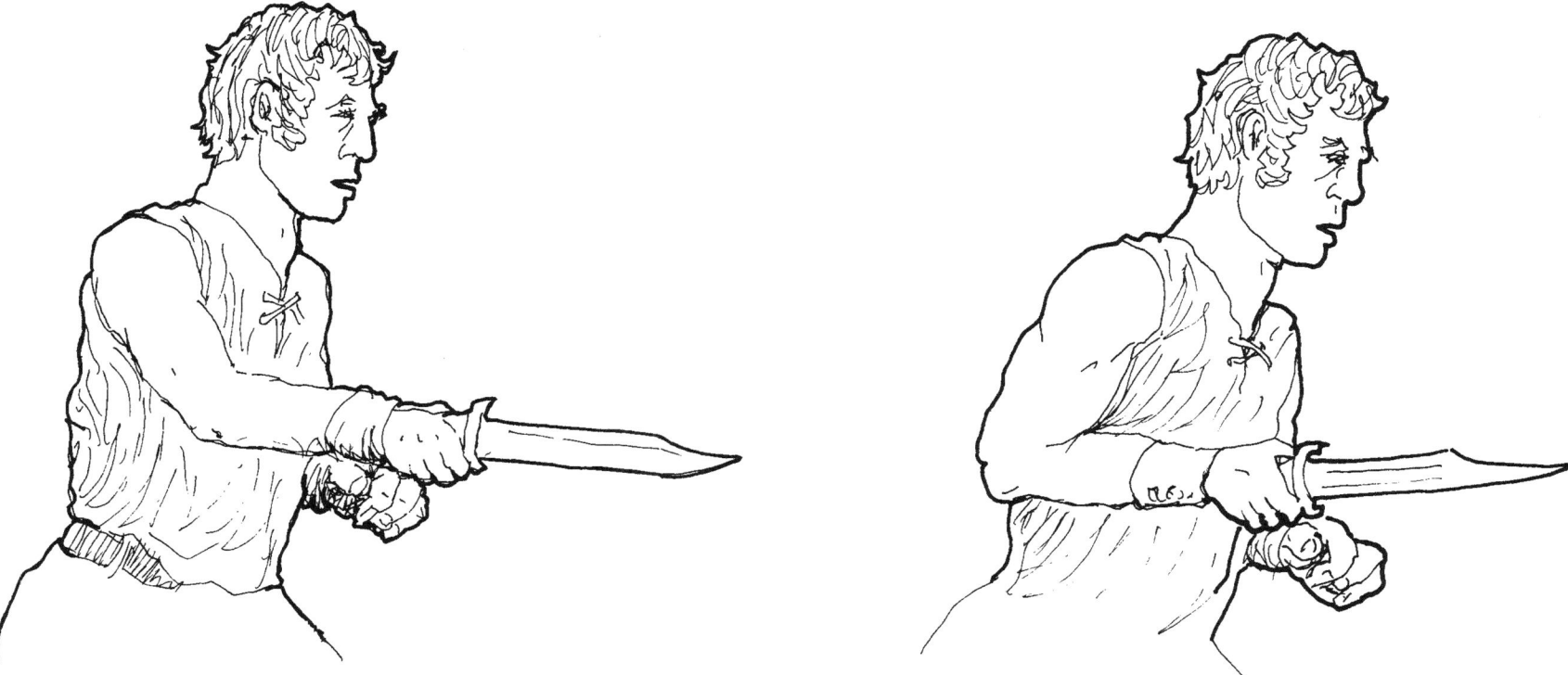

Figure 40. Flex and extended.

Figure 41. Chambered.

"GIVING POINT" (POINT OF IMPACT)

The moment the point makes contact with the target area on an opponent is an important factor in the execution of a correct thrust. At the point of impact no penetration of flesh has occurred, and no body movement (other than the extension of the weapon arm) has taken place.

The next element of giving point is the coordinated turning of the body and shifting of the hips into the direction of the point. This action provides the force to drive the blade deeply into the target area.

The action of the opposite or empty hand here is very important to push the blade through the point of impact and deep into the opponent. The empty hand is pulled back across the chest in line with the shoulder. Thus, we have two actions performed almost simultaneously.

Figure 42. Styers' full-extension thrust.

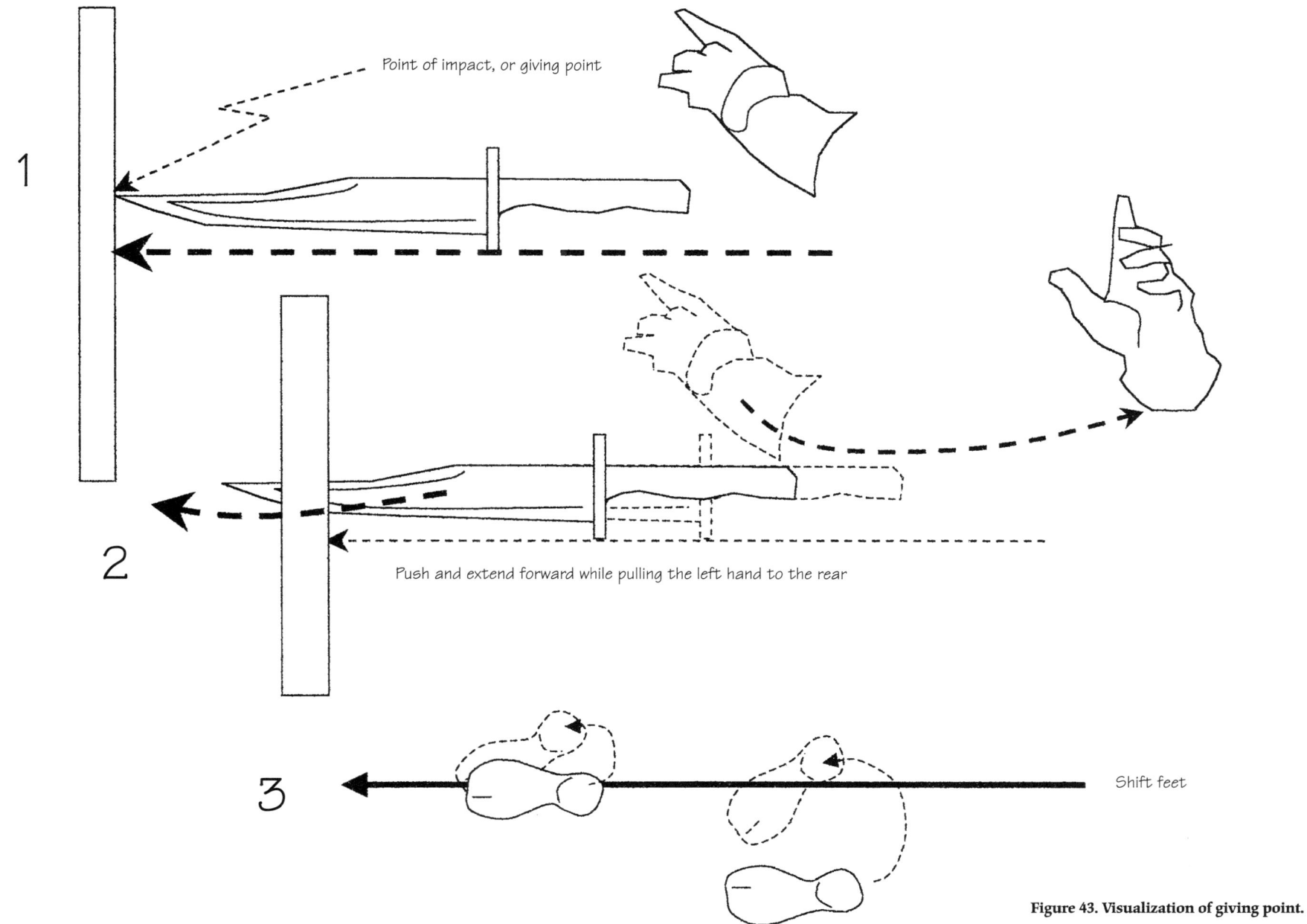

Point of impact, or giving point

1

2

Push and extend forward while pulling the left hand to the rear

3

Shift feet

Figure 43. Visualization of giving point.

STRAIGHT THRUST

Again, the straight thrust is performed in the following sequence: (1) giving point, (2) pivoting the body, and (3) shifting the feet. This is a simultaneous motion that is executed with dynamic speed. This thrust is accomplished with a simple body pivot or major movement of the feet to the left rear. Figure 44 illustrates the first and second movements.

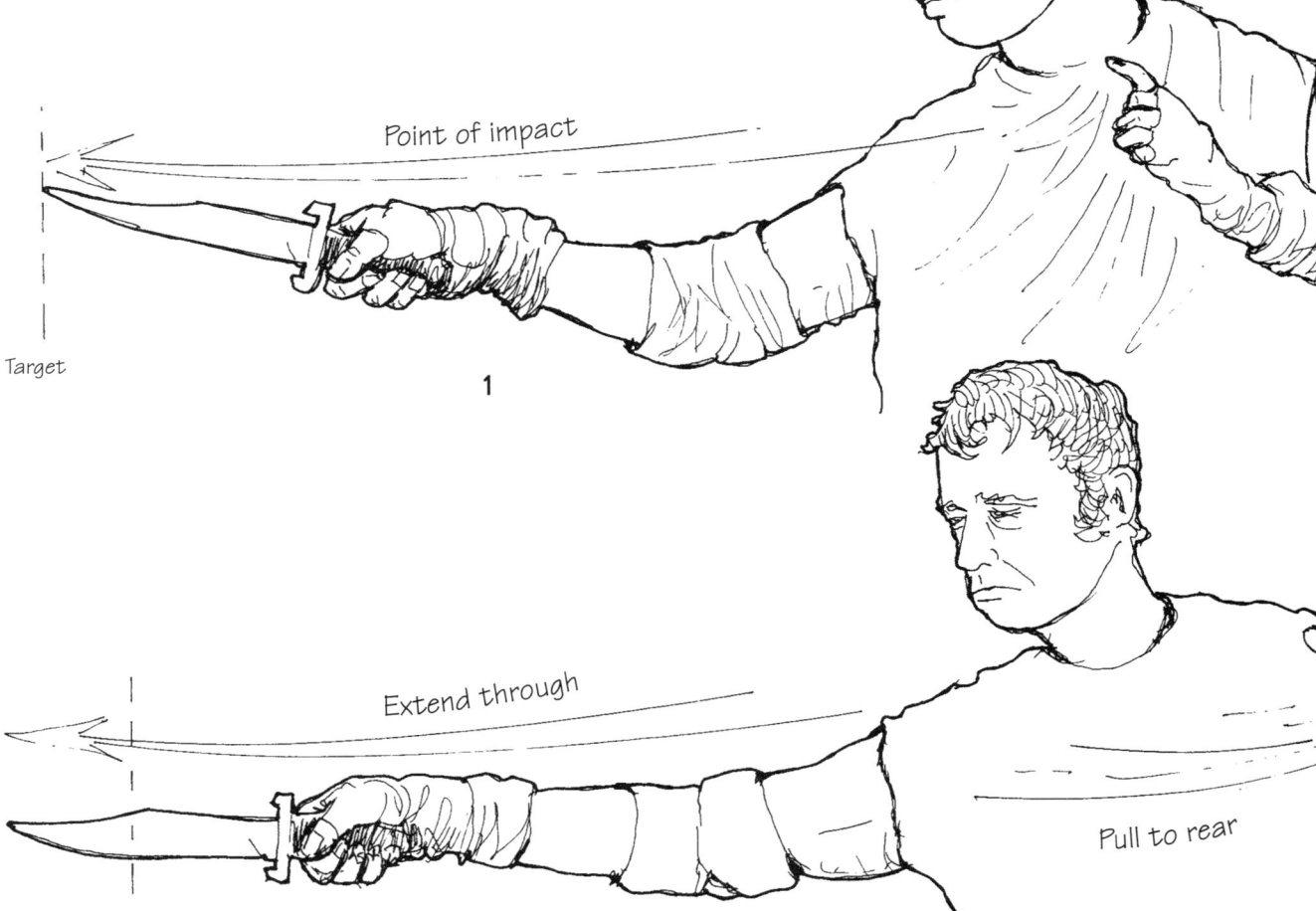

Figure 44.

Figure 45 depicts the foot movement with a larger shift to the rear while the fighter performs a straight thrust with a larger movement of the back foot to the left rear. This movement is particularly beneficial in avoiding an opponent's thrust and presenting an opening for a simultaneous counterattack thrust to the opponent's throat or torso.

HISTORICAL NOTE: In Renaissance fighting terms in Italy and Spain, this action would be referred to as the *quartatta (incartata)*.

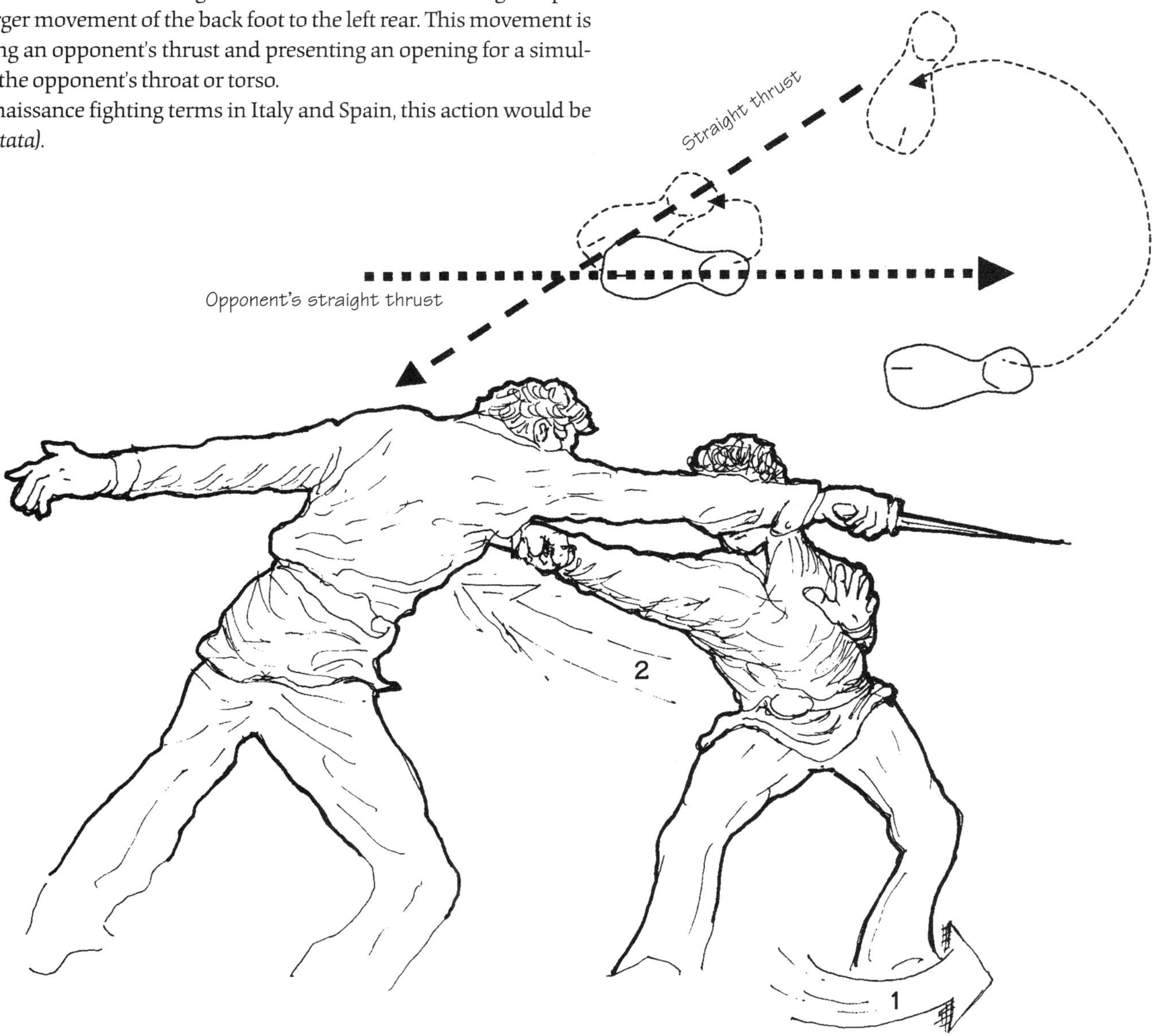

Straight thrust

Opponent's straight thrust

2

1

Figure 45. The *quartatta*.

PUNTA MANDRITTA

The next thrust variation involves a thrust to the opponent's left, outside his guard. This is a rapid, arching attack where the blade rotates approximately 45 degrees until the flat of the blade is horizontal with the ground. The *punta mandritta* can be executed with the same pivoting body action and foot shifting discussed in the section on the straight thrust.

TERMINOLOGY NOTE: From this point on, I will frequently use Italian-Spanish Renaissance fencing terms to describe many of the techniques and methods, primarily for brevity's sake. The historical manuals of that period often described techniques and actions with one or two words, whereas the English translation would require almost a sentence. The Renaissance terms also serve as excellent "memory joggers" for remembering the technique.

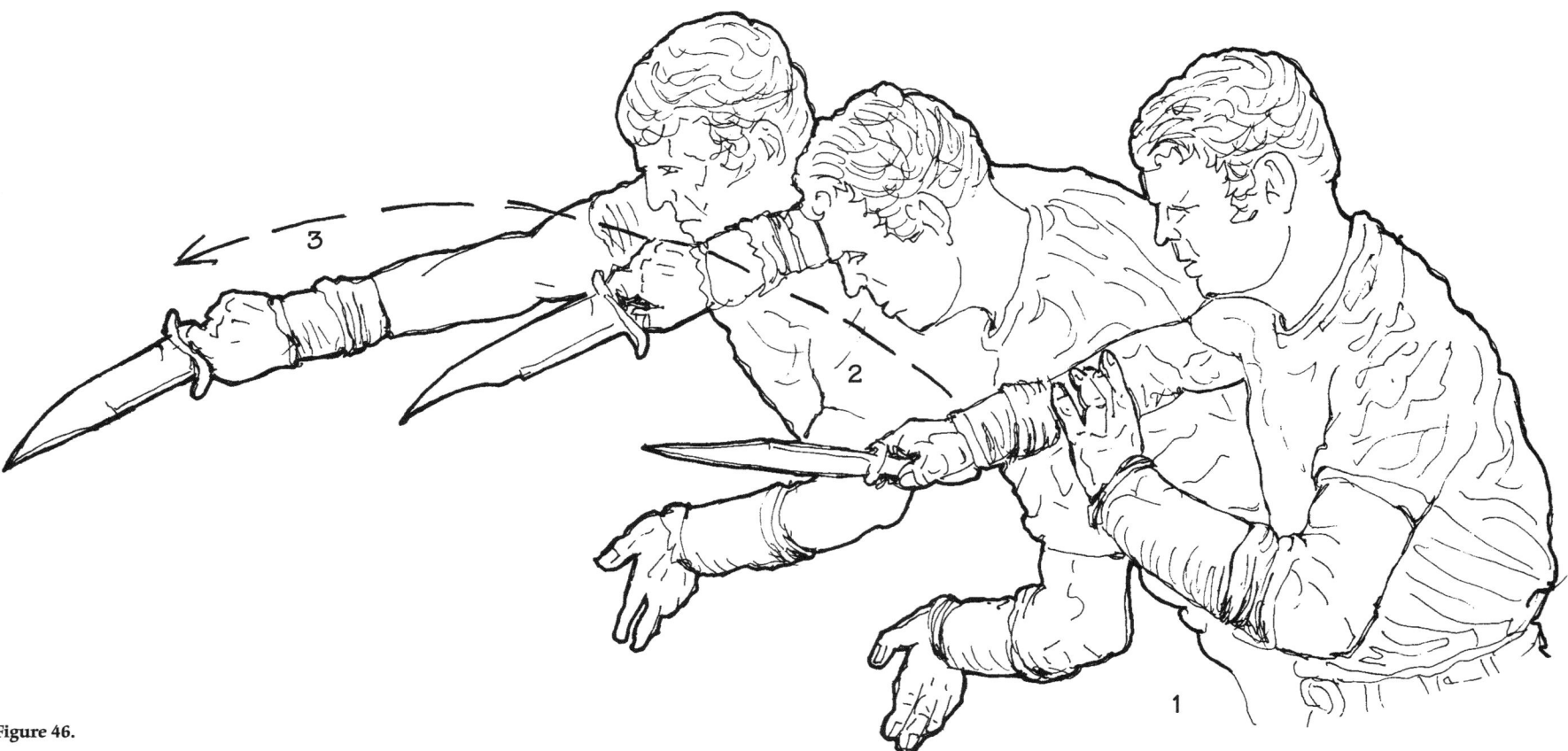

Figure 46.

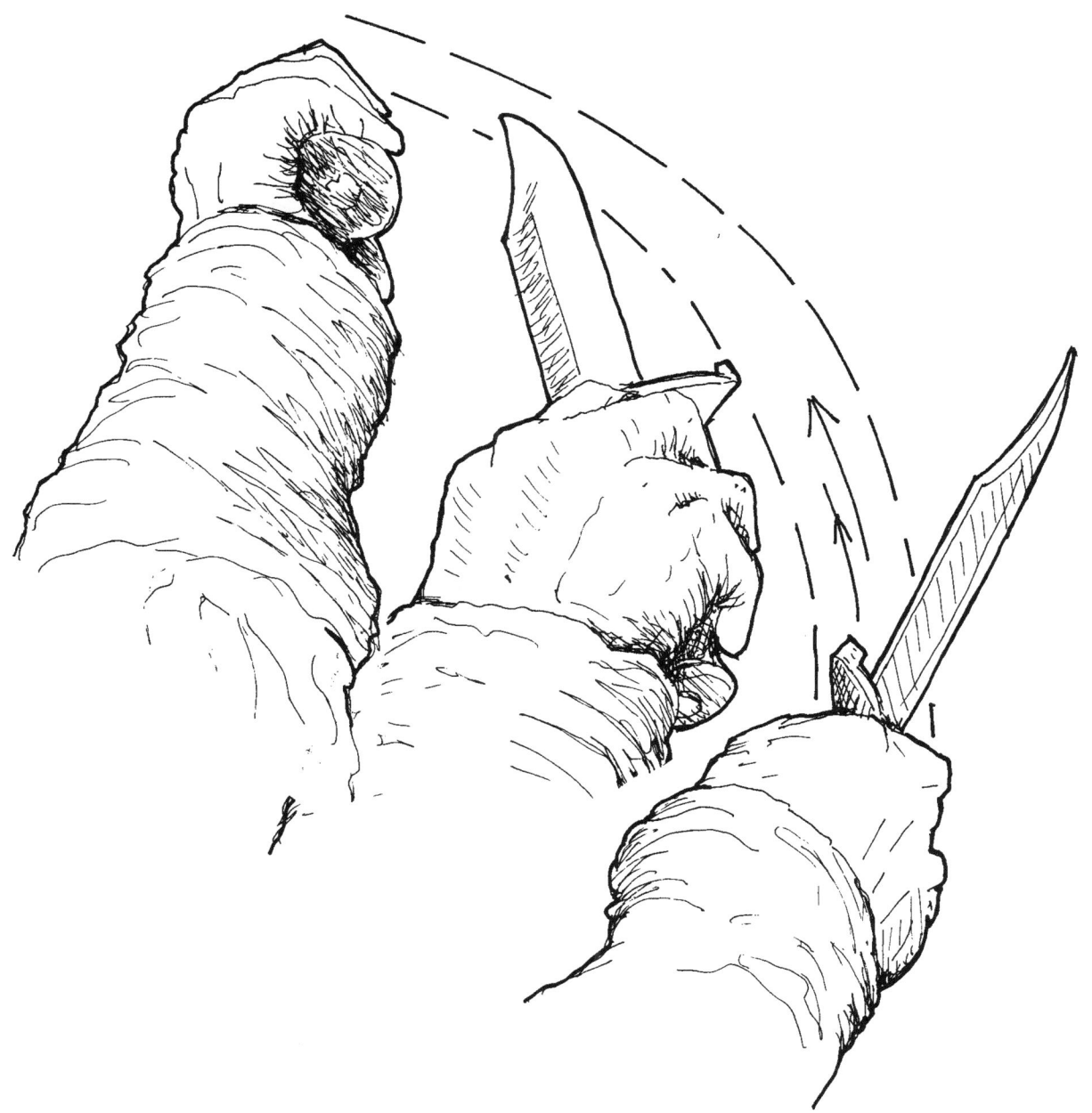

FIGURE 47. Attacker's eye view: the arching attack of the punta mandritta.

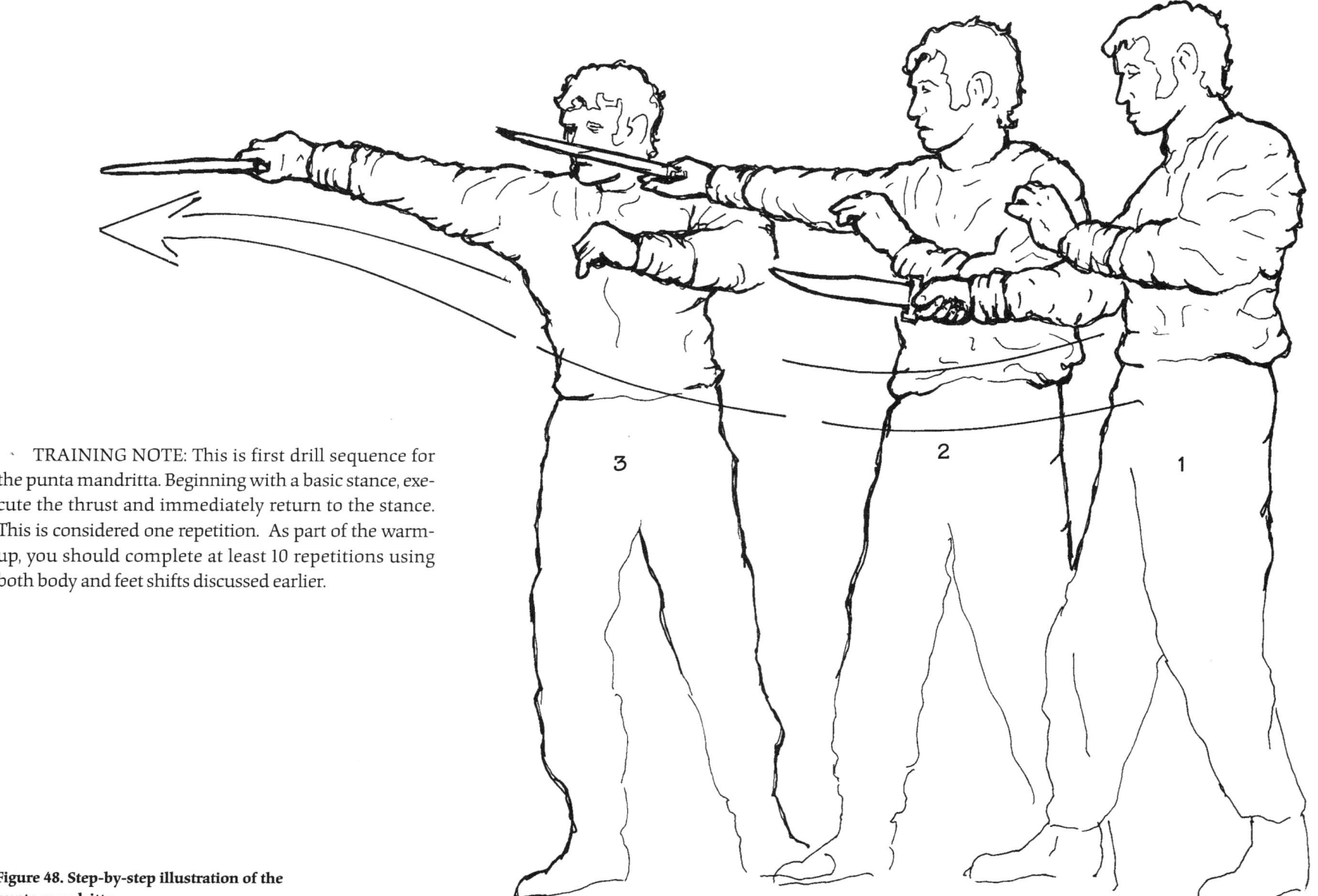

TRAINING NOTE: This is first drill sequence for the punta mandritta. Beginning with a basic stance, execute the thrust and immediately return to the stance. This is considered one repetition. As part of the warm-up, you should complete at least 10 repetitions using both body and feet shifts discussed earlier.

Figure 48. Step-by-step illustration of the punta mandritta.

PUNTA REVERSA

The *punta reversa* thrust variation takes the attack to the opponent's right, usually over his guard. This is usually used after avoiding an opponent's low thrust to the groin or legs. Like the punta mandritta, the punta reversa is a rapid, arching attack where the blade rotates approximately 45 degrees, or until the flat of the blade is horizontal with the ground. It best executed with the pivoting body action and deep passing of the left leg to the rear, as discussed in the section on the straight thrust.

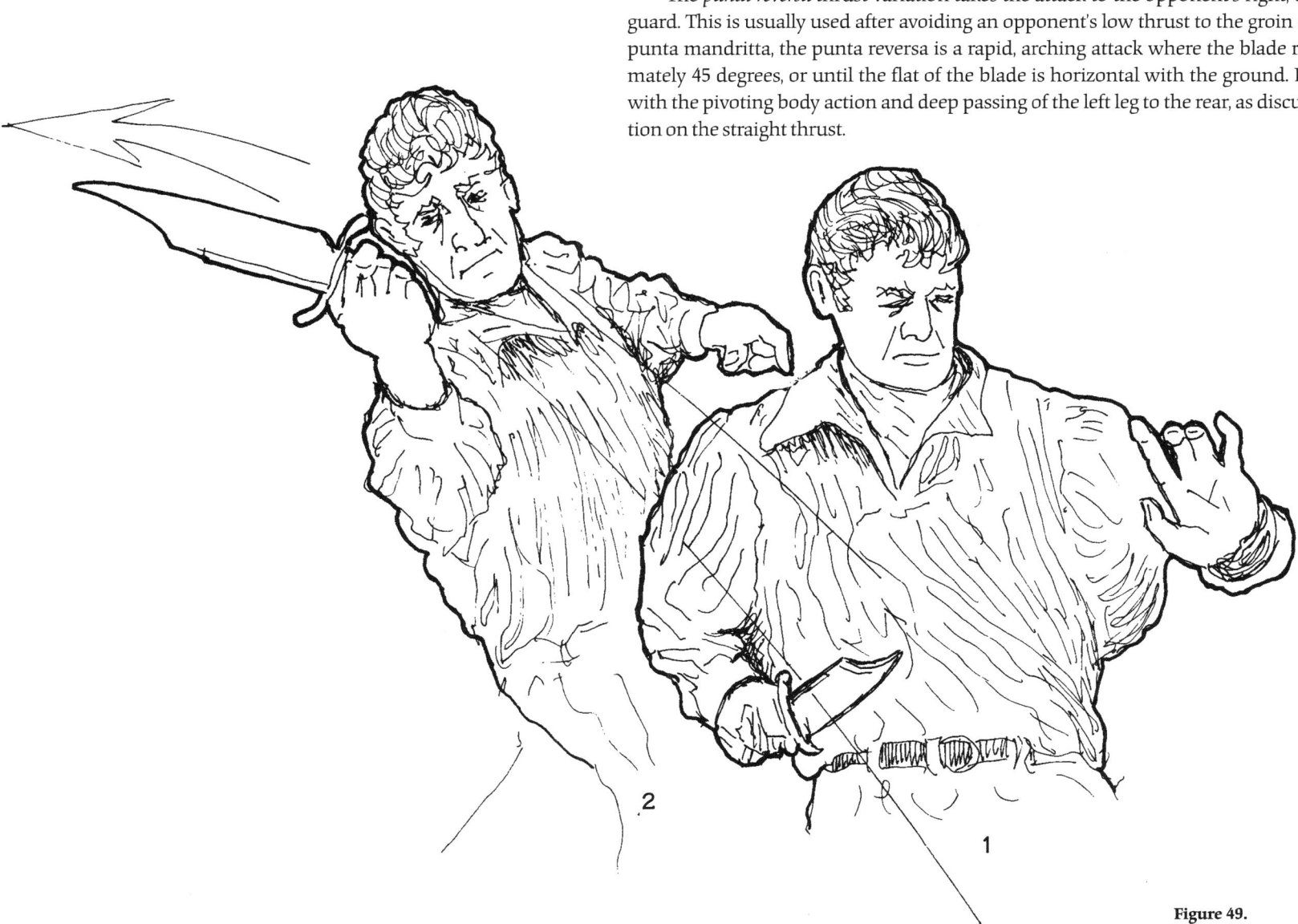

Figure 49.

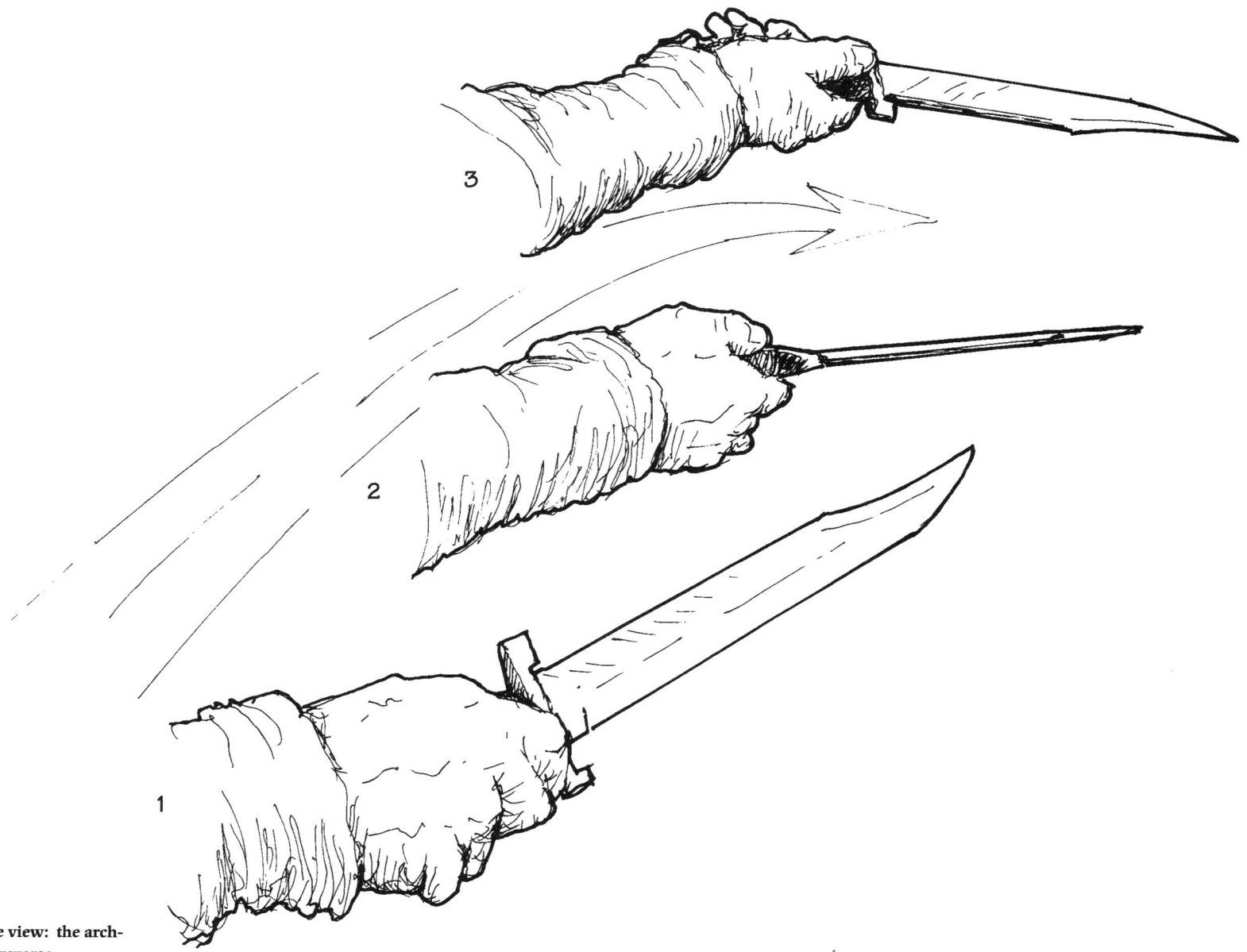

Figure 50. Attacker's eye view: the arching attack of the punta reversa.

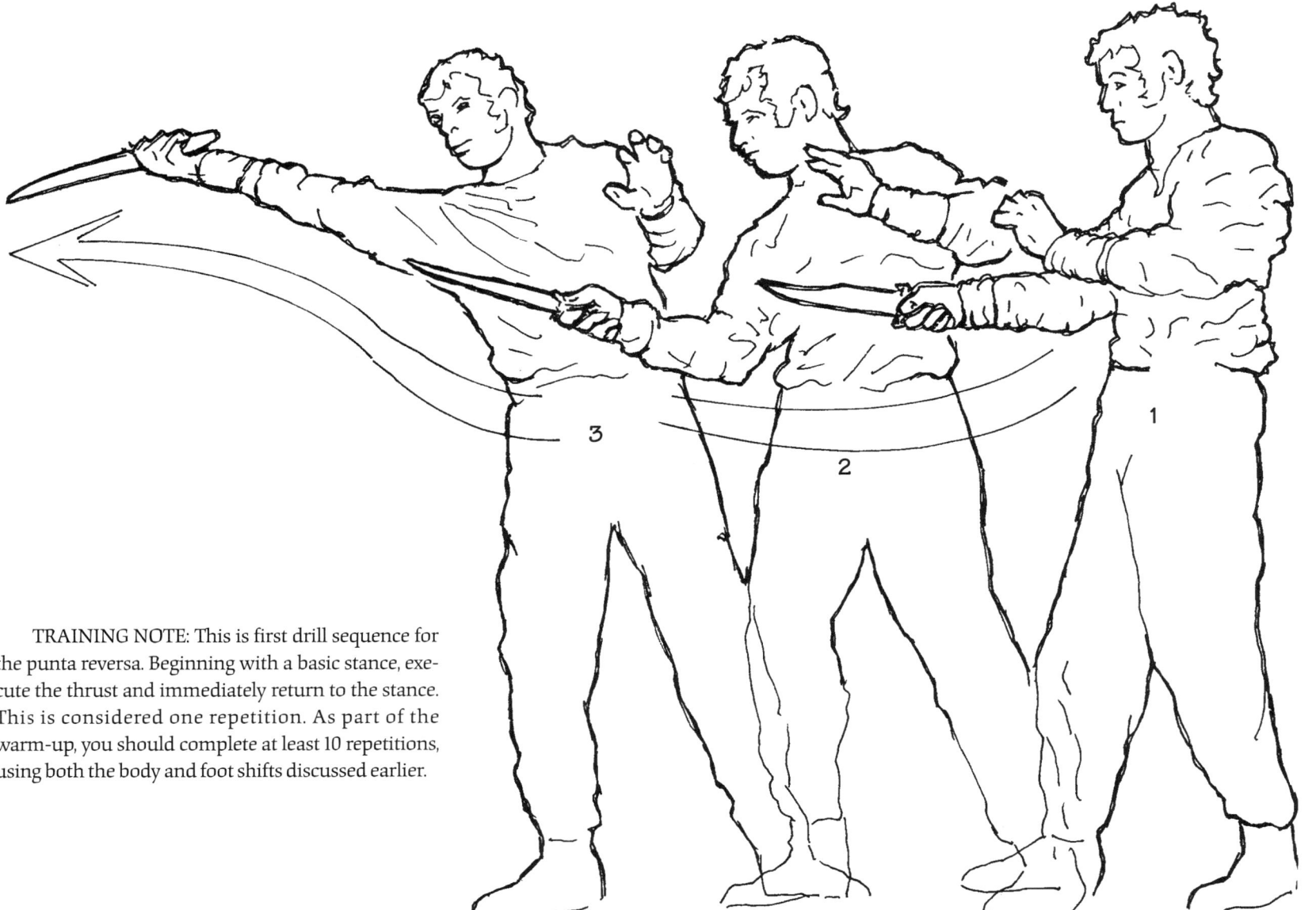

TRAINING NOTE: This is first drill sequence for the punta reversa. Beginning with a basic stance, execute the thrust and immediately return to the stance. This is considered one repetition. As part of the warm-up, you should complete at least 10 repetitions, using both the body and foot shifts discussed earlier.

Figure 51. Step-by-step illustration of the punta reversa.

REVERSE-STEP THRUST

The reverse-step thrust is an effective technique that can be used when an opponent attempts a mad rush to close. Starting with a standard strong-side-forward stance, the defender steps his forward leg to the rear while simultaneously thrusting his knife forward and achieving point.

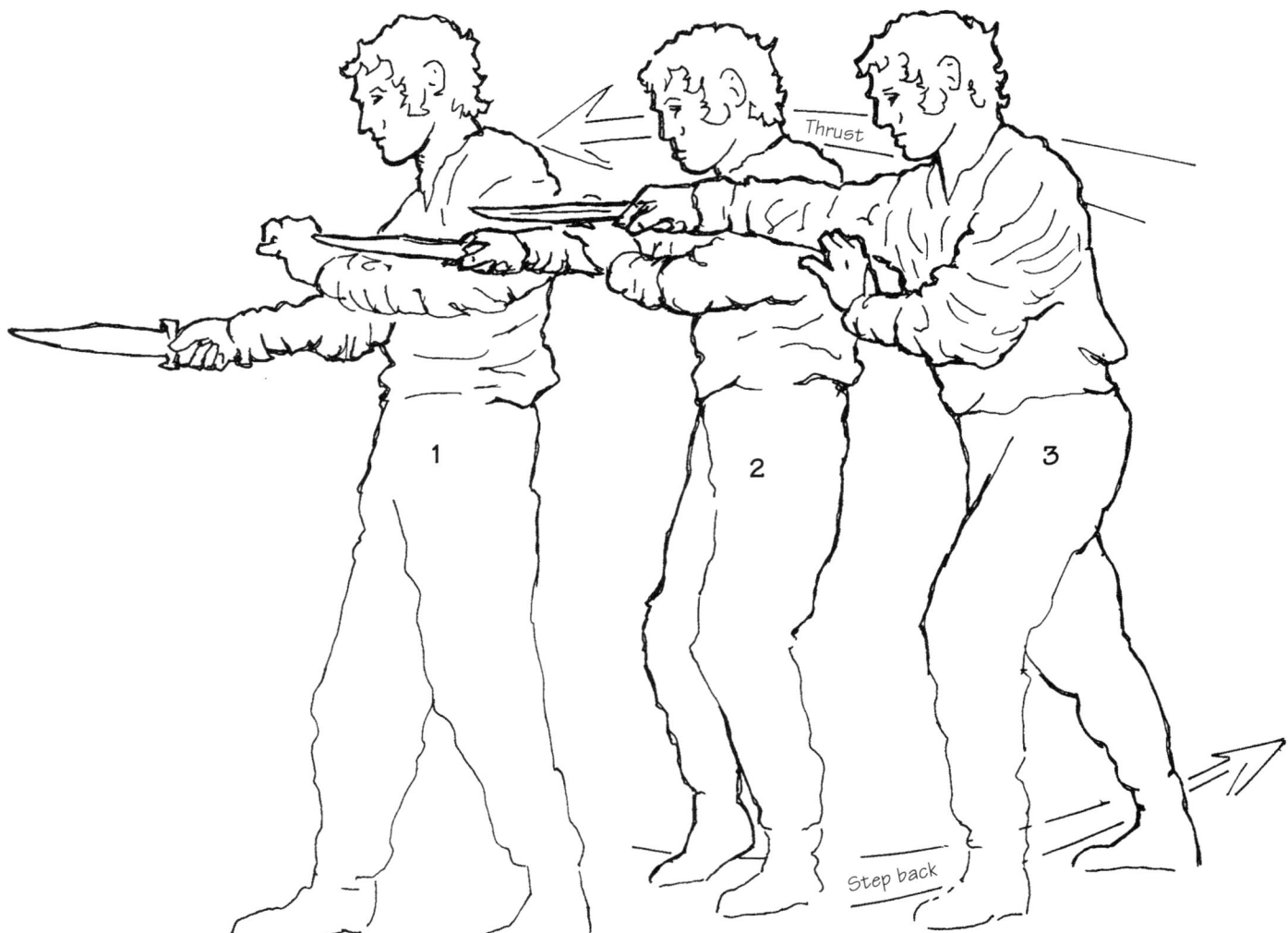

Figure 52.

MATADOR THRUST

The matador thrust is of Spanish origin and is similar to the technique of some bullfighters in going over the horns of a charging bull to deliver the kill between the shoulders. This is effective in avoiding an opponent who is attempting to cut, thrust, or grapple the legs. From a strong-side-forward stance, the fighter leaps backward, landing and bending at the waist and simultaneously thrusting forward.

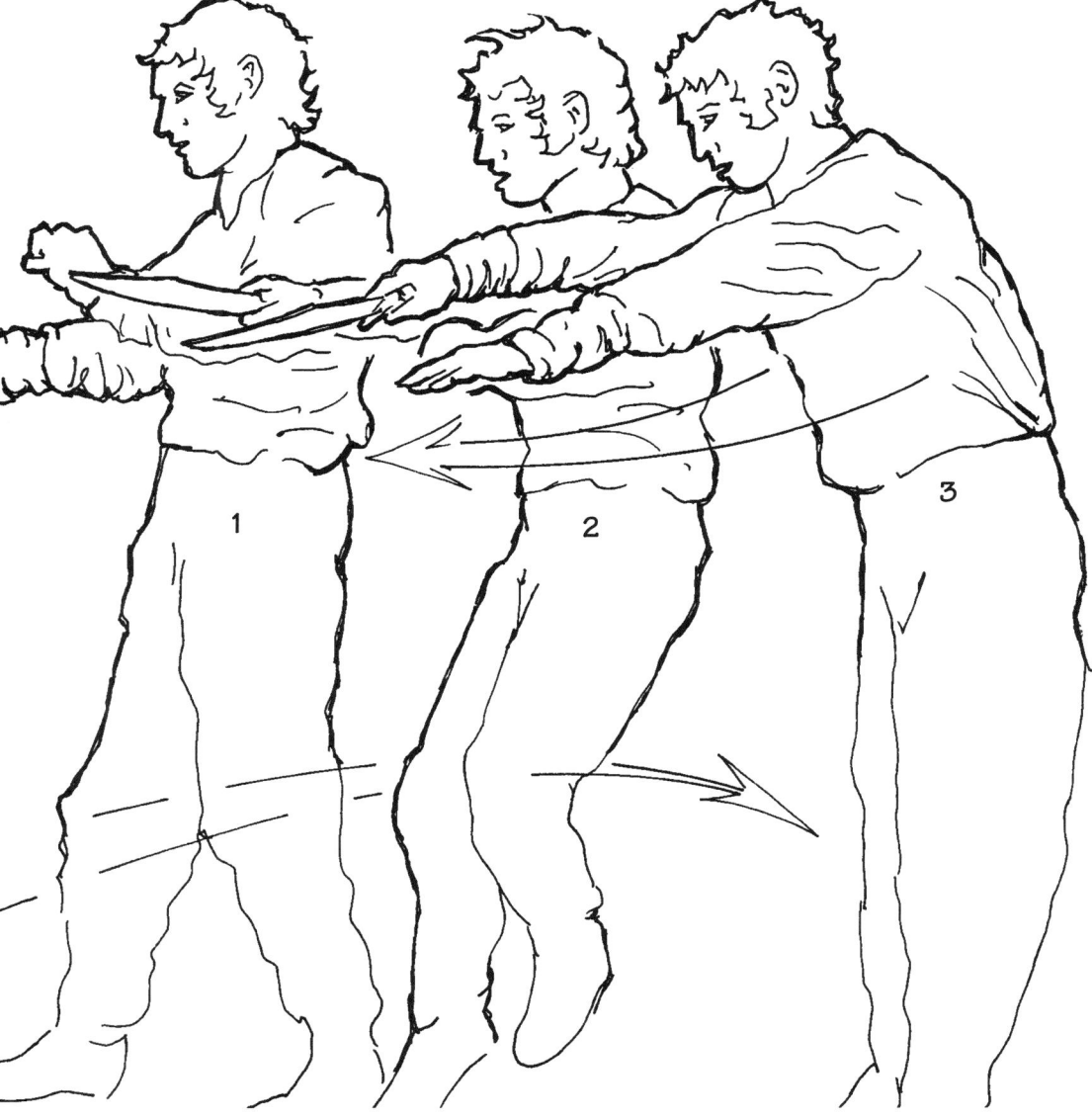

Figure 53.

PUNTA LUNGA (LUNGE)

The thrust variations that we have demonstrated so far did not involve much forward movement. The *punta lunga* does. You might say that this technique offers a means of reaching the opponent at range. In Italian rapier terminology, the *stocatta lunga* is a long-range thrusting attack that involves a forward step with the lead leg while simultaneously and dynamically pushing off with the rear foot.

The punta lunga covers ground, but it can also be executed by simply straightening the rear leg and executing a very deep extension of the weapon arm. The historical trace of this technique goes back to Marozzo's *Opera Nova* of 1536 for his cut-and-thrust system and refined in Agrippa's 1568 manual. One of the clearest examples of a typical lunge is also found in the illustrations of Ridolfo Capoferro from 1610. Figure 55 demonstrates the adaptation of the punta lunga to the big fighting knife.

Figure 54. Capoferro's classic rapier lunge.

TRAINING NOTE: This is the first drill sequence for the punta lunga. Beginning with a basic stance, execute the thrust and immediately return to the stance. That is considered one repetition. As part of the warm-up, you should complete at least 10 repetitions using both the body and feet shifts we discussed earlier.

Figure 55. Step-by-step illustration of the punta lunga.

PRIMARY TARGETS FOR THE THRUST

When looking for targets where the thrust will be most effective, you must look for those where the hydrodynamics of the human body will be most affected. To be blunt, you are looking for "the plumbing": those areas that have major blood vessels or organs. Figure 56 illustrates some of the primary targets for the thrust.

SAFETY NOTE: Under no circumstances should practice against these areas be initiated without proper protective equipment, whether using wooden, metal, or padded training weapons. Never practice strikes against these target areas using live steel. Check the section on protective equipment before conducting any training.

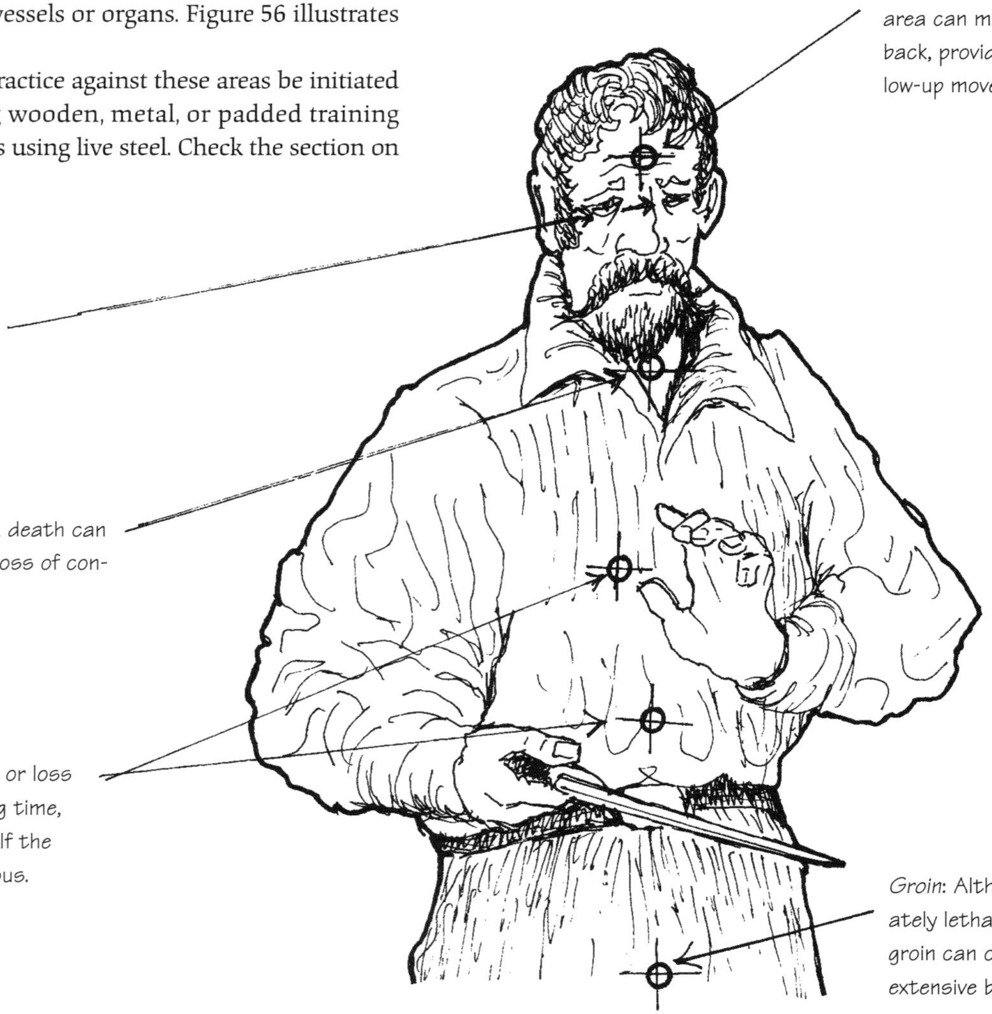

Forehead: Although not immediately lethal, a thrust to this area can make the head rock back, providing time for a follow-up movement.

The eyes: Although not immediately lethal, a thrust to the eyes can blind the opponent and limit his reaction time.

Throat: If the carotid artery is cut, death can occur within 10 or 12 seconds and loss of consciousness within 5 or 6 seconds.

Abdomen: If the stomach is hit, death or loss of consciousness can take quite a long time, depending on the depth of the wound. If the heart is hit, death can be instantaneous.

Groin: Although not immediately lethal, a thrust to the groin can cause shock and extensive bleeding.

Figure 56.

KNIFE-FIGHTING CONCEPT A:
THE TARGET AREAS

Now that we have finished with the basics of the grip, stance, and thrust, it is time to introduce some of the concepts that tie all of the fundamentals together. Concept A addresses the three areas into which both cuts and thrusts can be delivered. You must also think of these areas in terms of your opponent's being able to attack into the same area.

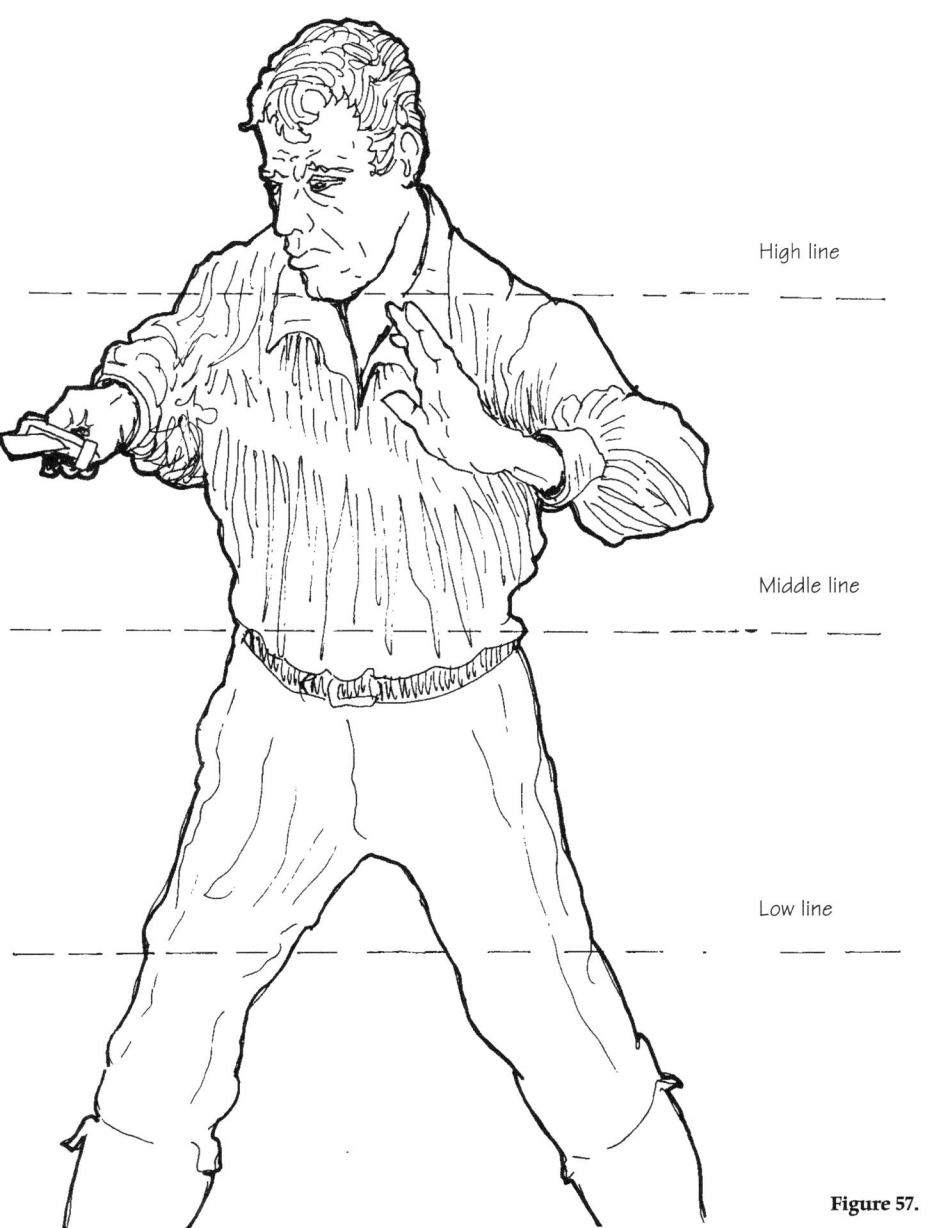

High line

Middle line

Low line

Figure 57.

TRAINING NOTE: The following series of illustrations depicts a fundamental thrust drill that can be performed solo in front of a mirror, on a target, or with a partner who executes a parry against the respective thrusts. The sequence begins with the fighter doing a straight thrust and then pulling back into a low guard. From the low guard the fighter executes a punta mandritta and then shifts back to the low guard. He follows with a punta reversa. The thrusts in this series are directed into the high-line area, but your training should also include the mid- and low-line areas. The key to this exercise is to make all of the thrusts flow from one engagement to the next. As the thrusts are made, the lead leg shifts forward and back.

Figure 58.

Thrust Flow Drill Action #1

Straight thrust

Approximate foot position

2

1

Figure 59.

Thrust Flow Drill Action #2

Approximate foot position

Figure 60.

Thrust Flow Drill Action #3

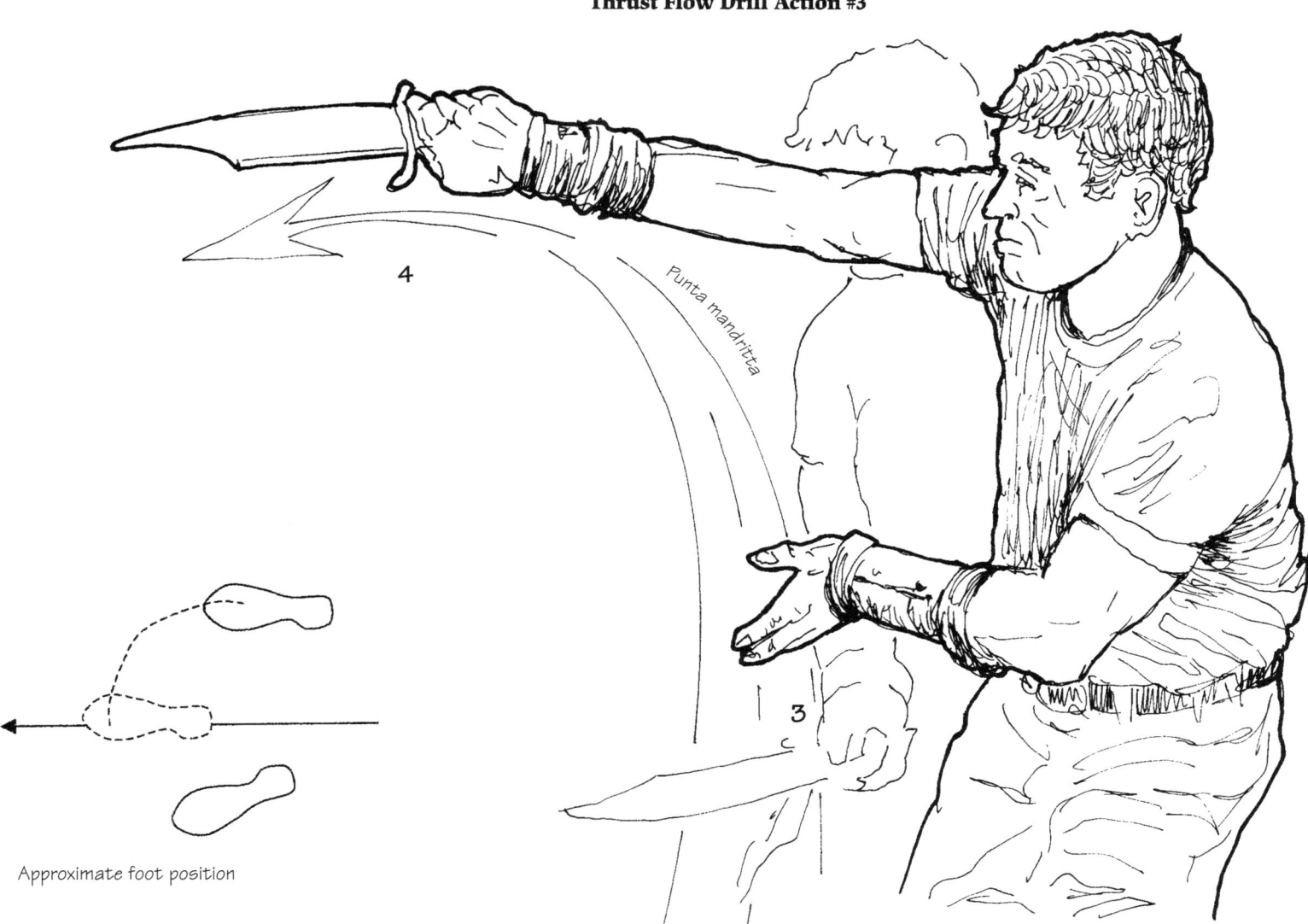

4

Punta mandritta

3

Approximate foot position

Figure 61.

Thrust Flow Drill Action #4

Approximate foot position

Figure 62.

Thrust Flow Drill Action # 5

6

Punta reversa

5

Approximate foot position

Figure 63.

KNIFE FIGHTING CONCEPT B: TIMETABLE FOR DEATH

Col. W.E. Fairbairn is known as one of the fathers of close-quarter combat. In *Get Tough*, he made an important contribution to knife fighting by adding training in the identification of those body areas vulnerable to the knife attack. He advocated six target areas: brachial artery, carotid artery, subclavian artery, radial artery, heart, and stomach. Figures 64 and 65 show Fairbairn's depiction of these target areas and the time frame between injury and unconsciousness or death. Although medical technological advances have since revealed that the data on these tables is inaccurate (nor do the figures account for the shock that occurs from severed tendons, ligaments, and nerves), the information serves as a good beginning point for relating anatomy to the science of the blade.

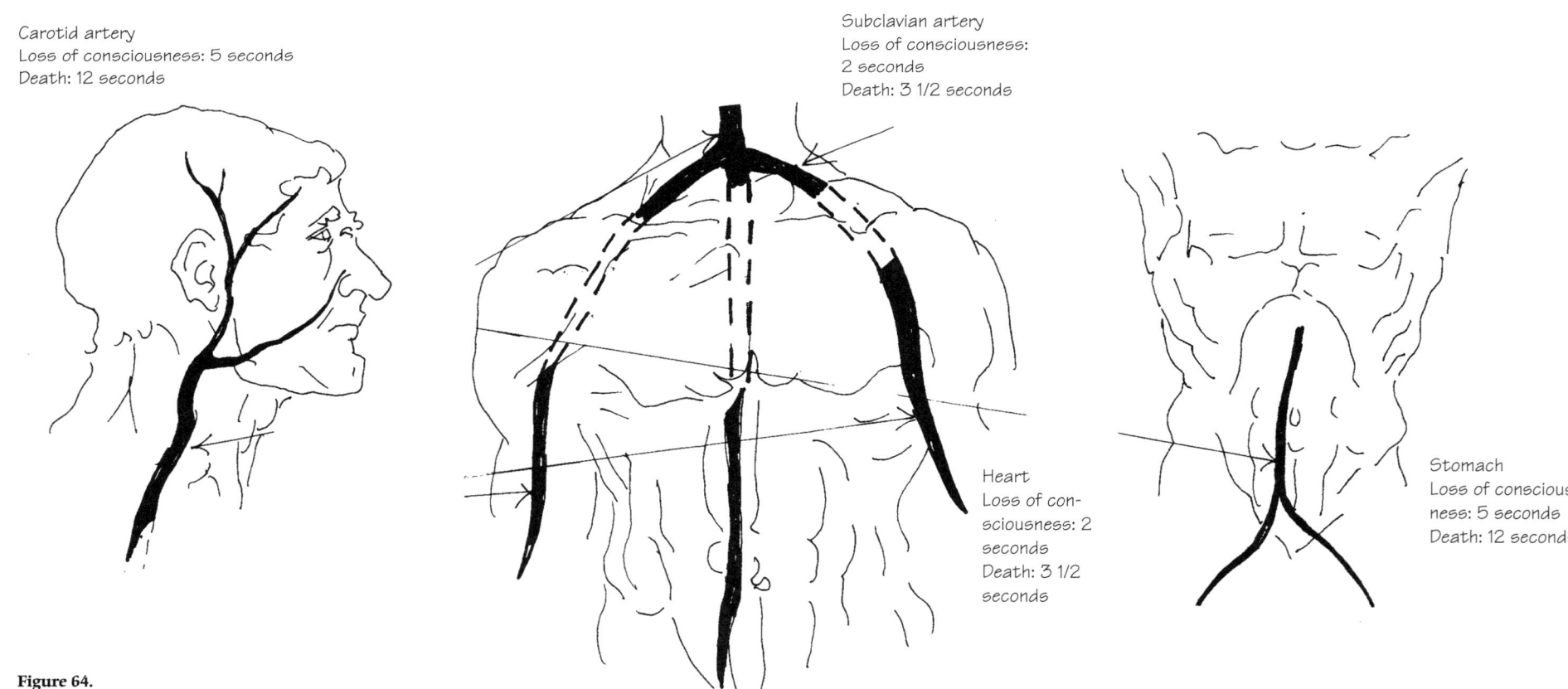

Carotid artery
Loss of consciousness: 5 seconds
Death: 12 seconds

Subclavian artery
Loss of consciousness:
2 seconds
Death: 3 1/2 seconds

Heart
Loss of consciousness: 2 seconds
Death: 3 1/2 seconds

Stomach
Loss of consciousness: 5 seconds
Death: 12 seconds

Figure 64.

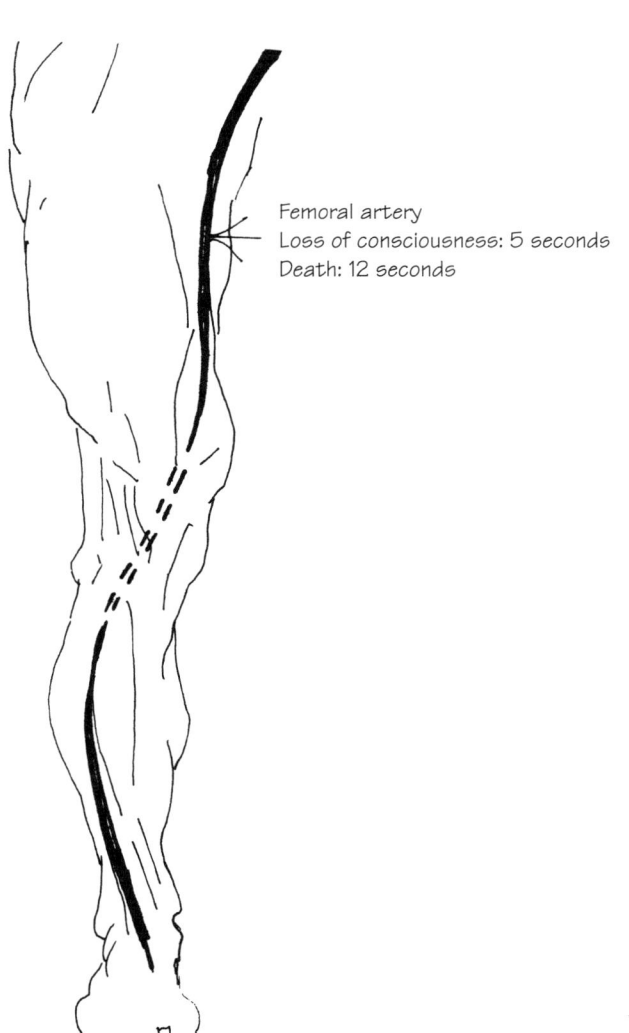

Femoral artery
Loss of consciousness: 5 seconds
Death: 12 seconds

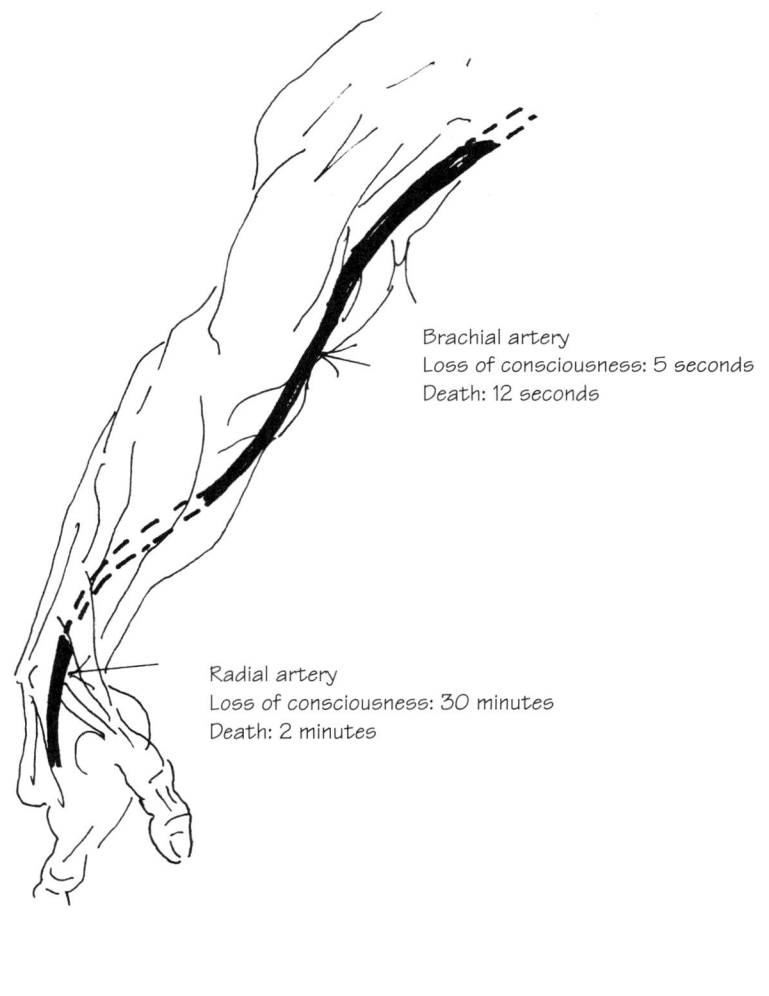

Brachial artery
Loss of consciousness: 5 seconds
Death: 12 seconds

Radial artery
Loss of consciousness: 30 minutes
Death: 2 minutes

Figure 65.

SECTION THREE: THE CUT

To introduce the cut let's look again at what our expert Bill McConnell says in his paper "The Cut & Thrust of Blade Combat":

> Forget about trying to cut someone with a light civilian sword. However, if you do have a military-weight blade, you are better off hacking than poking for the most part.
>
> Although a cut is less likely to kill outright, your chances of doing enough mechanical damage to render the opponent harmless are pretty good. Cuts to the hands, arms, elbows, or shoulders can finish a fight outright. The opponent might now be dead, but if they can't hold a sword, they can't fight. Cuts to the chest and abdomen are more likely to be superficial (and painful) unless you have a heavy (and sharp) blade. Cuts to the thigh, knee, and lower leg reduce mobility and also limit the opponent's ability to continue the engagement. For swift death, blows to the head and neck are the obvious choice. Those carrying heavier, sharper blades may opt for cutting an opponent in two maneuvers, but this is probably best reserved for executions, not duels. You may well get poked a few times in your wind-up anyway.
>
> That a cut is much slower than a thrust can be argued to hell and back. Of course a lighter weapon can be moved faster, but in a cut or thrust invariably the hand is moved through the same distance, and so the execution is similar in time for each maneuver. Also it must be pointed out that since most combat begins with opponents a step or so out of range with each other, the blow can never be faster than the step into combat anyway. This is what George Silver calls the time of the foot. It might be worth noting here that most people's reaction time (when a decision needs to be made) is rarely better than about half a second. A sword blow (cut or thrust) can often be delivered well under half a second. If two opponents are already in range of each other each other, then the first to deliver a blow will most likely succeed. Mr. Silver makes reference to this in saying that the hand is quicker than the eye.

CUTTING TECHNIQUES

There are essentially three cutting techniques applicable to the Bowie and big knives: the cut (slash), snipe (hack), and classic back cut.

Cut

In *The Knife Fighting Encyclopedia*, World Black Belt Hall of Fame member W. Hock Hochheim provides an excellent, though simplistic description of this technique.

> You strike across and through the target, raking or drawing the blade. Try to imagine an apple hanging from a string. Try to slash through the apple without the apple moving.

> Once you have engaged the target, don't allow the blade to drop too far beyond the target.

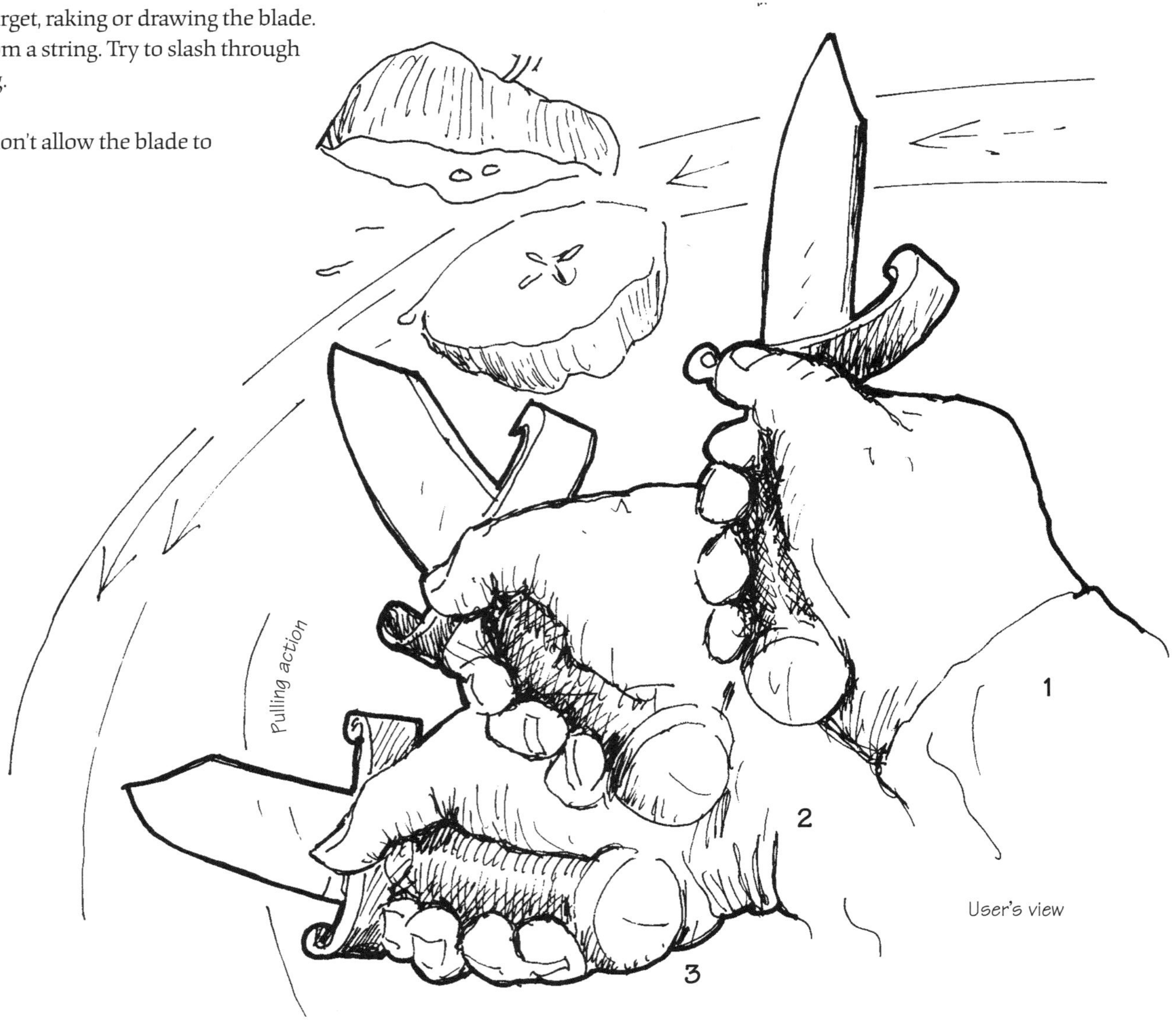

Pulling action

1

2

3

User's view

Figure 66.

Figure 67 provides a side view of a more expansive version of the cut. Here it is proceeded by an upward clearing (or blocking) action, where the wrist rotates over into a descending cut through the target and across the body of the opponent.

Figure 67.

Snipe (Hack)

The snipe is delivered with a powerful, chopping-like motion similar to the techniques used with a battle ax or tomahawk. The massive Bowie blades with a clipped point deliver stunning blows that can cripple a hand or split a skull.

The snipe is executed with a powerful forward push with the point held high. As the blade nears the target area, the point is violently snapped down with a slight rearward pull. Legend has the snipe as a classic Bowie technique.

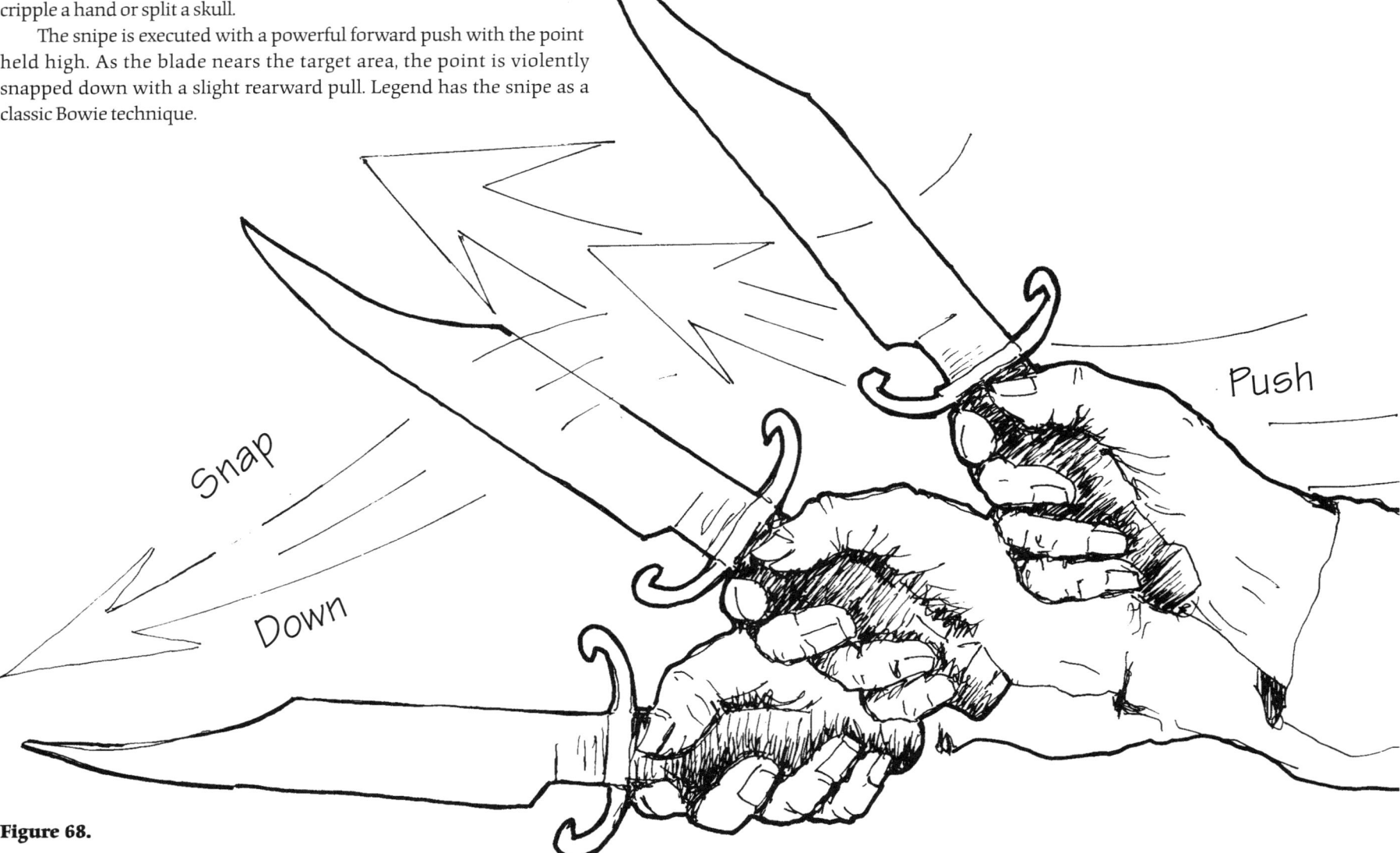

Figure 68.

Figure 69. Frontal view of the snipe being thrown from the arm in chamber. Note that this technique involves a push followed by a snap of the wrist, with the blade striking slightly before the point.

Back Cut

Whether historically accurate or not, the term back cut has come to be associated with the Bowie knife. In his 1949 book, *The Bowie Knife*, Raymond Thorpe, without using the term, painted a word picture of the back cut that he had gained from researching the numerous recorded knife fights of the 1800s: "The knife is usually held sidewise in the hand, the thumb alongside the blade just beyond the guard. The fighter is now in position to deliver a slashing, sidewise blow or a ripping uppercut."

It is interesting to note that Thorpe is describing the foil grip, which permits one of the more efficient applications of this technique. For generations the back cut technique was thought to be uniquely American and associated with the Bowie knife. The reality is that it was originally practiced with both Renaissance cut-and-thrust war swords and backswords. Similar applications are also seen in some of the European saber manuals of the 1800s. A good example is found in Joseph Swetnam's 1617 treatise, *The Schoole of the Noble and Worthy Science of Defence*:

> Thy enemie lying in this guard, soddenly plucke in the pummell of thy sword to thy breast, and with all turne thy knuckles inward and the present lie proffer a thrust towards thy enemies breast, but turne it over with a blow to his right eare, with the which blow thou maist hit a god plaier, if he bee not aware of it before hand, for hee must bare his sword against the thrust for the defense thereof, now if he do over carrie him never so little further then he ought to doe for his true defence, then hee cannot bring him back time enough to defend the blow you have hit him, as beforesaid.

The weapon Swetnam is referring to is the backsword ("back swerd"). This was a single-edged Renaissance battle sword of the cut-and-thrust variety. There were many variations made of these weapons. Some, like the Bowie, had a false or real edge running for about 7 inches from the point. The technique Swetnam describes could also be applied to most of the double-edged cut-and-thrust swords of the time.

The Midline Back Cut

The midline back cut is performed in a quick "snap-like" motion against a thrust to the torso or a snipe to the hand. This is a very tight movement in a small arc that is the foundation motion for all other back cut aspects. The back cut depicted in Figure 70 is delivered while the fighter simultaneously shifts the body outside the zone of attack. It begins with a rotation of the wrist in a tight 180-degree arc to present the back edge. Simultaneously, he raises his elbow as the hand pulls the back edge into the opponent's wrist or arm. Remember, this is a pulling action, not a fanning motion.

Figure 70.

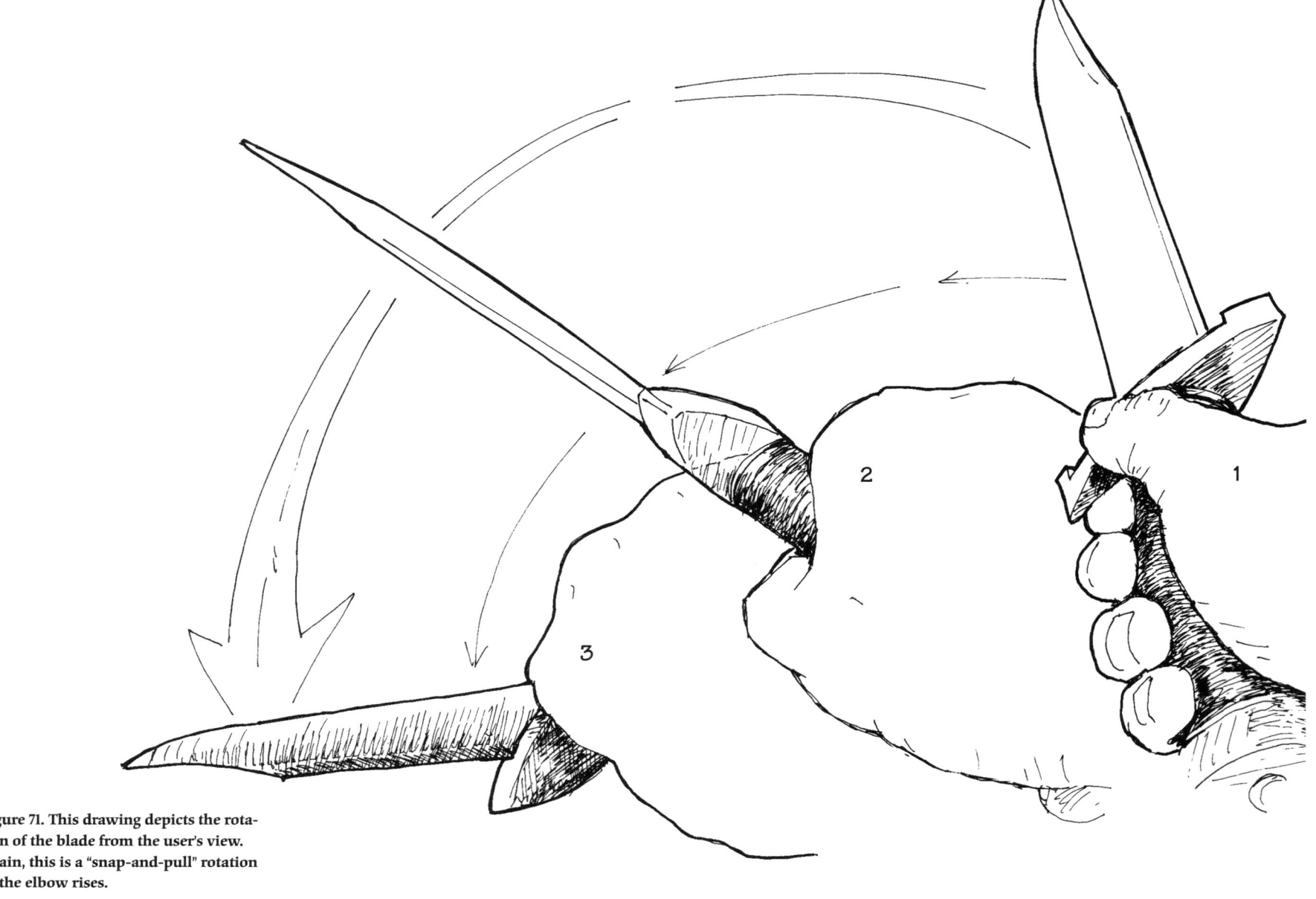

Figure 71. This drawing depicts the rotation of the blade from the user's view. Again, this is a "snap-and-pull" rotation as the elbow rises.

The High-Line Back Cut

The high-line back cut is performed with the same quick, "snap-like" motion as the mid-line back cut. The target here is the temple or the throat. This wrist movement is not as tight and is primarily offensive in its application. The back cut shown in Figure 72 is delivered while the fighter simultaneously shifts his body outside the zone of attack. It begins with a slight lifting of the wrist and pulling of the back edge into the target area. In application it is very similar to the punta mandritta except that the wrist is leading and pulling the edge instead of pushing the point.

Figure 72.

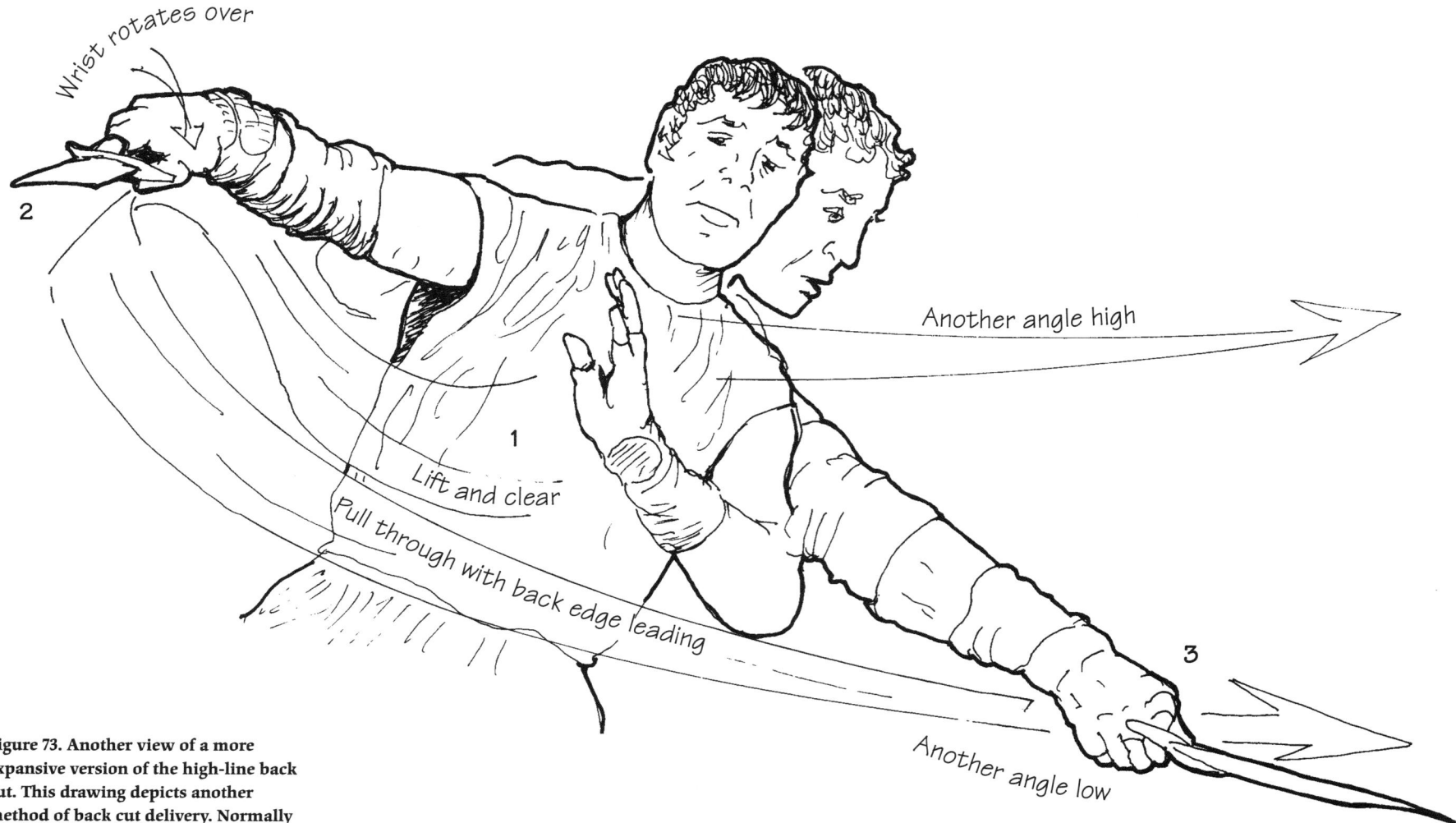

Wrist rotates over

2

Another angle high

1

Lift and clear

Pull through with back edge leading

3

Another angle low

Figure 73. Another view of a more expansive version of the high-line back cut. This drawing depicts another method of back cut delivery. Normally this wide swinging action is performed when outside the opponent's guard or weapon arm. Targets can be the temple, throat, arm, or back of the leg. It is executed in the same manner as the one previously shown except that the arm is extended more.

The Low-Line Back Cut

Figure 74 depicts the low-line method of back cut delivery. This can be a tight pulling motion with the blade held close to the body or a wide expansive action with the arm extended. This back cut is usually performed with a rolling motion of the wrist rather than the overhand snap we saw with the high-line version. Rather than lifting the elbow the point of the weapon is dropped slightly, and the hand rolls up with a pulling action. The back edge is dragged across the body into the target areas of the torso or hand.

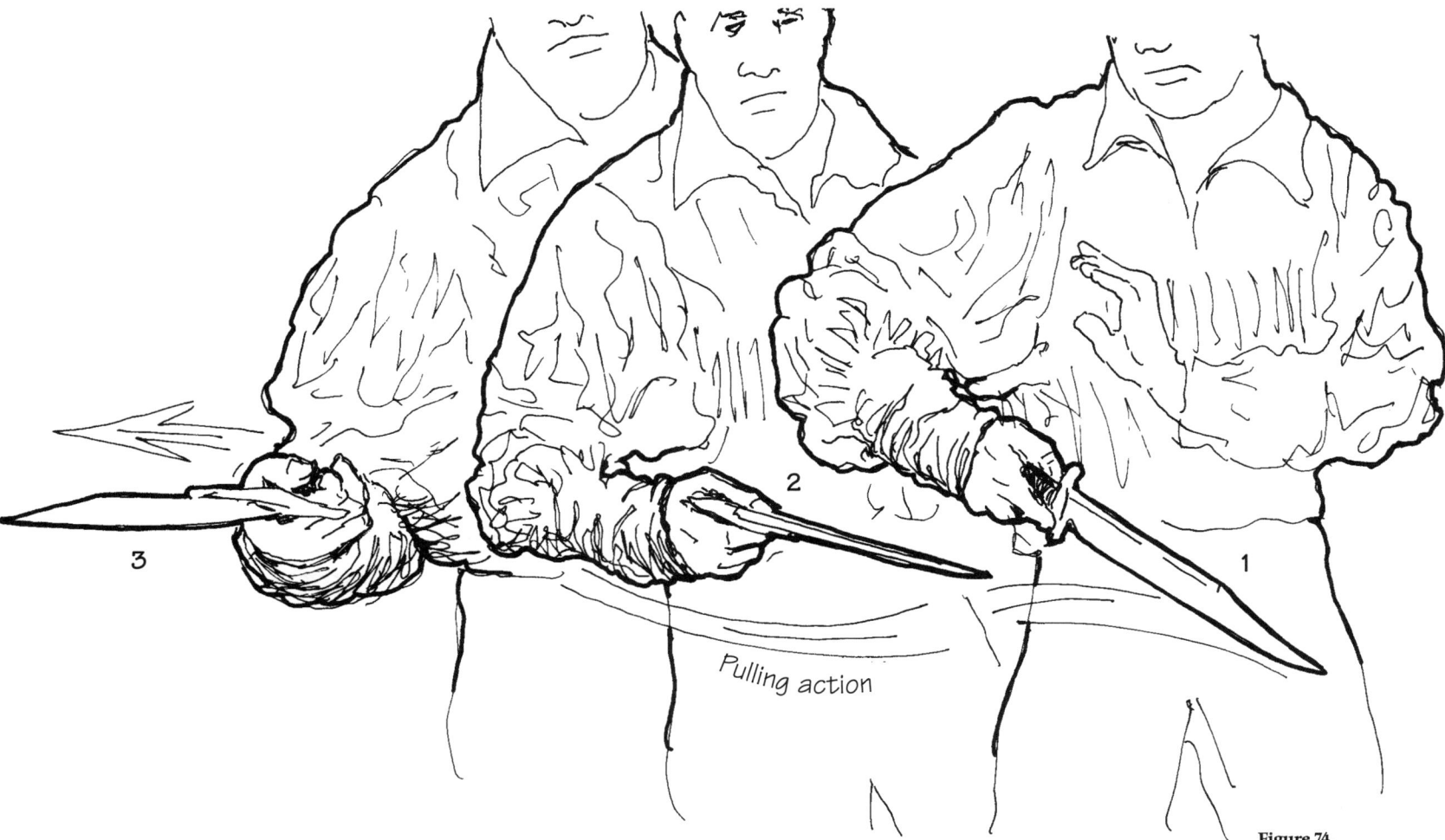

Figure 74.

Figure 75. A side view of this back cut. (Later I will examine this same technique used as a protective parry to set up a counterattack.) NOTE: For identification purposes, I have labeled the back cut depicted as high and low. In actuality, these are far more flexible in use against a variety of targets within the window of combat.

APPLICATION OF THE CUT

Before looking at some drills for the application of cutting techniques, we need to review another of the enduring knife fighting concepts essential to acquiring any degree of skill: the window of combat.

KNIFE FIGHTING CONCEPT C: WINDOW OF COMBAT

Figure 76 shows what the American Fighting Congress refers to as the *window of combat*. This is an imaginary rectangle roughly bounded by the shoulders and hips of the fighter and his opponent. Some of the Renaissance masters of defense defined this concept as a circle that contained the opponent's vulnerable points. On the dark side, this is also the area from which your opponent can fire both accurate thrusts and cuts at you.

When you are inside the box or window, you must be aware that you have to "deal with the steel" by parry or feint to obtain an attack opening inside the window. Inside this window you are exposed to attacks from left, right, above, and below.

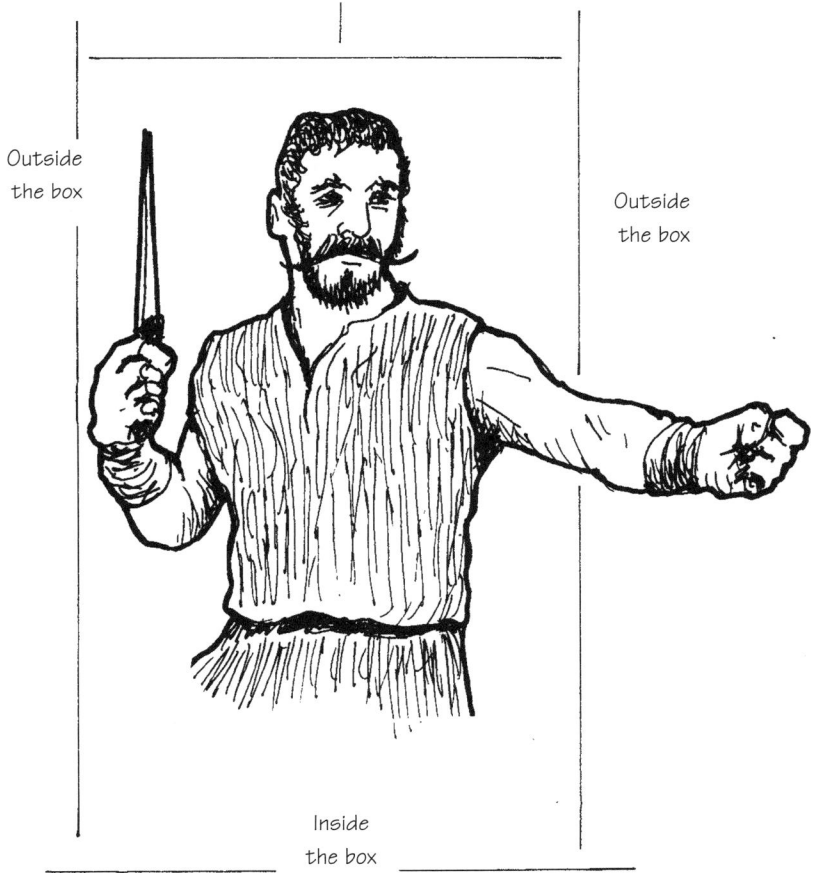

Outside the box

Outside the box

Inside the box

Figure 76.

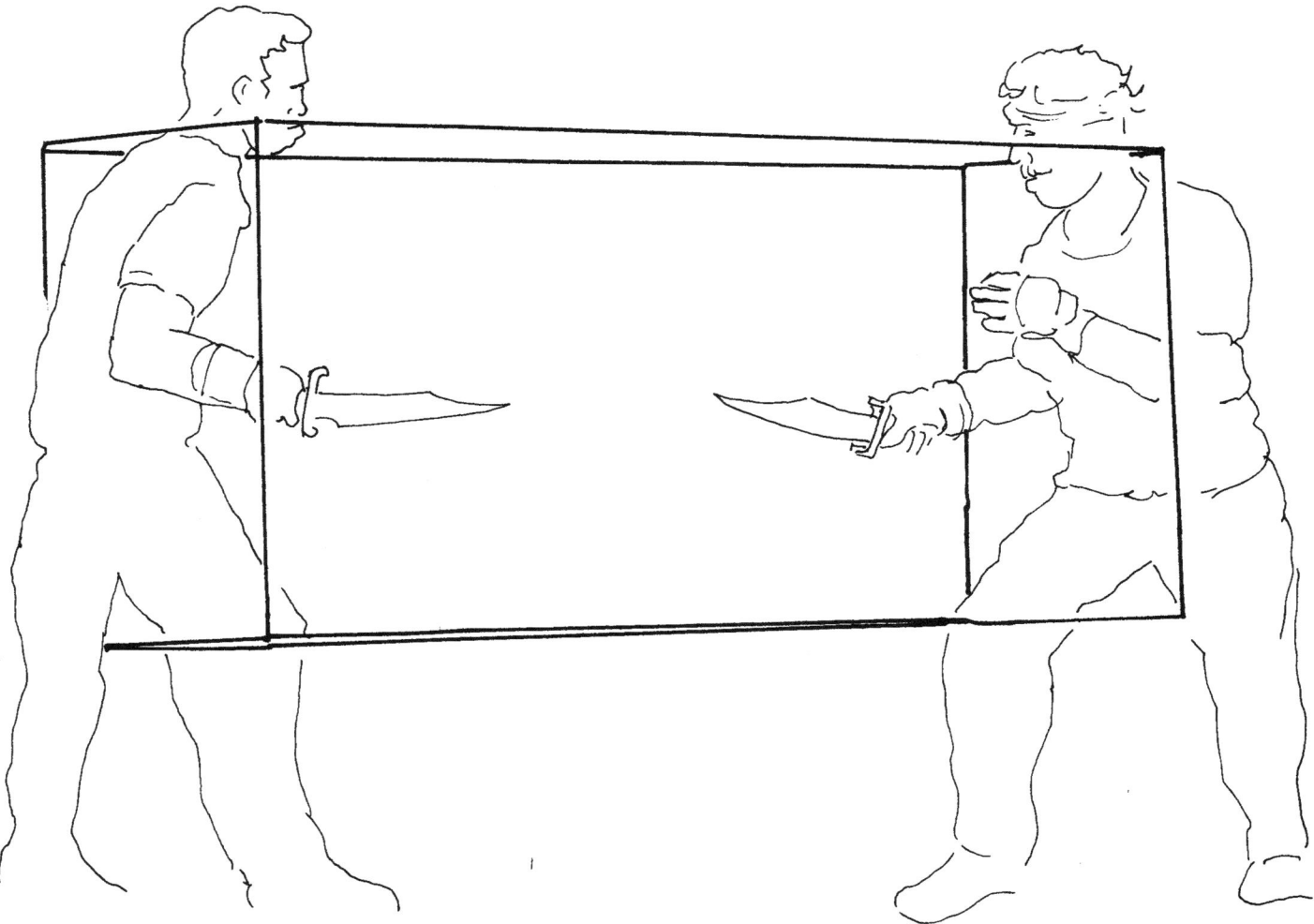

Figure 77. Here is another look at the application of the window of combat, or the principle of inside and outside the box. Both fighters are inside the box in this diagram.

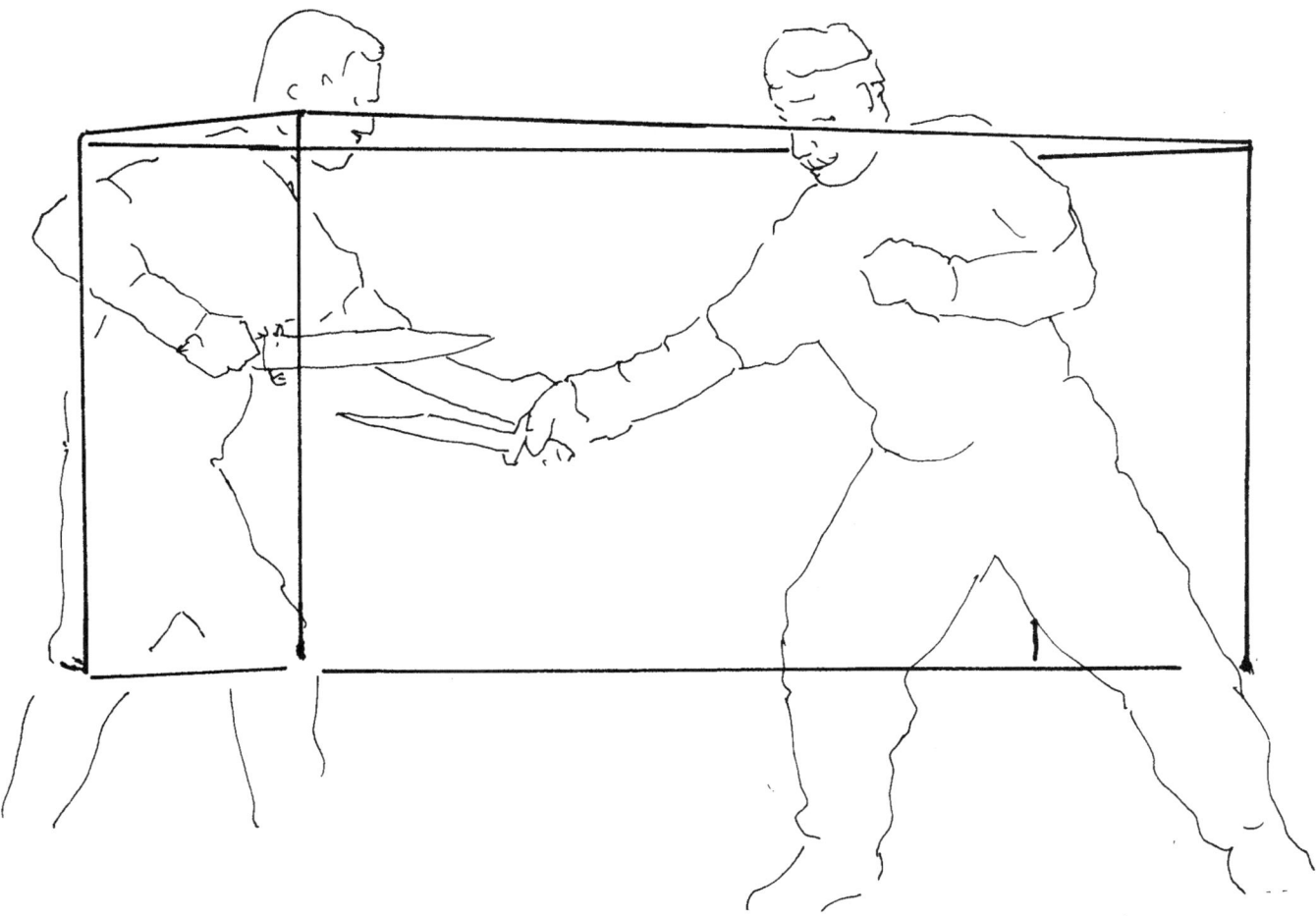

Figure 78. In this drawing a fighter has passed his opponent's thrust to the inside and stepped to the left. From this position (outside the box) the attacks can be delivered without interference from the opponent's left hand.

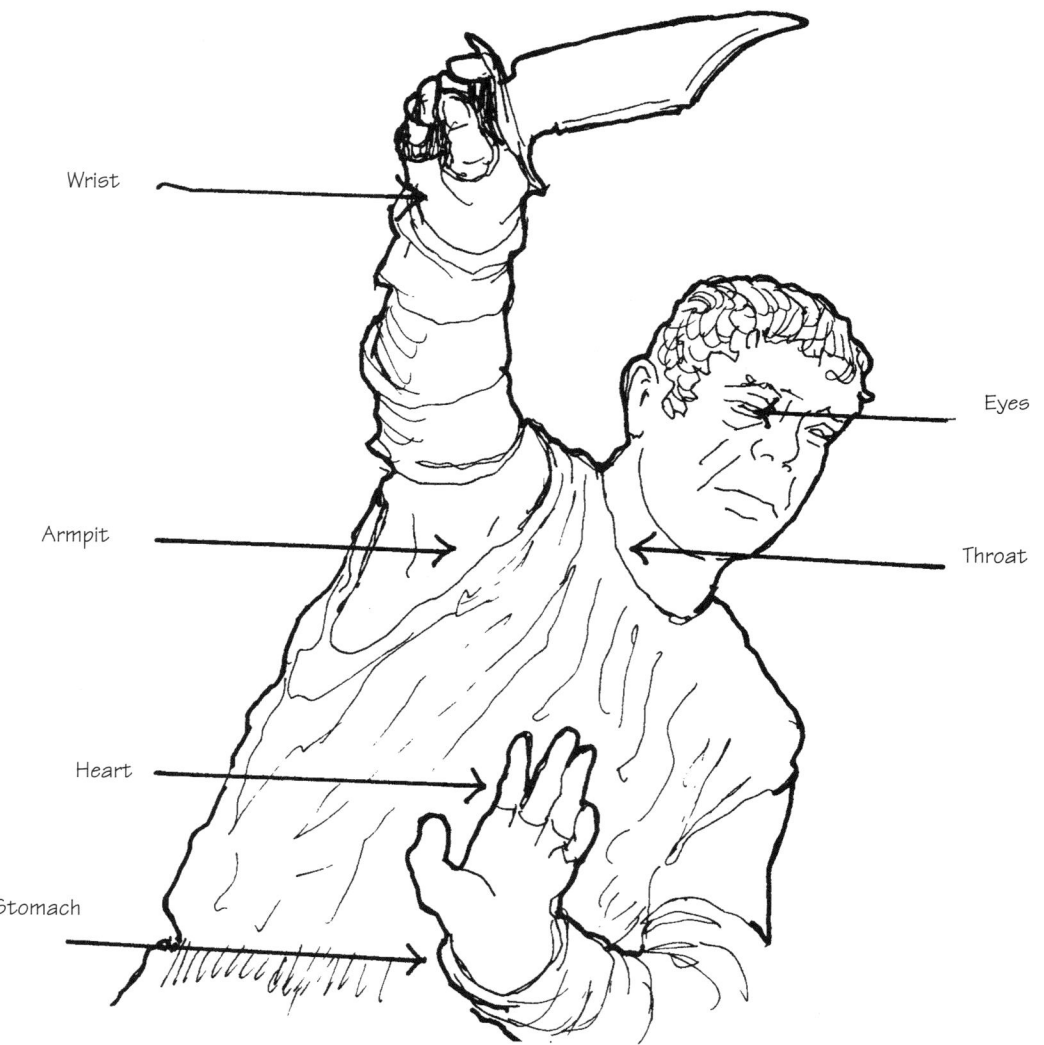

Wrist

Eyes

Armpit

Throat

Heart

Stomach

Figure 79. Here we view the target opportunities from inside the box. Our opponent is executing a punta mandritta. While his weapon hand is our primary concern, we must be aware that the left hand can come into play by striking, blocking vision, or attacking with another weapon from this position. Our opponent may also use kicks. Note the target areas as labeled.

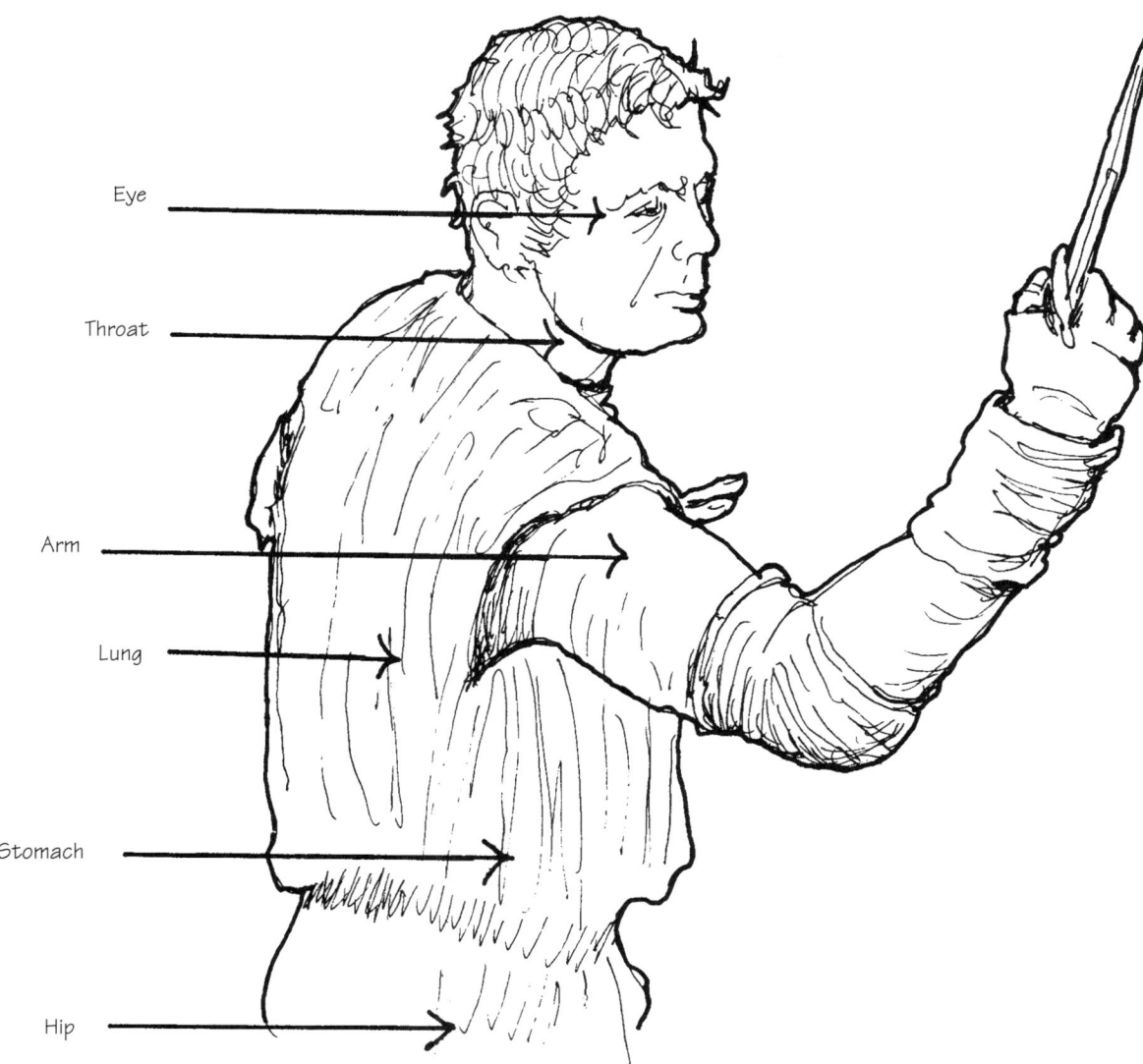

Eye

Throat

Arm

Lung

Stomach

Hip

Figure 80. In this outside-the-box view, our opponent is executing a punta reversa. Note that from this position the left, or back-up, hand cannot be immediately brought into play to attack, yet the same target areas are available to our attack. Maybe this is the position to be in.

KNIFE FIGHTING CONCEPT D: ANGLES OF ATTACK

Through the ages weapons instruction has been based on the use of a series of angles of attack as the starting point for communicating proper cutting techniques (associated target areas) to the student.

- In 1536 Achille Marozzo used large wall figures that identified the angles by specific terms.
- Joachim Meyer in 1570 depicted these angles alphabetically on a large, framed wooden board. There is evidence of use of these angles throughout the European continent from the 1400s to the 1600s. The saber manuals from the 1700s and 1800s contained similar angles.
- Some historians contend that the masters of the fencing (dueling) schools of Old New Orleans, who had basic European training backgrounds, continued this tradition and applied it not only to sword training but also to the Bowie and dagger training they taught.
- Today, we see these similar angles used in the Filipino martial arts. This influence can be traced back to the Spanish occupation of the Philippines.

Figure 81. This drawing shows Joachim Meyer's cutting-angle board being used as a thrust target.

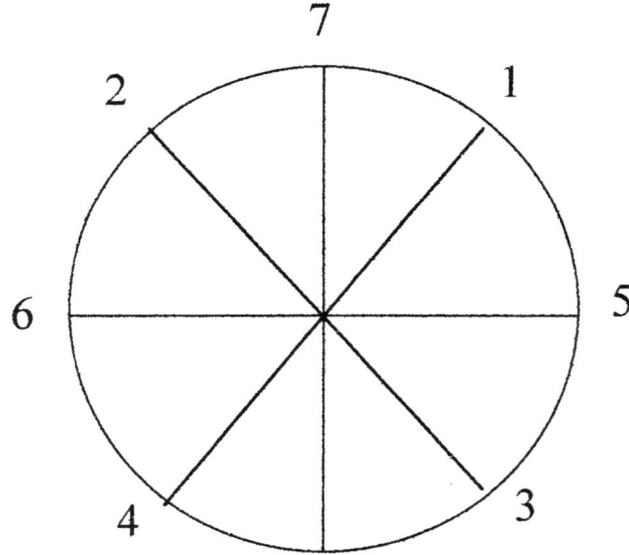

Figure 82. Angles from 1821 *Light and Horse Artillery Saber Exercise Manual.*

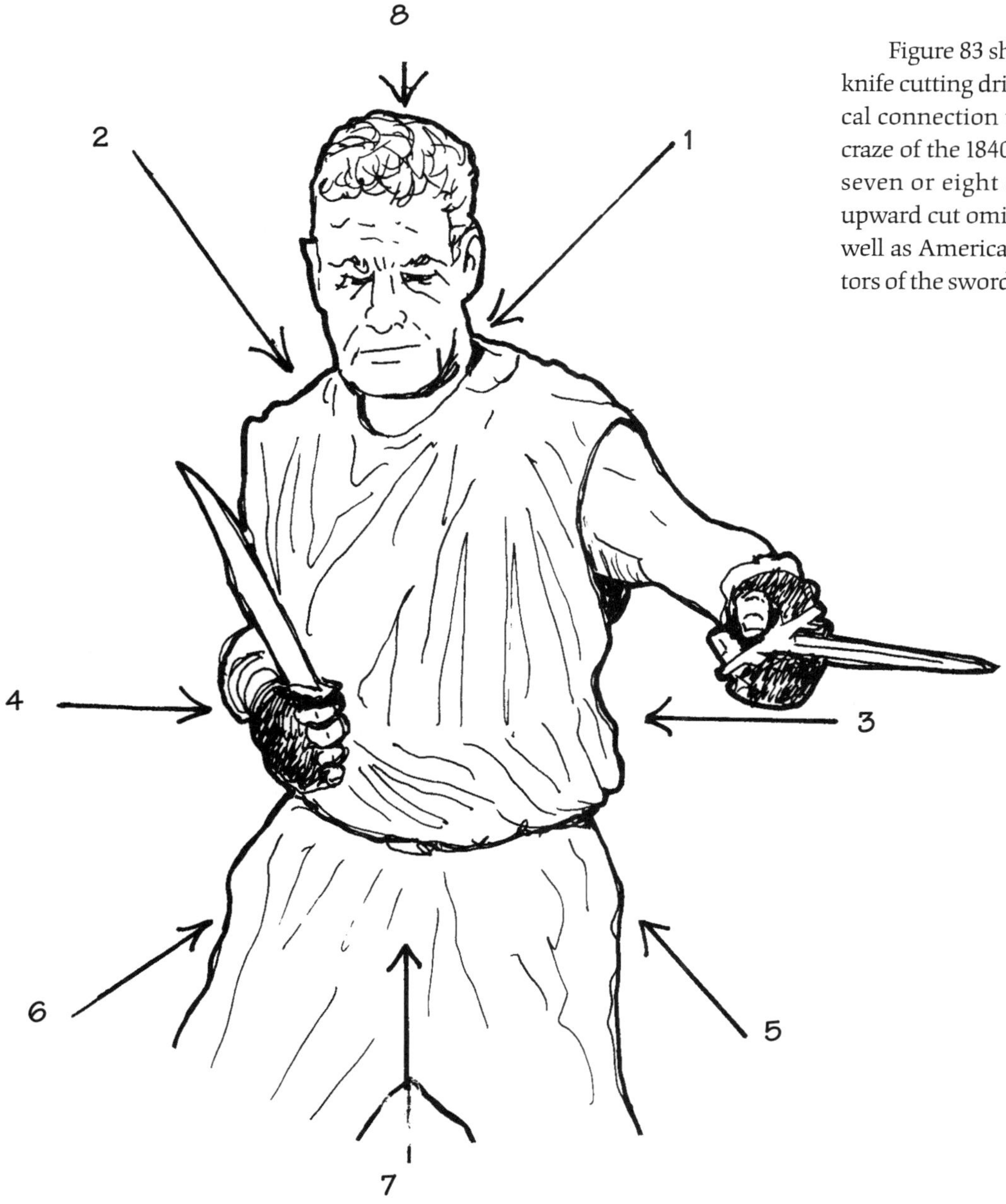

Eight Angles of Attack

Figure 83 shows the eight angles of attack upon which the basic Bowie knife cutting drills are based. This picture was chosen because of its historical connection to what would have been taught during the Bowie knife craze of the 1840s. The saber and sword manuals of the 1800s reflect either seven or eight angles of attack (the former having the low centerline upward cut omitted for mounted combat). These were taught in Europe as well as America and probably would have been available to most instructors of the sword of that period.

Figure 83. The eight angles of attack.

Drill 1: Eight Angles of Attack

Historically the eight angles of attack have been linked in a drill sequence that can be repeated over and over to enhance retention of technique (muscle memory). The drill is normally done in a figure-eight pattern, which ultimately translates into a flow exercise.

When combined with body and foot movement, the eight angles of attack closely approximate those of an actual knife fight. The *Knife Fighting Encyclopedia* provides a detailed description of how this drill is accomplished.

> The drill consists of four figure-eight patterns. When performed in succession, every two angles create a "figure eight" configuration: flat figure eight when slashing horizontally and a vertical figure eight when working angles number 7 and number 8.... The backup hand remains in motion.... One must use this free hand for guard, trapping, follow-up strikes, or body manipulations such as grabbing, pushing, or pulling. Keep the free hand moving in the window of combat while you do these exercises. Do not drop to your side or glue it to your chest.

TRAINING NOTE: When using the Bowie these angles are not cut as tight (inside the box) as in the Filipino styles; rather the motion is more expansive to allow the weight of the weapon to assist in carrying through the target area. Figures 85 through 100 show other views of the eight angles of attack drill.

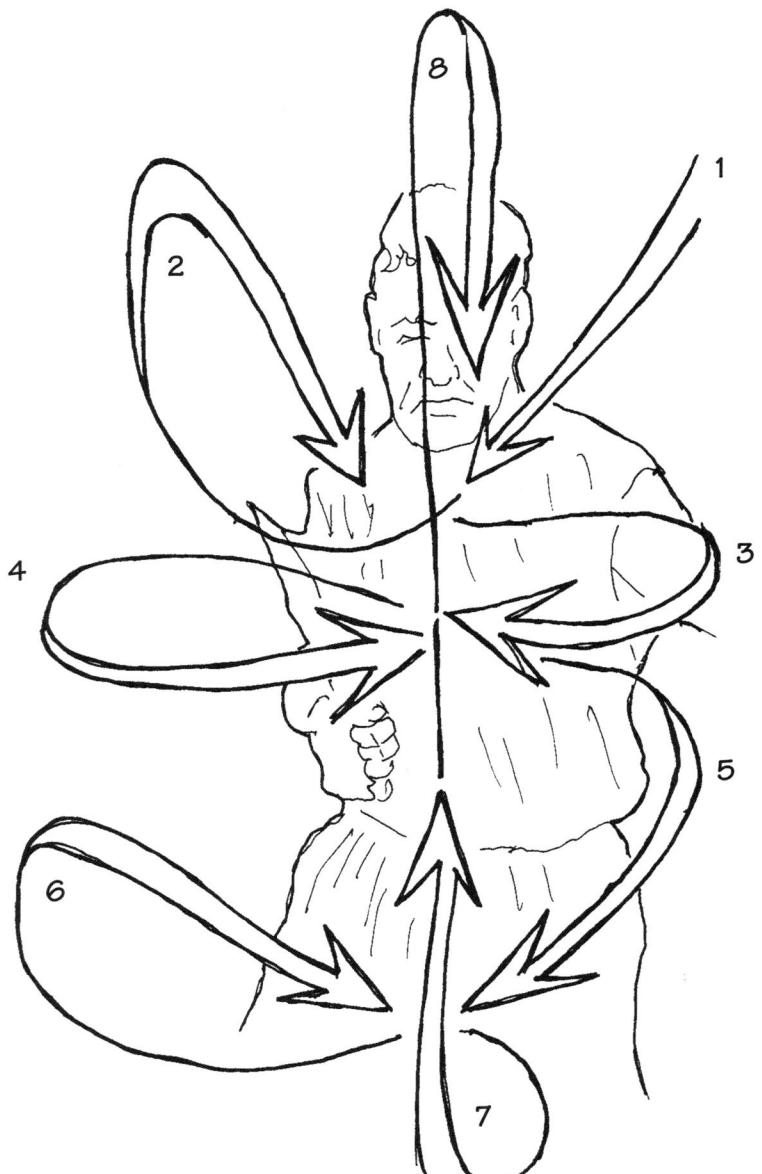

Figure 84. The flow of the eight angles of attack.

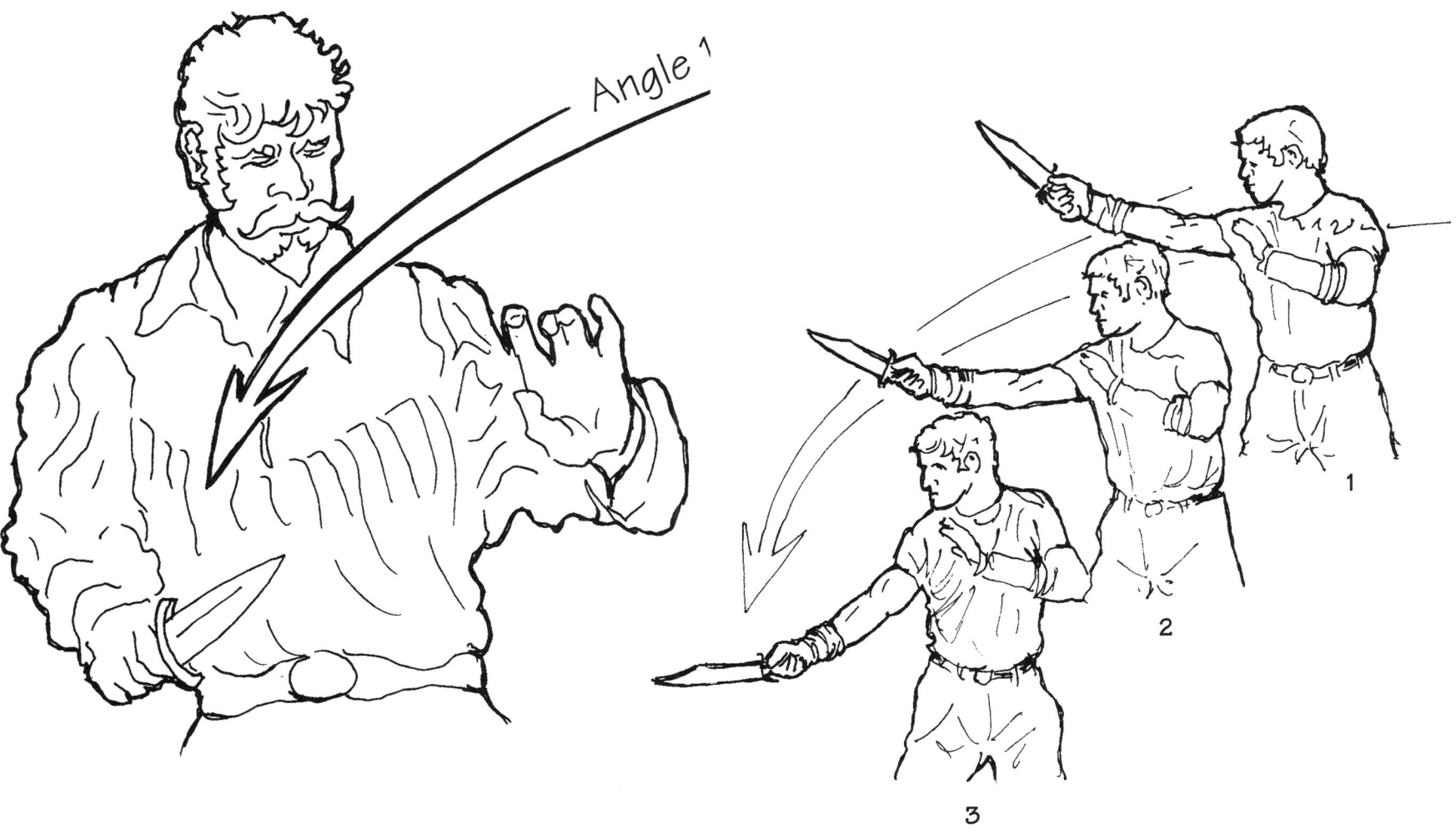

Figure 85. View of the angle one on the opponent.

Figure 86. View of angle 1 from the side.

Angle 2

1

2

3

Figure 87. View of angle 2 on the opponent.

Figure 88. View of angle 2 from the side.

Figure 89. View of angle 3 on the opponent.

Figure 90. View of angle 3 from the side.

Figure 91. View of angle 4 on the opponent.

Figure 92. View of angle 4 from the side.

Figure 93. View of angle 5 on the opponent.

Figure 94. View of angle 5 from the side.

Figure 95. View of angle 6 on the opponent.

Figure 96. View of angle 6 from the side.

Figure 97. View of angle 7 on the opponent.

Figure 98. View of angle 7 from the side.

Figure 99. View of angle 8 on the opponent.

Figure 100. View of angle 8 from the side.

Angles of Attack to the Hand

Historically, the angles of attack were not limited to the torso. Some of the old saber manuals of the 1800s applied this aspect to the hand in both attack and defense. Figure 101 shows the vulnerable areas of the hand as well as how a slight rotation of the wrist can shift the blade to protect the hand.

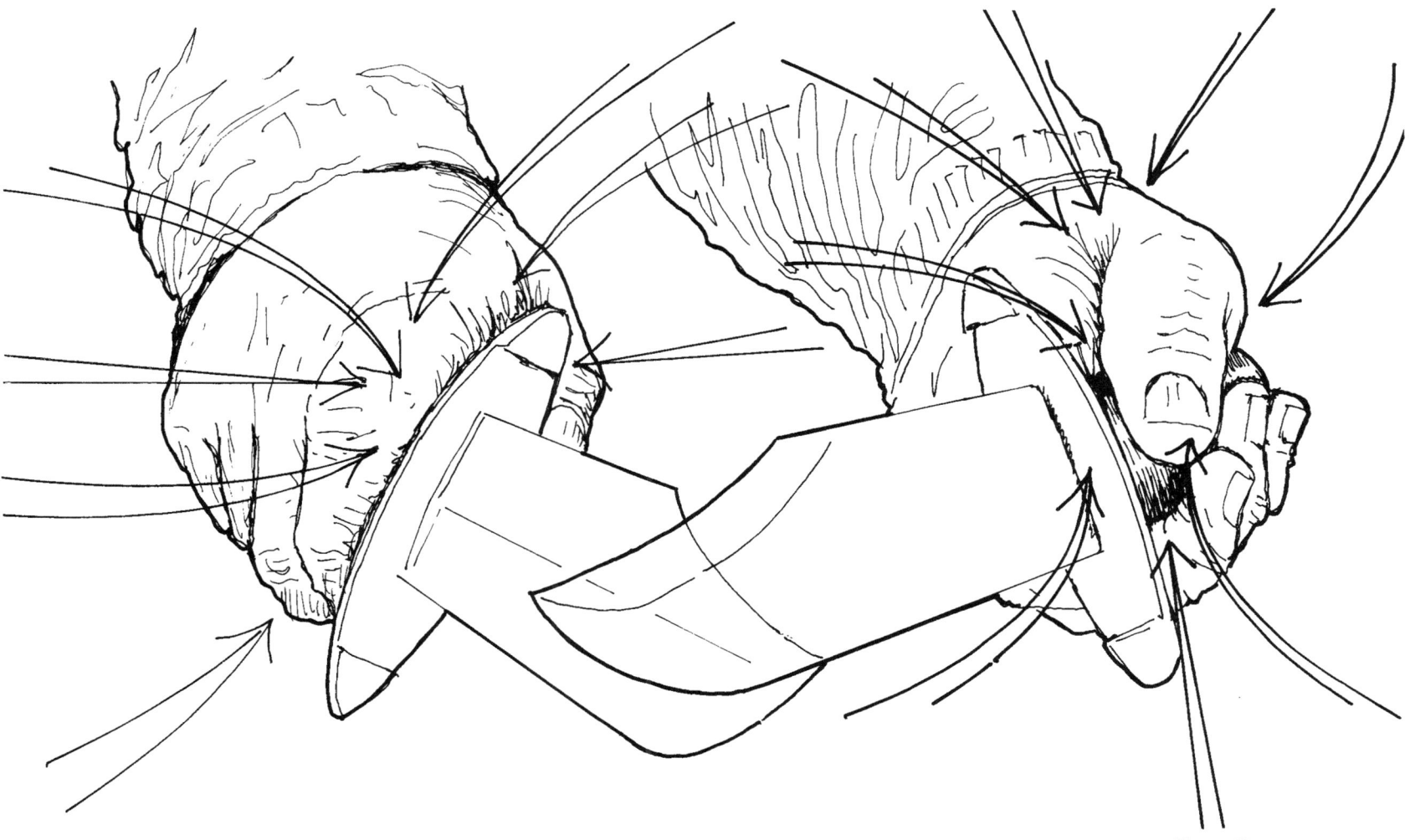

Figure 101.

TRAINING NOTE: Training in the use of the back-up hand when performing the eight-angle cutting drill is essential. Driving the back-up hand into the window of combat after each cut (or each two cuts) simulates a strike, seizure, or pass of the opponent's arm/head. The technique serves as an excellent training base for development in the use of two weapons.

FOOT MOVEMENT: Movement of the feet during this drill may be accomplished by simply shifting the feet back and forth from a stationary position. The right foot is forward when the cut is initiated, and the left foot moves forward when the back-up hand is used. This action can be enhanced by walking forward or backward during the process or angling to the left and right.

Figure 102.

TRAINING NOTE FOR THE EIGHT-ANGLE ATTACK DRILL: As mentioned earlier the eight-angle drill has been around a long time, dating back to the Renaissance and Medieval periods. The reason this drill was so common undoubtedly rests with its effectiveness in teaching proper cutting coordination thorough repetition. Simply speaking, we call this process "building muscle memory." The eight angles of attack should be practiced routinely as part of any training period.

It is a good warm-up for the wrists and arms, beginning initially with slow-motion techniques and gradually increasing the speed until the cut can be executed with full, accurate force. Practice of this drill should consist of a minimum of three sets that contain all eight angles. Practice the cut, snipe, and back cut using both left and right hands. Initially, practice the drill with no target. The objective here is to achieve the correct cutting angle, grip, and follow-up action.

Remember that all the angles should flow as if in a figure-eight pattern with each cut in smooth transition into the next. It is a good idea to practice the drill in front of a mirror at first to help with the proper form. Again, start slowly to ensure that all cutting angles are accurate and correct before speeding up your movements. Only after you have mastered the angles in the open air should you begin practicing on a target.

A wooden log (pell) anchored in the ground or any standard boxing heavy bag can be used. The training knife for this activity should be made of wood. Frequently beginners associate cutting with striking hard, assuming that a hard, chopping-like action produces a more efficient cut. Taking care at this time to ensure that proper cutting techniques are used to prevent this bad habit from being developed. "Strike fast, strike smooth" is a good rule for avoiding this bad habit.

During the cutting of all angles be sure you know where the edge is in relation to the target—this is being "edge aware." Again a minimum of three sets of each of the three cutting techniques is needed to attain proficiency.

The next step is practicing with a live blade. Here the wooden pell is required.

Figure 103. One training drill for your eight-angle attack drill is working the pell with live steel.

Figure 104. A valuable training aid to is a hanging log with limbs positioned strategically to simulate an opponent's hands.

Twelve Angles of Attack

Another flow drill that greatly builds reaction time and muscle memory for the cut is the 12-angle attack. Basically this drill incorporates the thrusting techniques into the eight-angle cutting drill. Figures 105 and 106 depict this drill.

Figure 105. Angle 1.

Figure 106. User's view of angle 1.

Figure 107. Angle 2.

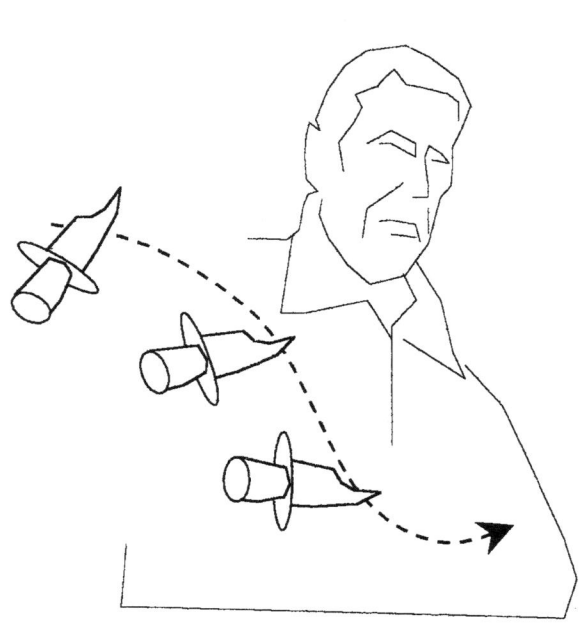

Figure 108. User's view of angle 2.

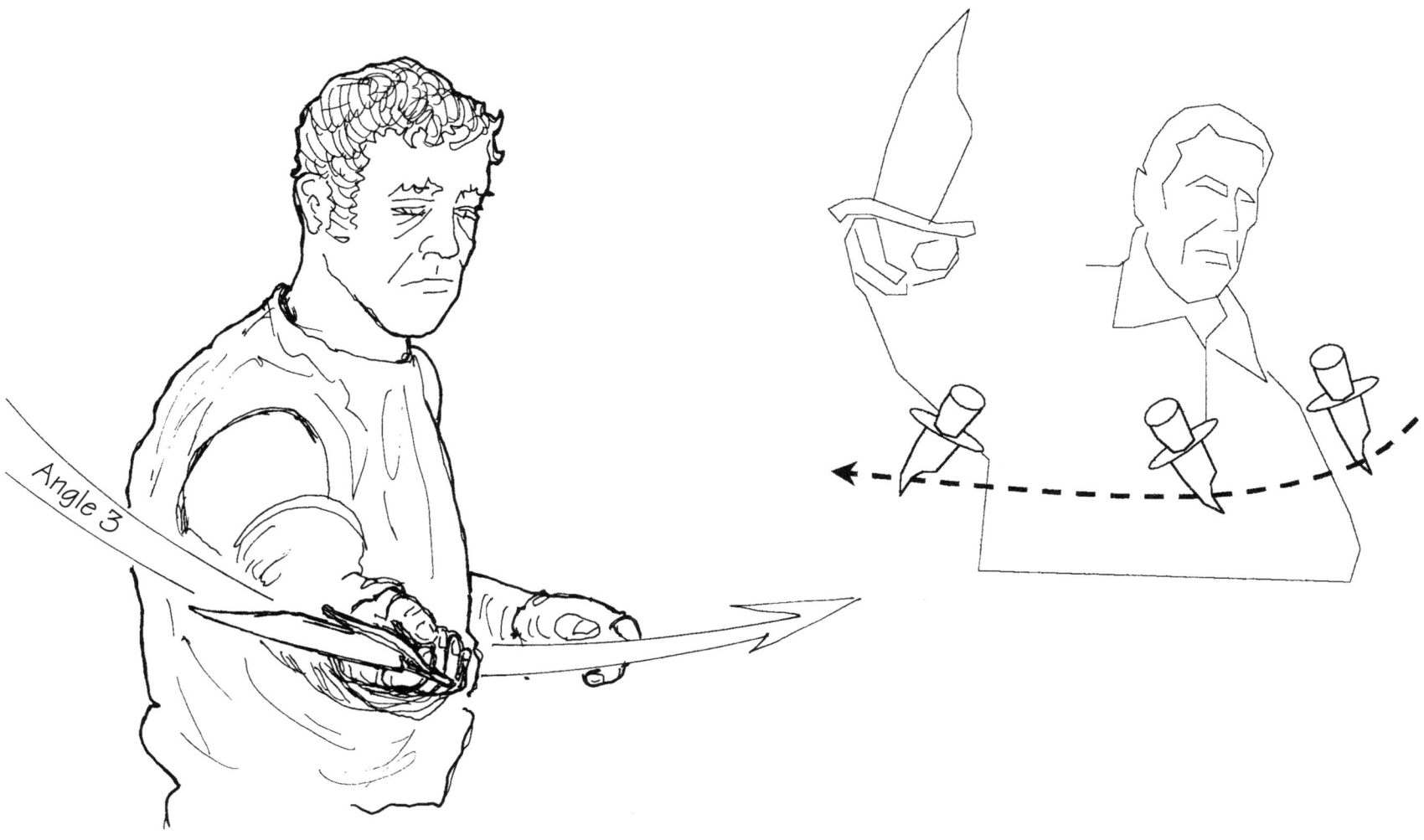

Angle 3

Figure 109. Angle 3.

Figure 110. User's view of angle 3.

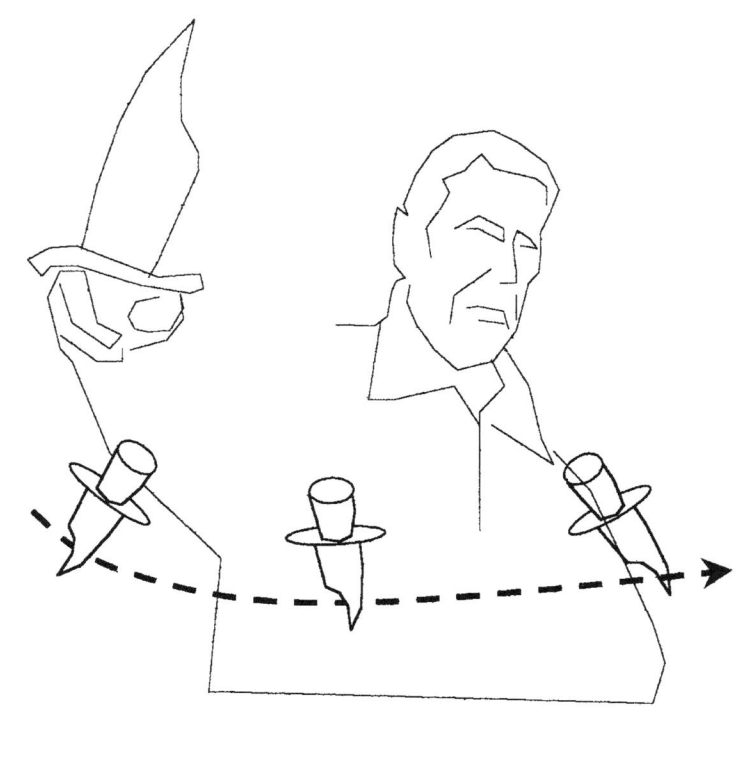

Figure 111. Angle 4.

Figure 112. User's view of angle 4.

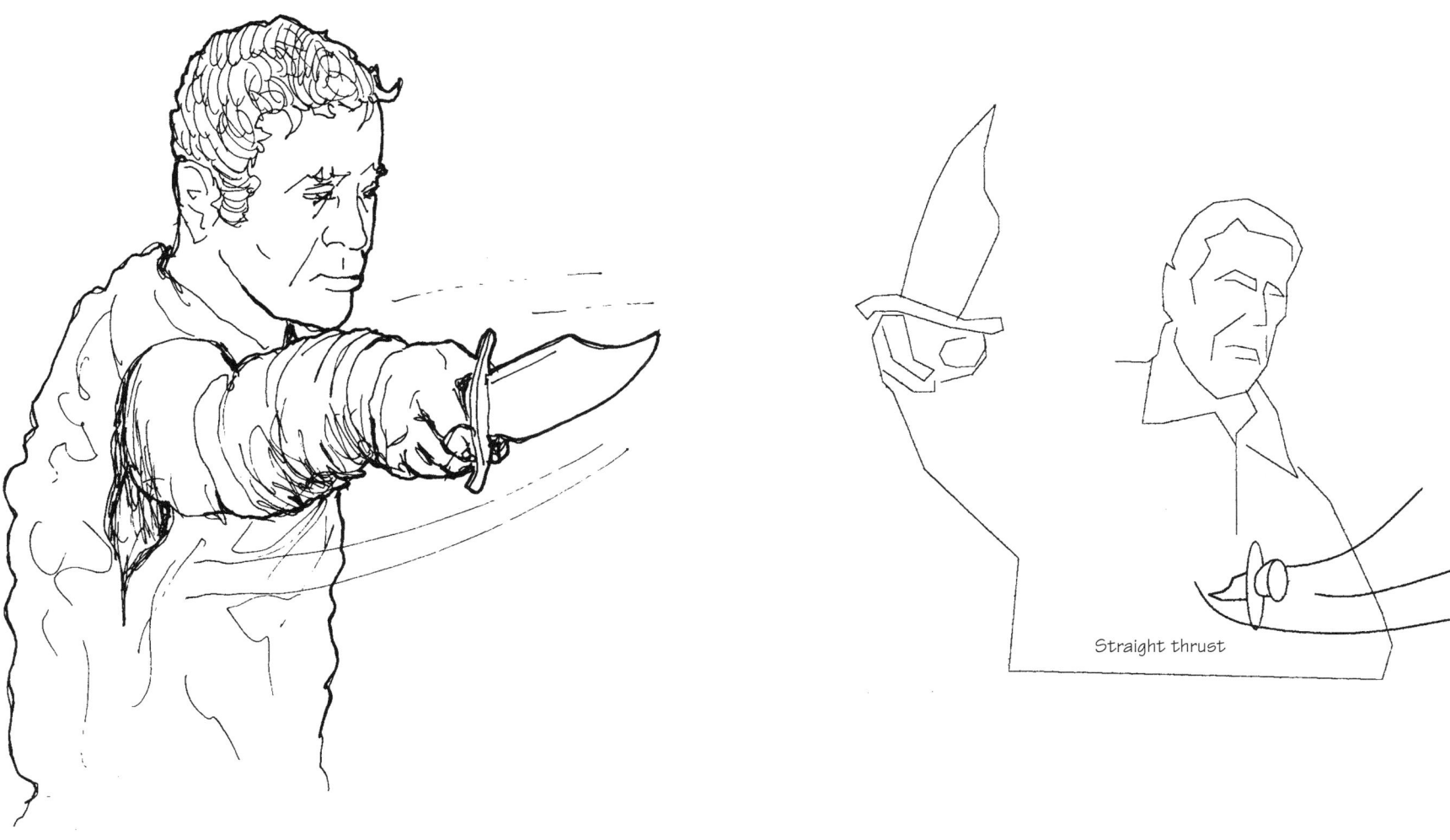

Figure 113. Angle 5, the thrust.

Straight thrust

Figure 114. User's View of angle 5.

Figure 115. Angle 6, punta mandritta.

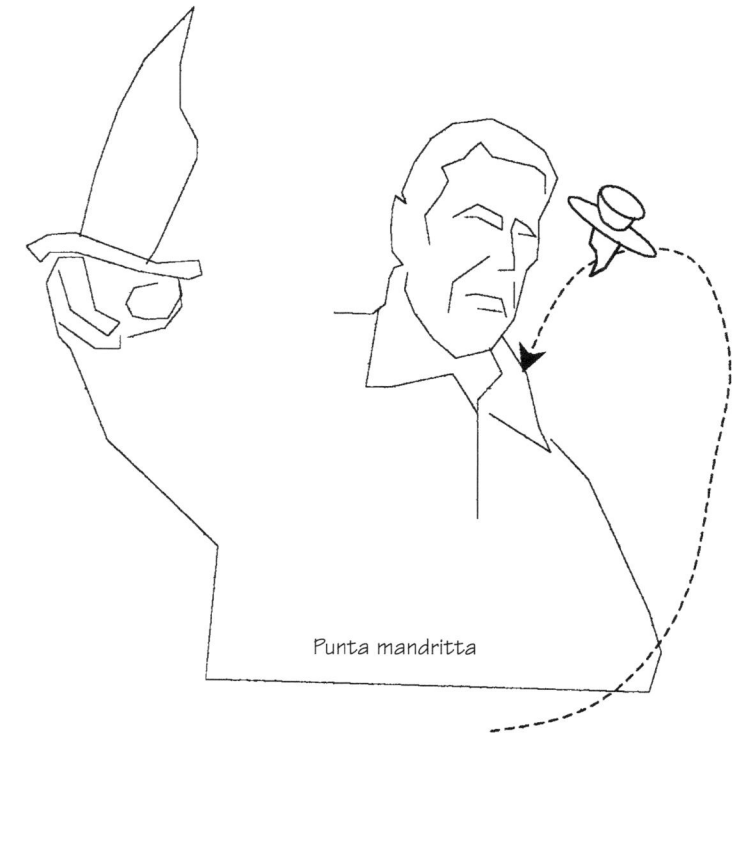

Punta mandritta

Figure 116. User's view of angle 6.

Figure 117. Angle 7, punta reversa.

Punta reversa

Figure 118. User's view of angle 7.

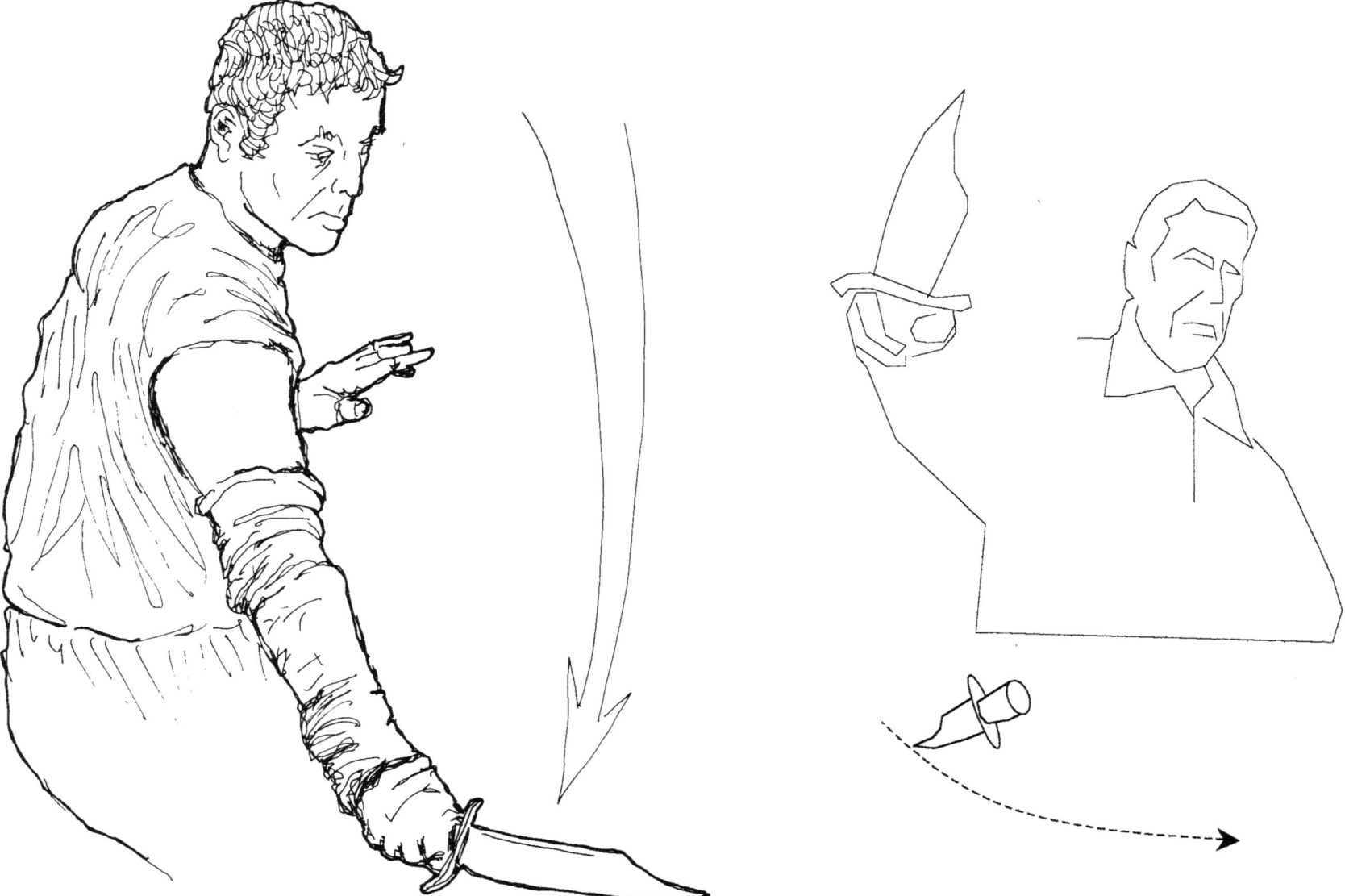

Figure 119. Angle 8.

Figure 120. User's view of angle 8.

Figure 121. Angle 9.

Figure 122. User's view of angle 9.

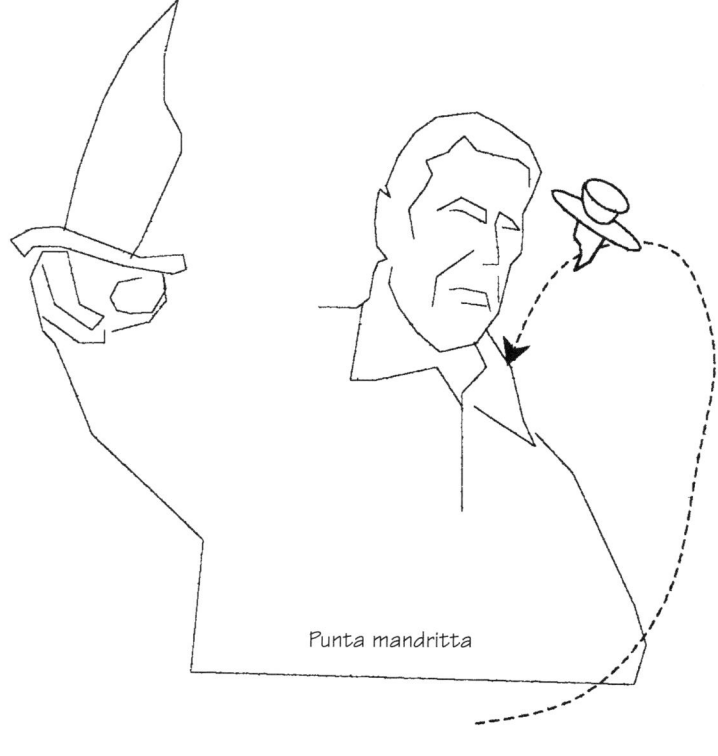

Punta mandritta

Figure 123. Angle 10, punta mandritta.

Figure 124. User's view of angle 10.

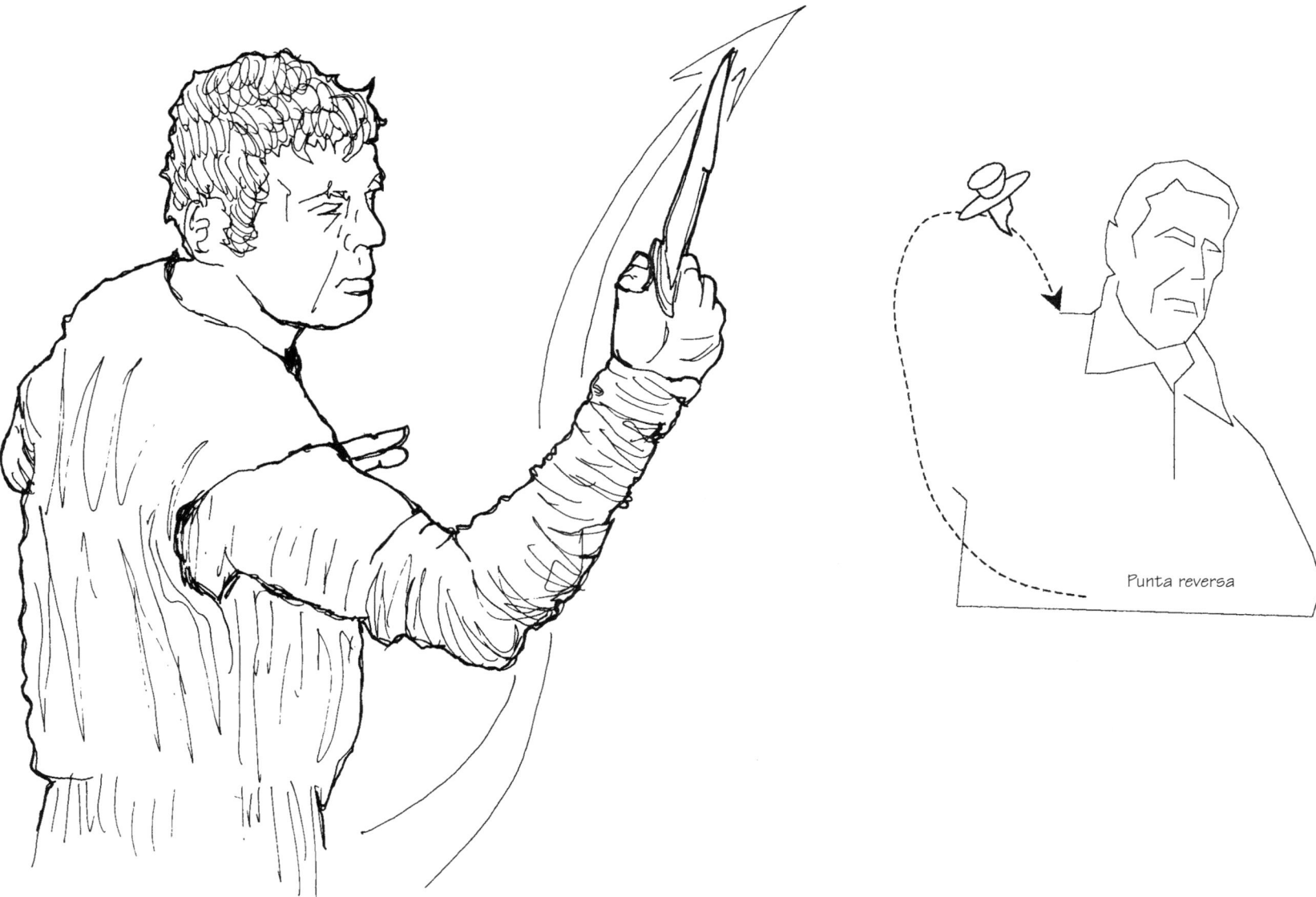

Figure 125. Angle 11, punta reversa.

Punta reversa

Figure 126. User's view of angle 11.

Figure 127. Angle 12, overhead cut.

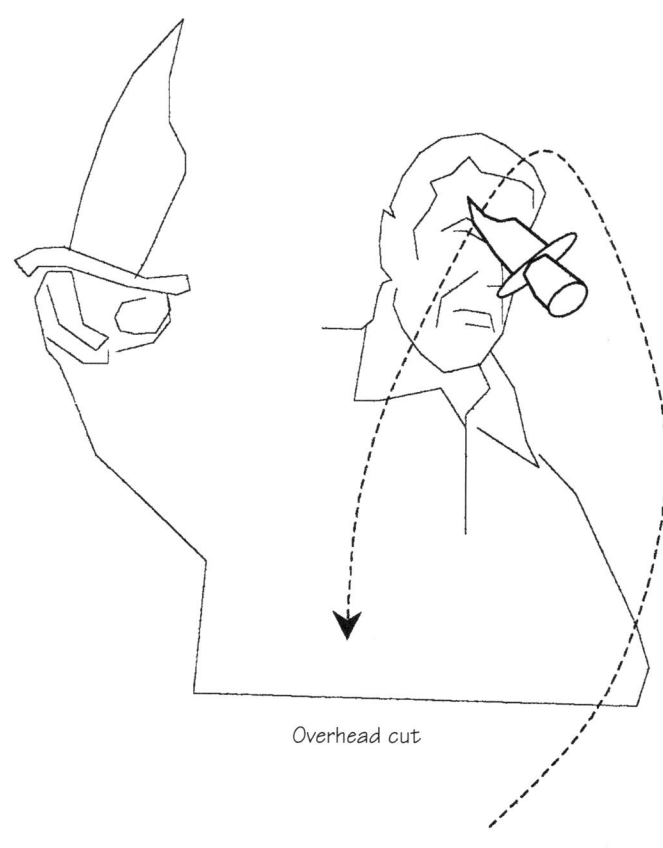

Overhead cut

Figure 128. User's view of angle 12.

KNIFE FIGHTING CONCEPT E: PARRY AGAINST ANGLES OF ATTACK

Throughout history there have been counters to the angles of attack to prevent one from getting hit. Depending on the weapon faced and the type used, there have been many variations of blocks or parries. Some historical sources lump these terms together under the following definition of block: to resist an attack by imposing blade against blade. For our purposes, we will use the following terms to apply to the concept.

- Block: Placing the blade along the angle of an opponent's attack and applying deliberate resistance (force) to stop the attack in place. Blocks are normally associated with longer swords and usually do not involve a lot of movement to avoid the strike.
- Parry: Using the blade to intercept and deflect the opponent's blade from the attacking angle. This involves a moderate degree of force and is often associated with movement techniques to avoid, as opposed to stopping, the attack.

NOTE: Blocks against high and midline attacks with big knives are very difficult to perform and require regular training. Against low-line attacks they are more effective, provided movement away from the attack is used. The parry is the recommended technique for the Bowie.

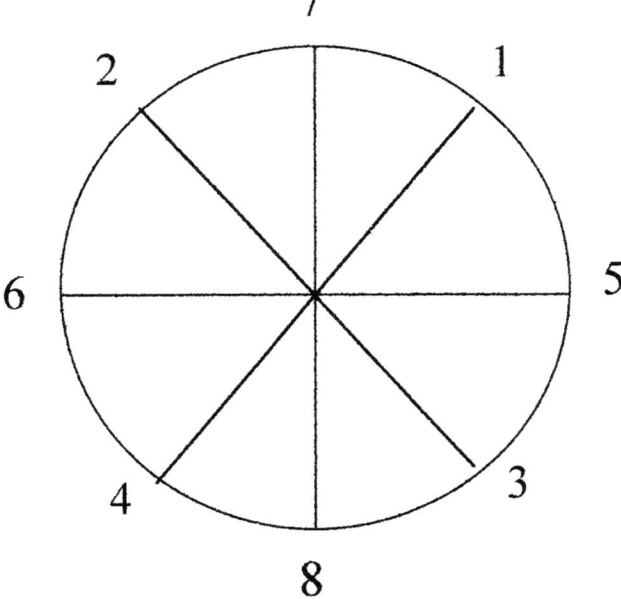

Figure 129. The eight angles of attack.

Parrying with the Edge, Flat, and Heel of the Blade

Historically, there has always been a debate over which part of the blade provides the most effective parry. The argument is usually over whether the edge or flat is superior. Four points need to be considered here when addressing this argument.

1.   The edge is most effective against high-line and low-line attacks when an immediate counterattack is planned. The heel of a big Bowie is best used to parry midline attacks; in some instances, with the proper force this action can be used to break an opponent's blade or disarm him.
2.   When the back cut is used as a parry, the edge usually makes contact first.
3.   It takes a considerable amount of training to perfect a flat-edge parry without some lateral "wobbling" of the blade taking place. It is probably not worth the investment of training time to perfect this technique with a Bowie just for the sake of "saving the edge."
4.   The more flexible the blade, the greater the requirement to parry with the edge or heel.

NOTE: Don't worry about detailed "foolishness" like this at first. When countering the eight angles of attack the rule is "first, get steel on steel and then get the hell out of the way!" The following drill visualizes the parry drill. As with the eight-angle attack drill, this parry drill is also designed to flow. It is composed of eight parries to counter each of the eight attack angles. The motion flows from side to side, with the fighter twisting his trunk and positioning the blade to deflect or parry his opponent's blade out of the way and set up an immediate counterattack. This flow should be practiced regularly to build muscle memory. Practice consists of three sets of the complete eight angles.

The Parry as a Single-Flow Drill

NOTE: For this demonstration we are using the edge-up presentation of the blade, which allows a more effective use of the Bowie heel to parry.

Figure 130. Parry 1.

Figure 131. Parry 2.

Figure 132. Parry 3.

Figure 133. Parry 4.

Figure 134. Parry 5.

Figure 135. Parry 6.

7

8

Figure 136. Parry 7.

129

Figure 137. Parry 8.

Now that we understand the flow, let's take a more detailed look at these parries from a three-quarters side view and that of an individual executing the parries against the eight angles of attack covered earlier.

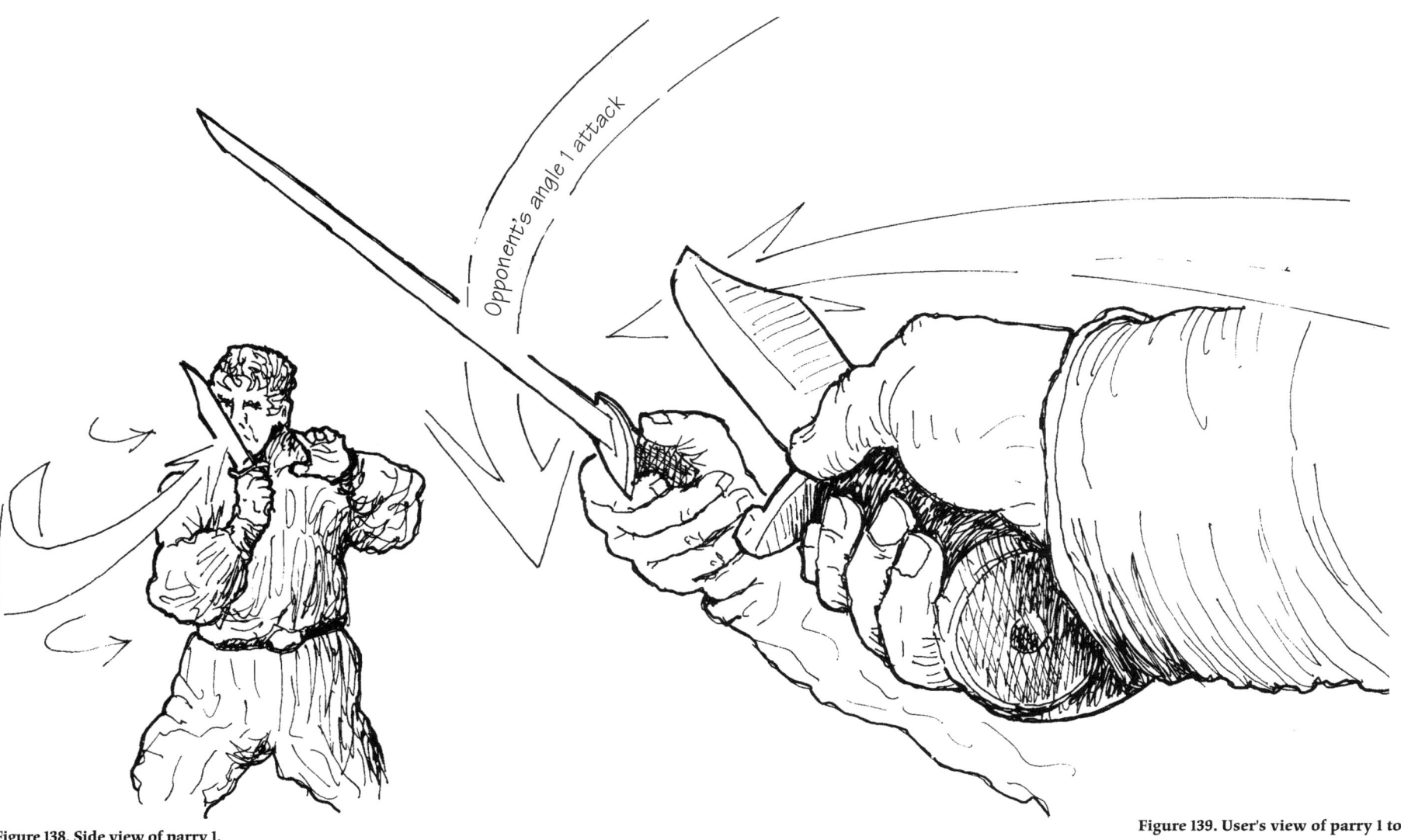

Figure 138. Side view of parry 1.

Figure 139. User's view of parry 1 to angle 1 attack.

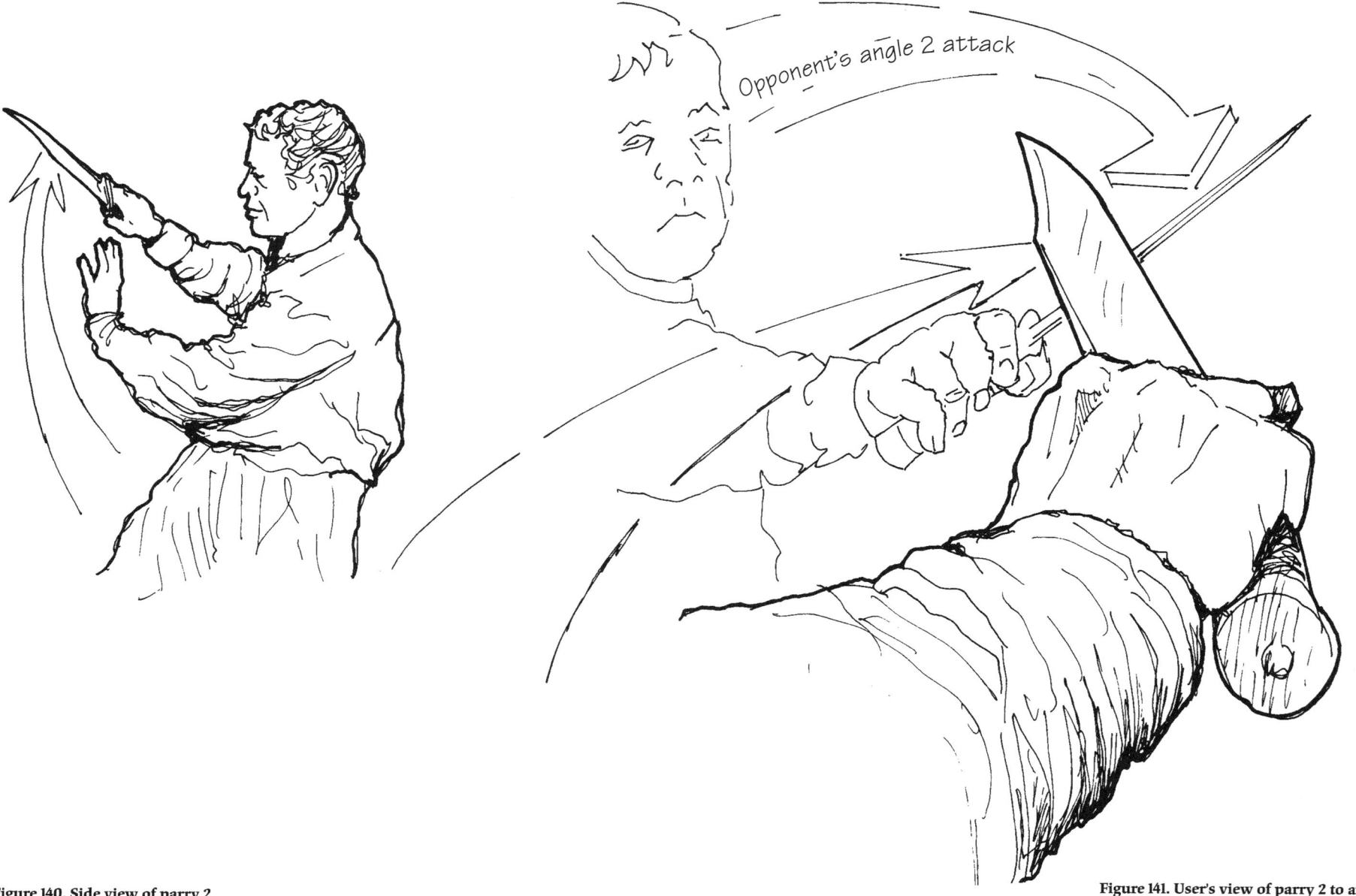

Opponent's angle 2 attack

Figure 140. Side view of parry 2.

Figure 141. User's view of parry 2 to angle 2 attack.

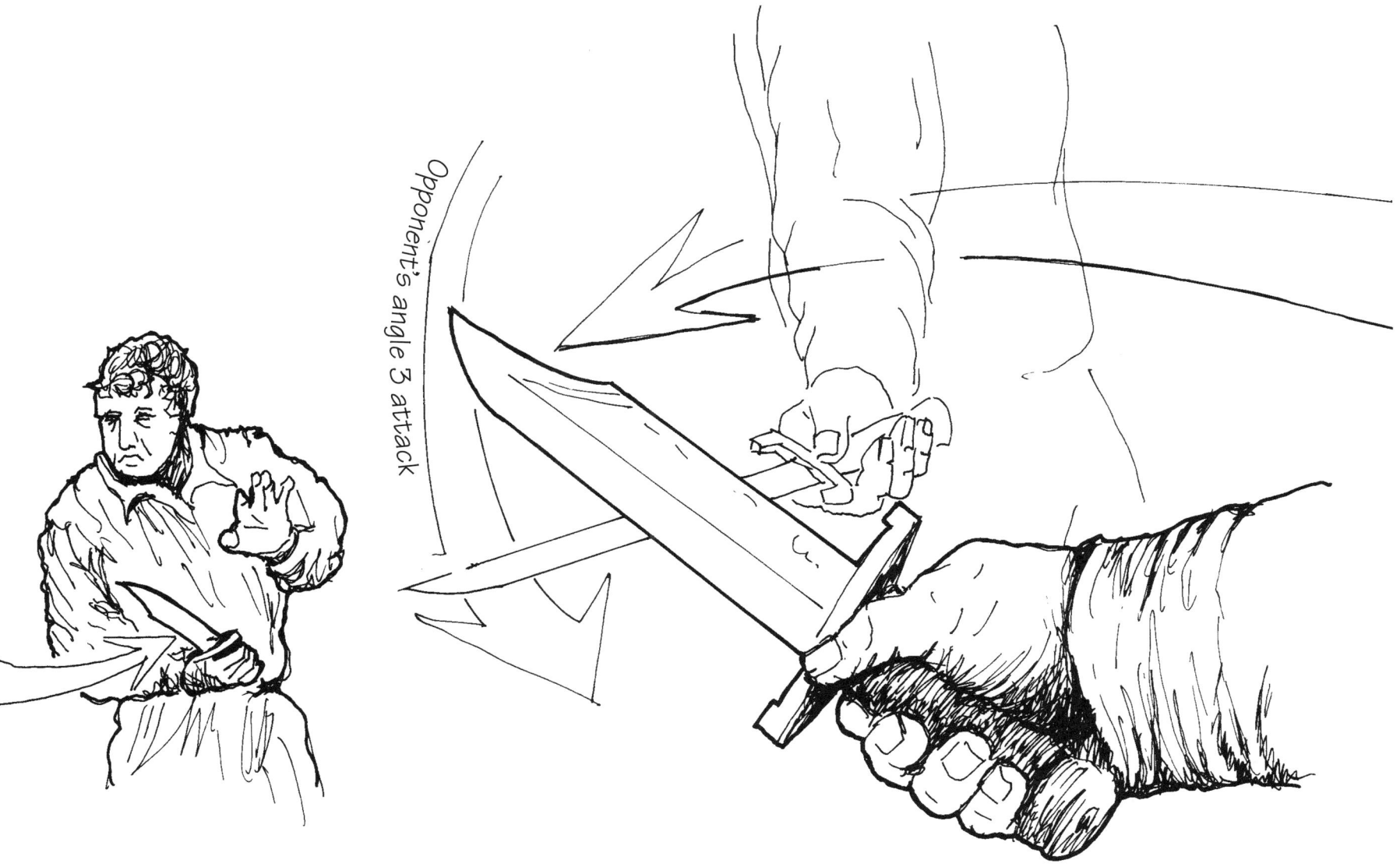

Opponent's angle 3 attack

Figure 142. Side view of parry 3.

Figure 143. User's view of parry 3 to angle 3 attack.

Opponent's angle 4 attack

Figure 144. Side view of parry 4.

Figure 145. User's view of parry 4 to angle 4 attack.

Figure 146. Side view of parry 5.

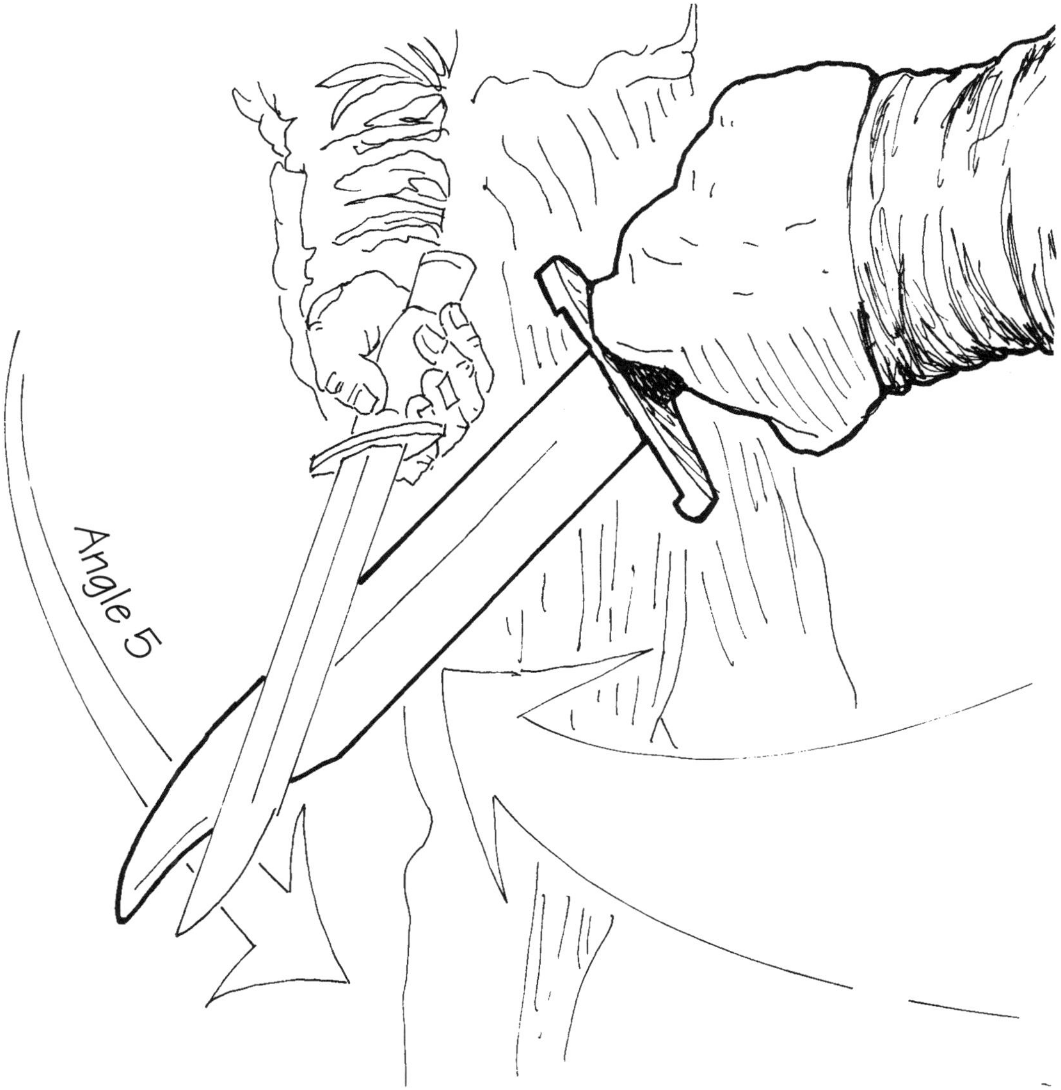

Angle 5

Figure 147. User's view of parry 5 to angle 5 attack (drawing not to scale).

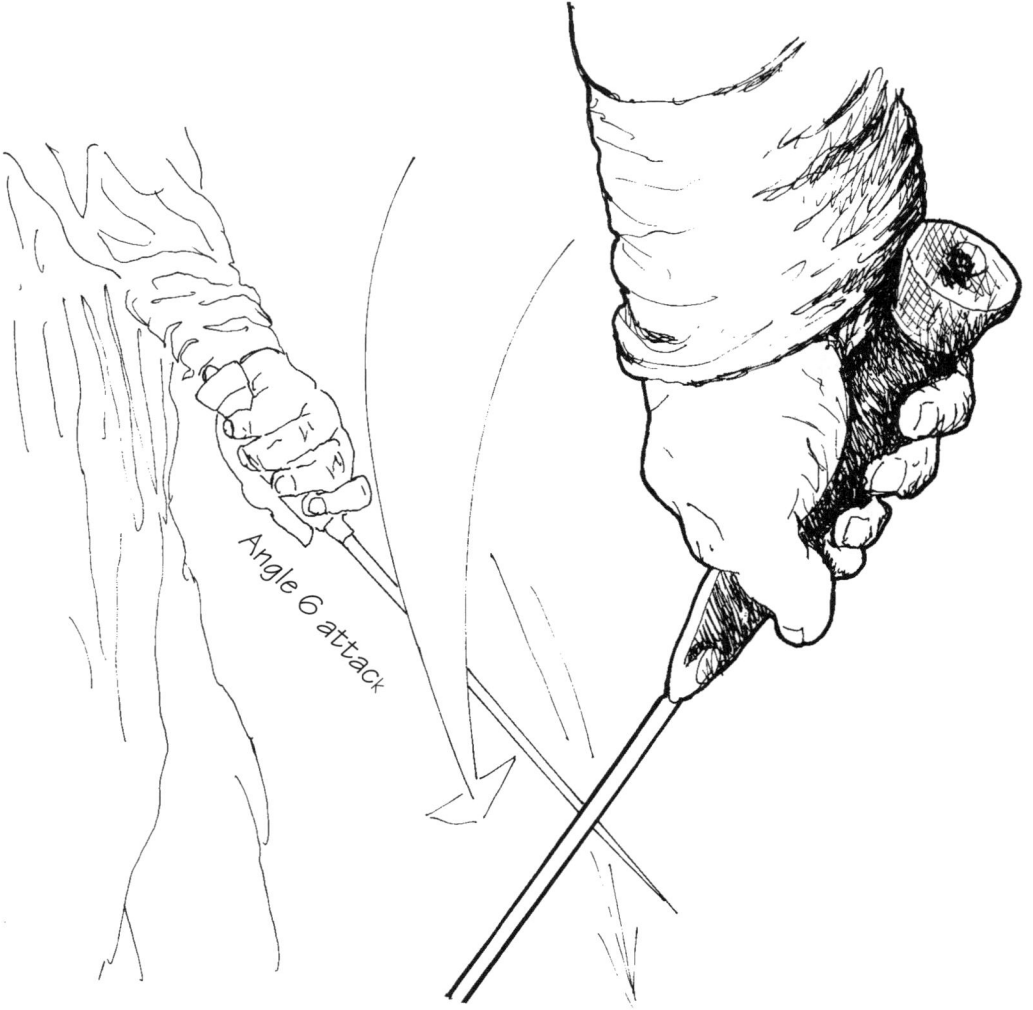

Angle 6 attack

Figure 148. Side view of parry 6.

Figure 149. User's view of parry 6 to angle 6 attack.

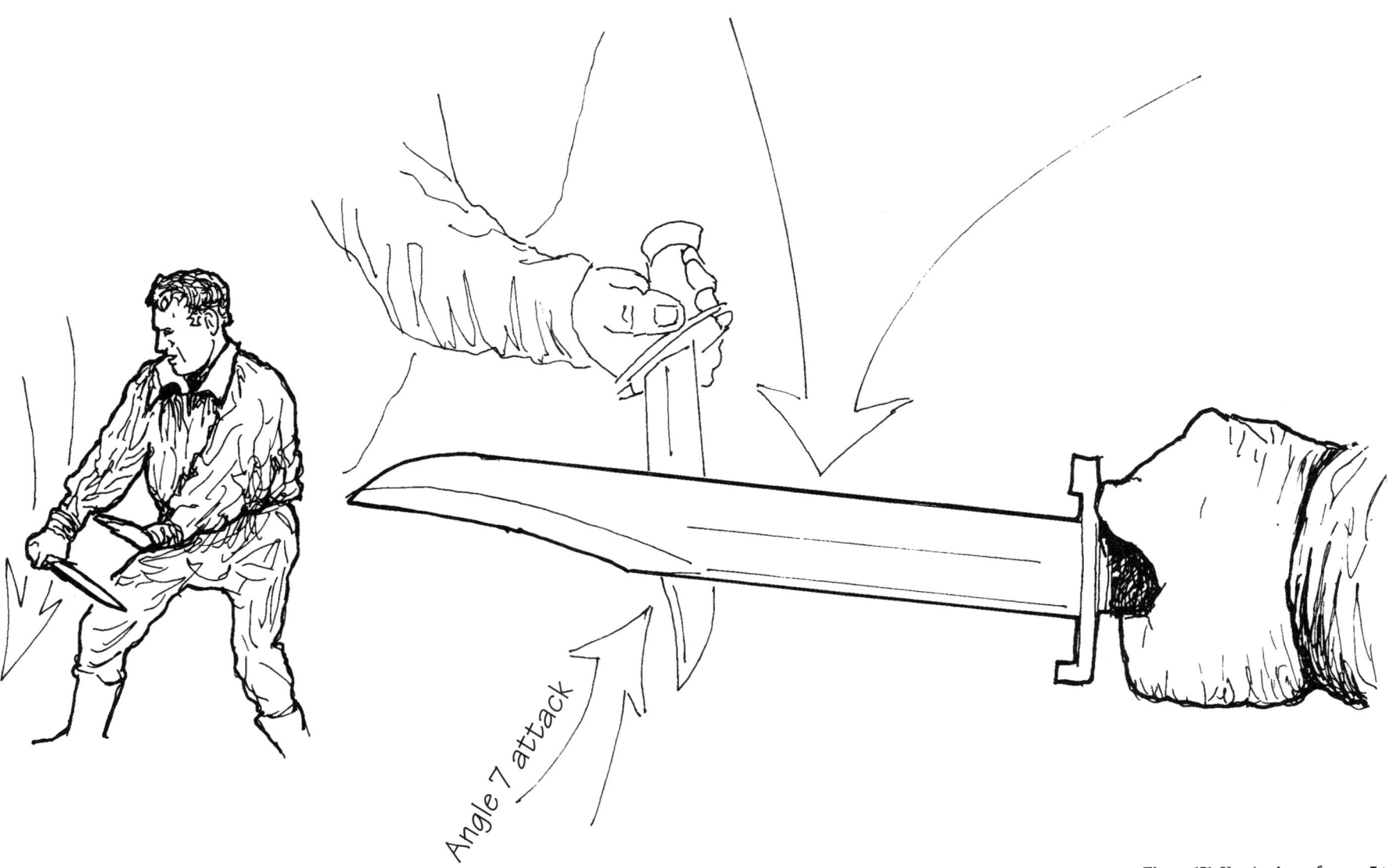

Angle 7 attack

Figure 150. Side view of parry 7.

Figure 151. User's view of parry 7 to angle 7 attack.

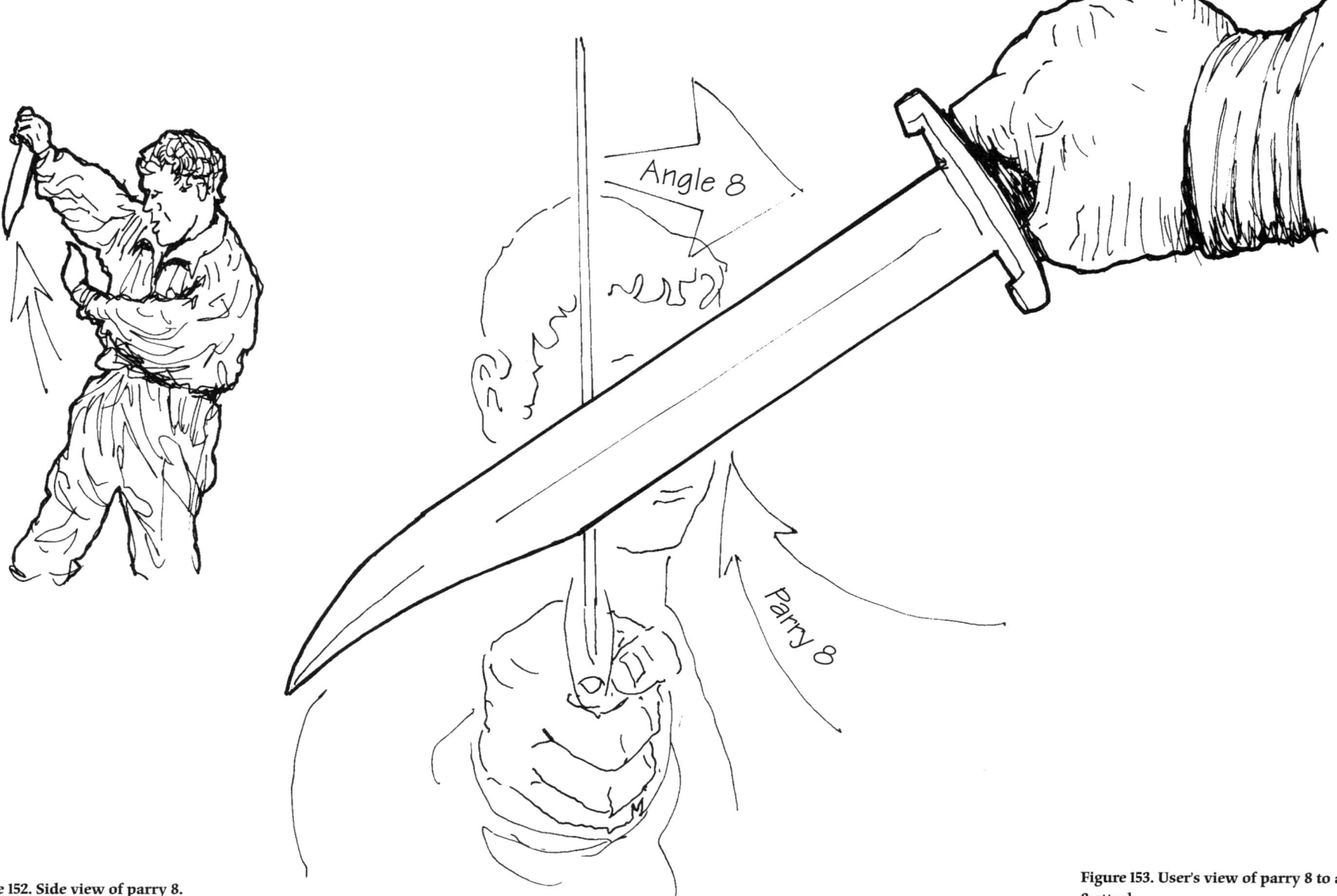

Figure 152. Side view of parry 8.

Figure 153. User's view of parry 8 to angle 8 attack.

HISTORICAL NOTE: One of the popular theories today is that the Bowie knife-fighting methods of the 1840s evolved from those of the saber. There is a lot of circumstantial evidence to support this, but we cannot be sure that this is indeed true. What most of the major Bowie historians will say is that there are many similarities between the use of the two weapons and there is great crossover training value for learning to use both weapons. Alliance Martial Arts Master of Arms Pete Kautz in his treatise *Connecting the Sword and the Bowie* comments that

the basics of the saber were quite direct and a man could learn them in a short period of time and then practice sparring, or assaulting as it was known. The basics of the saber consisted of three wards or guards, seven cuts, seven defenses, three thrusts, and a circular parry. With these basics, which could be learned in a few hours, a man could develop his skill. When practicing with the saber one quickly sees how much these two weapons have to teach. How wonderfully such movements as the back cut, moulinet, and so forth can be executed with either.

Figure 154 shows a copy of an 1864 saber drill target. As we mentioned earlier, this diagram is very similar to various sword diagrams throughout history. The lines drawn on the diagram represent the angles of attack that can be directed at an opponent, while the sword drawing represents the various guards or parries that can be used to protect oneself.

Figure 155 is a diagram of this same concept that has been adapted to the Bowie knife for your training enjoyment.

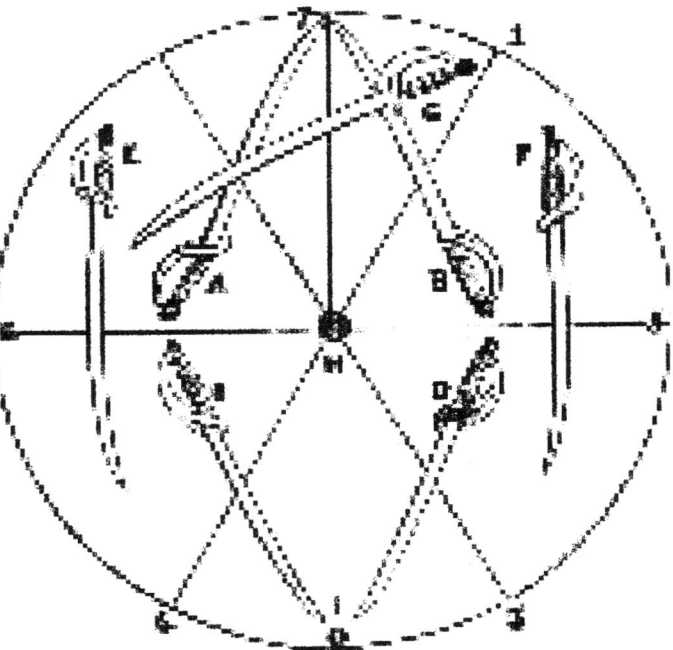

Figure 154. An 1864 saber target.

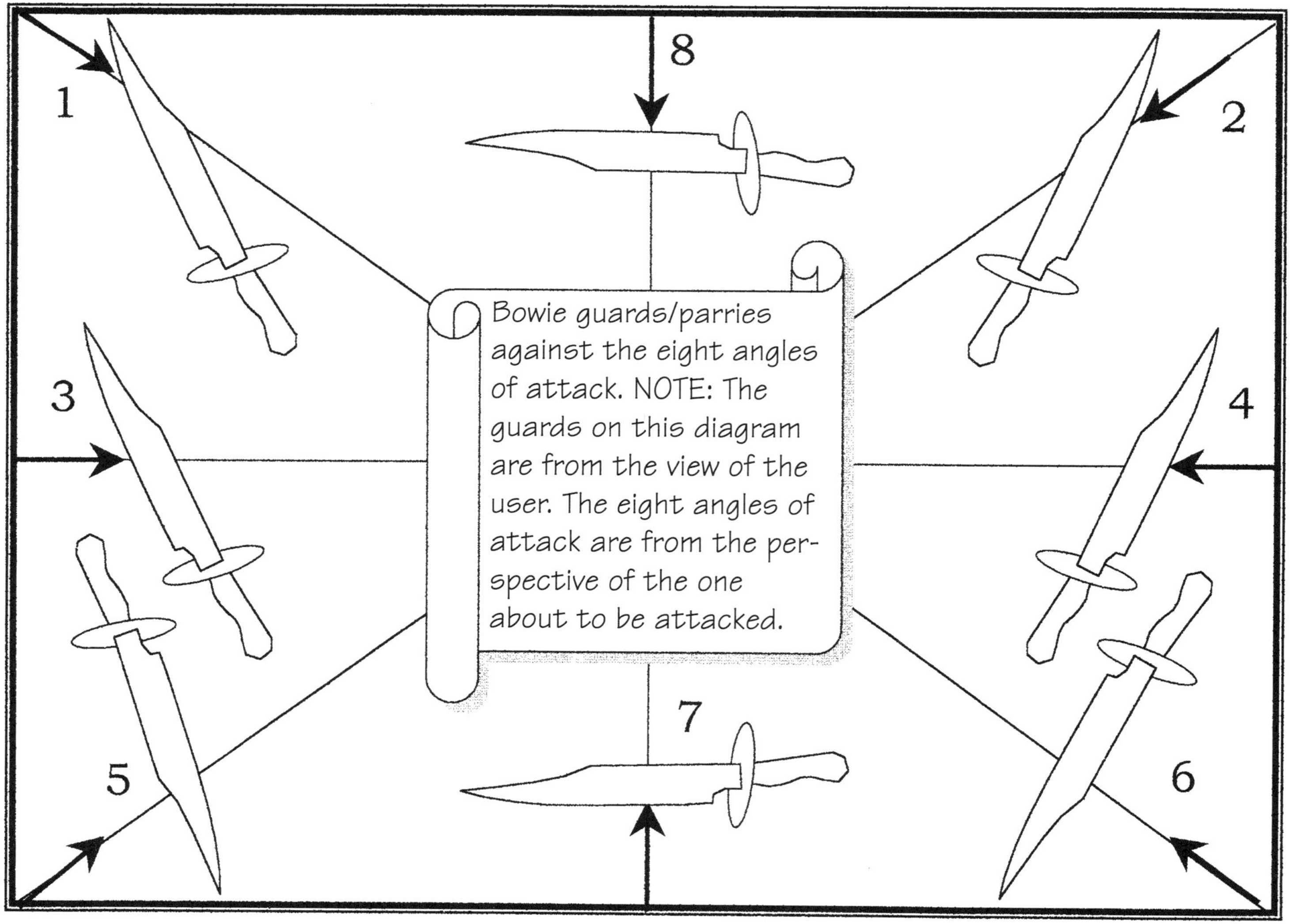
1
2
3
4
5
6
7
8
Bowie guards/parries against the eight angles of attack. NOTE: The guards on this diagram are from the view of the user. The eight angles of attack are from the perspective of the one about to be attacked.

Figure 155.

KNIFE FIGHTING CONCEPT F: DISRUPTION ATTACK (TAKING THE HAND)

In *Do or Die* Lieutenant Colonel Biddle emphasized attacking the hand as a primary target. We also see this same approach repeated down through history: several Polish saber manuals show the eight angles against the hand. The intent was to disrupt an opponent's attack with a decisive cut to the hand, wrist, forearm, or upper arm.

The weight, balance, and blade length of the Bowie are factors that make this a very devastating technique that will usually end the fight "here and now." This technique can be used not only from a defensive position but as a preliminary move to launch multiple attacks against an opponent. Figure 156 is an example of this.

Figure 156.

Twelve-Angle Drill versus Eight-Angle Disruption Attacks to the Hand

In *The Knife Fighting Encyclopedia*, W. Hoch Hochheim describes the disruption cut from the Filipino martial arts perspective as "defanging the snake." To enhance skills of this technique, Hoch uses a drill where the 12 angles of attack are used against a training partner employing the eight-angle disruption attacks.

Basically, one partner attacks with 12 angles while his partner immediately executes a disruption cut and moves. This is also called the "cut and get out of the way" drill movement, or out-of-the-box of combat. The drill is executed completely with the hand as a target; then the drill is repeated targeting the wrist, the forearm, and finally the upper arm. An additional sequence should be practiced by varying the target of each strike. For example, attack the wrist against angle 1 and then the forearm for angle 2.

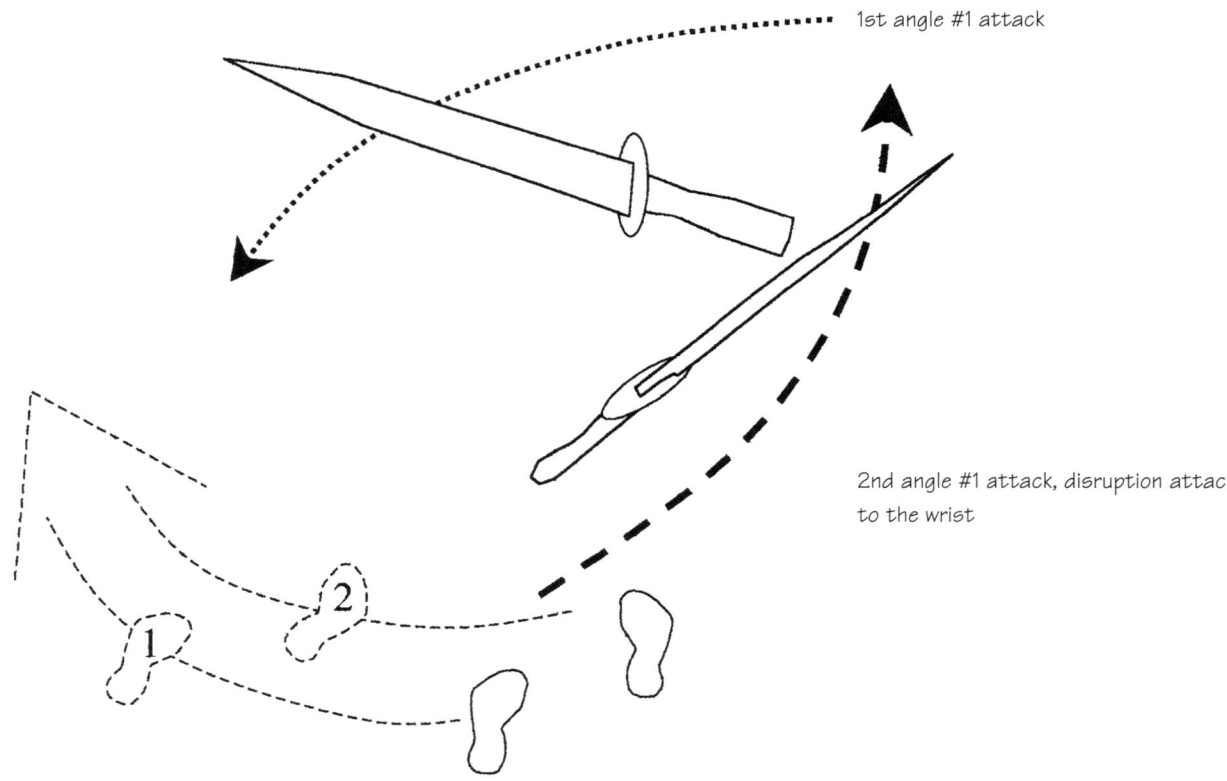

1st angle #1 attack

2nd angle #1 attack, disruption attack to the wrist

Figure 157. The figure to the right depicts both the flow of the drill from the user's perspective as he cuts and the direction of movement. Remember, these are conceptual memory aids designed to help clarify the action.

SAFETY NOTE: These exercises should be performed with padded sparring weapons and using hand, wrist, forearm, and elbow protection. Use of protective eyewear is also recommended. Conduct the exercise first at slow speed until you have mastered the movement and cuts and then increase to half-speed and eventually move into full-speed sparring.

Figure 158 shows an adaptation of this two-man drill with the Bowie knife. Note that the disruption cut is executed with immediate movement out of the box of combat.

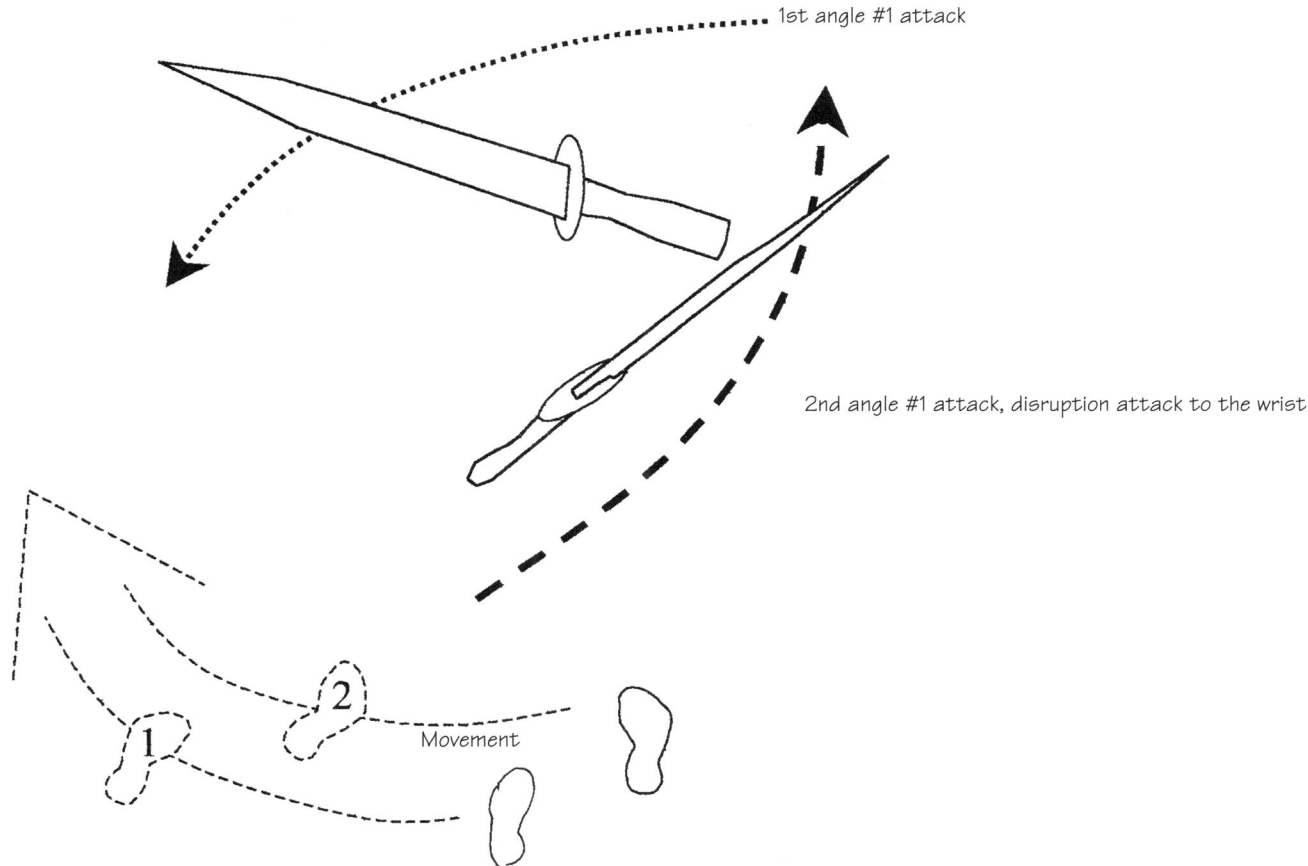

1st angle #1 attack

2nd angle #1 attack, disruption attack to the wrist

Movement

Figure 158. Action 1: The opponent executes angle 1 of 12-angle attack pattern; his partner makes an angle 2 cut to the wrist while shifting to the left outside the box.

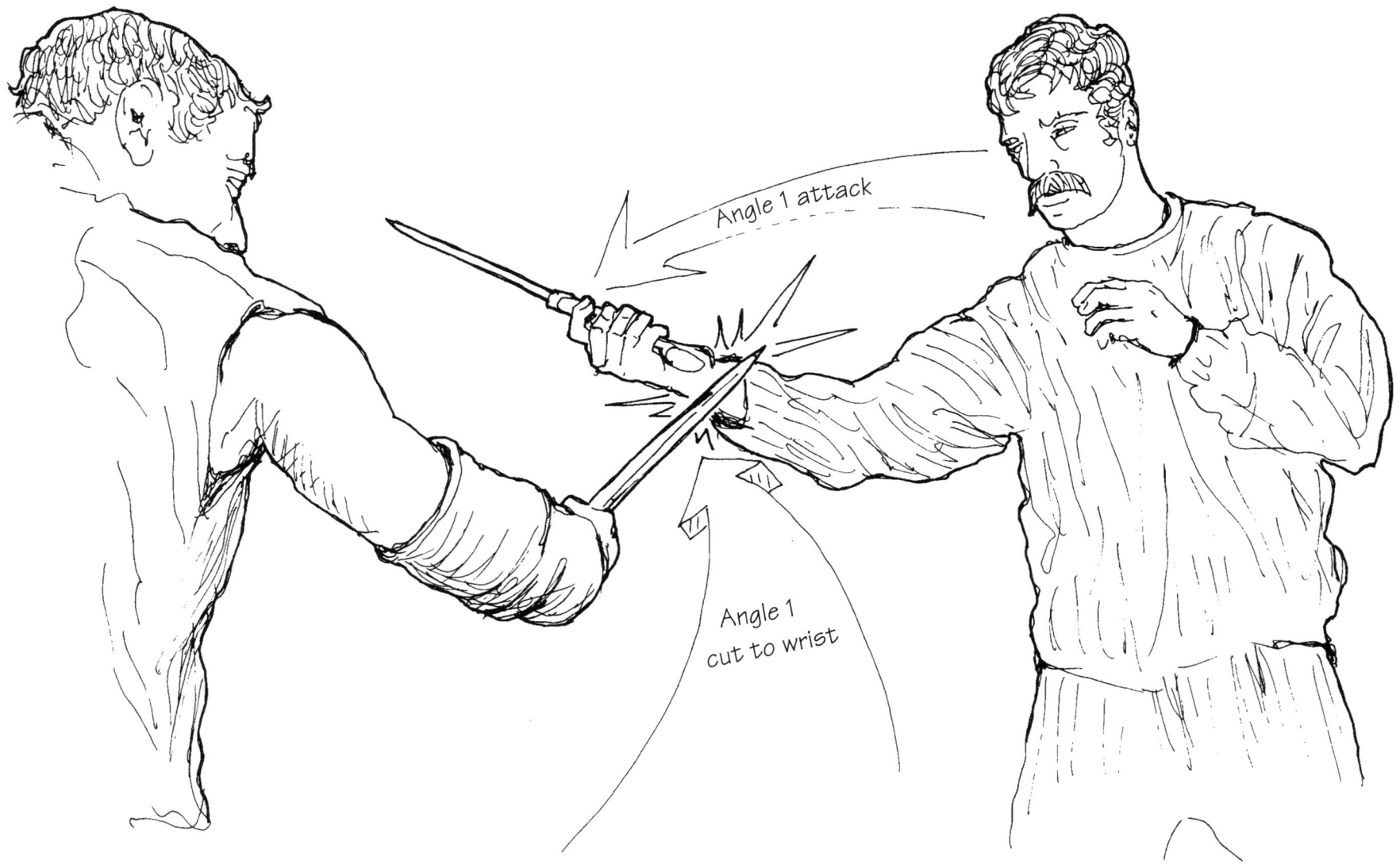

Angle 1 attack

Angle 1
cut to wrist

Figure 159. Action 1.

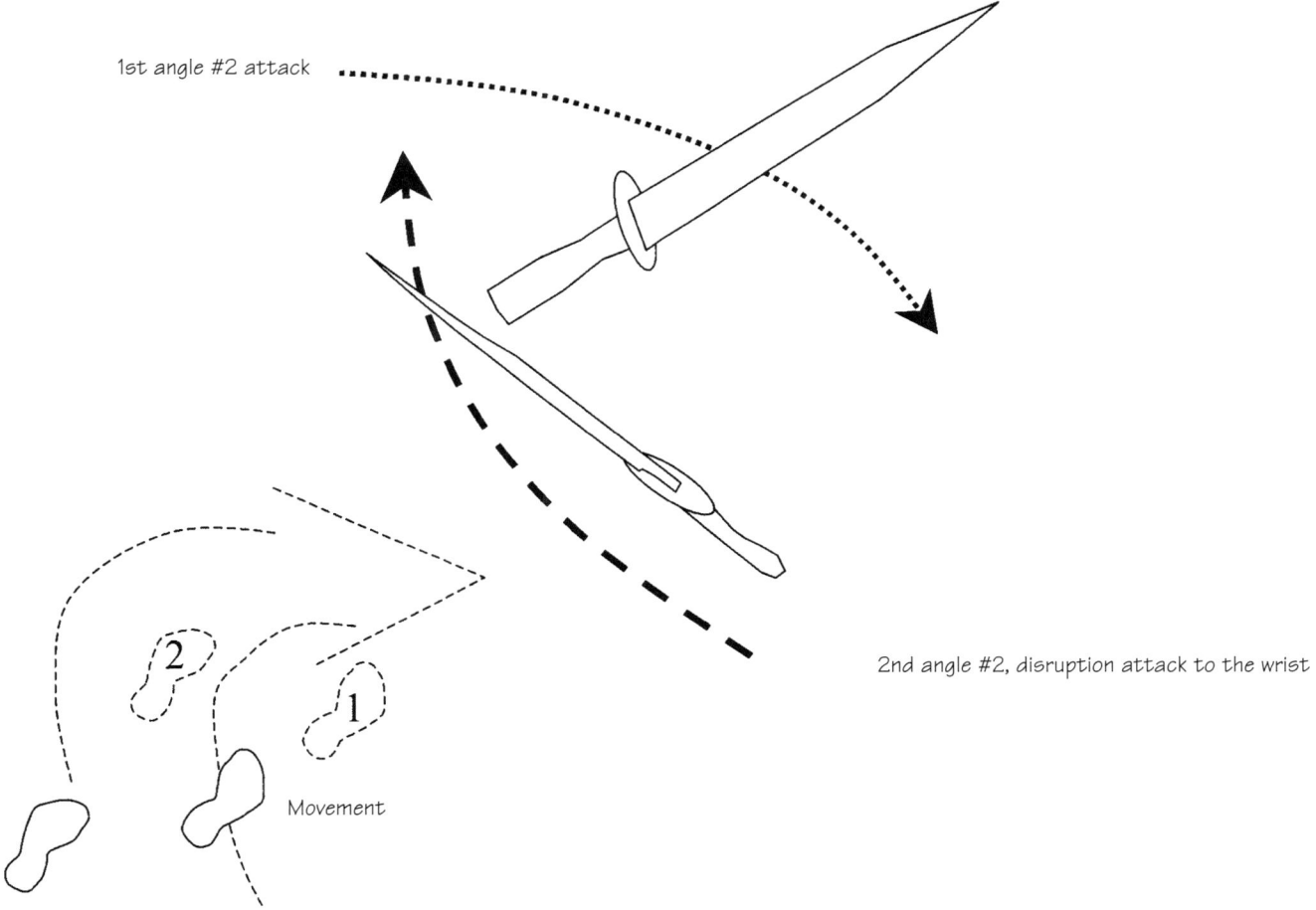

1st angle #2 attack

2nd angle #2, disruption attack to the wrist

2

1

Movement

Figure 160. Action 2: Opponent executes angle 2 of 12-angle attack pattern; his partner makes an angle 2 cut to the wrist while moving to the left outside the box and shifting forward slightly.

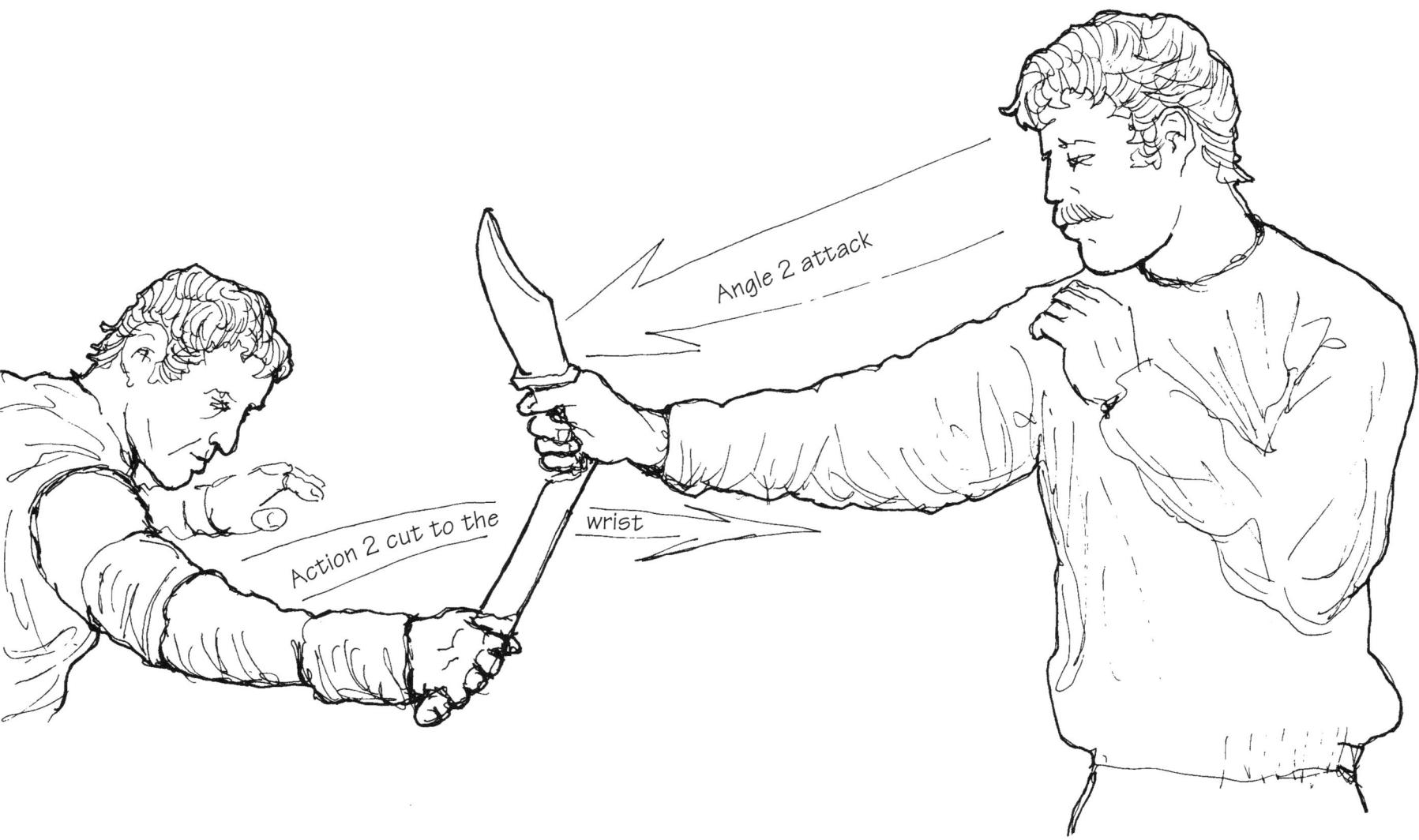

Figure 161. Action 2.

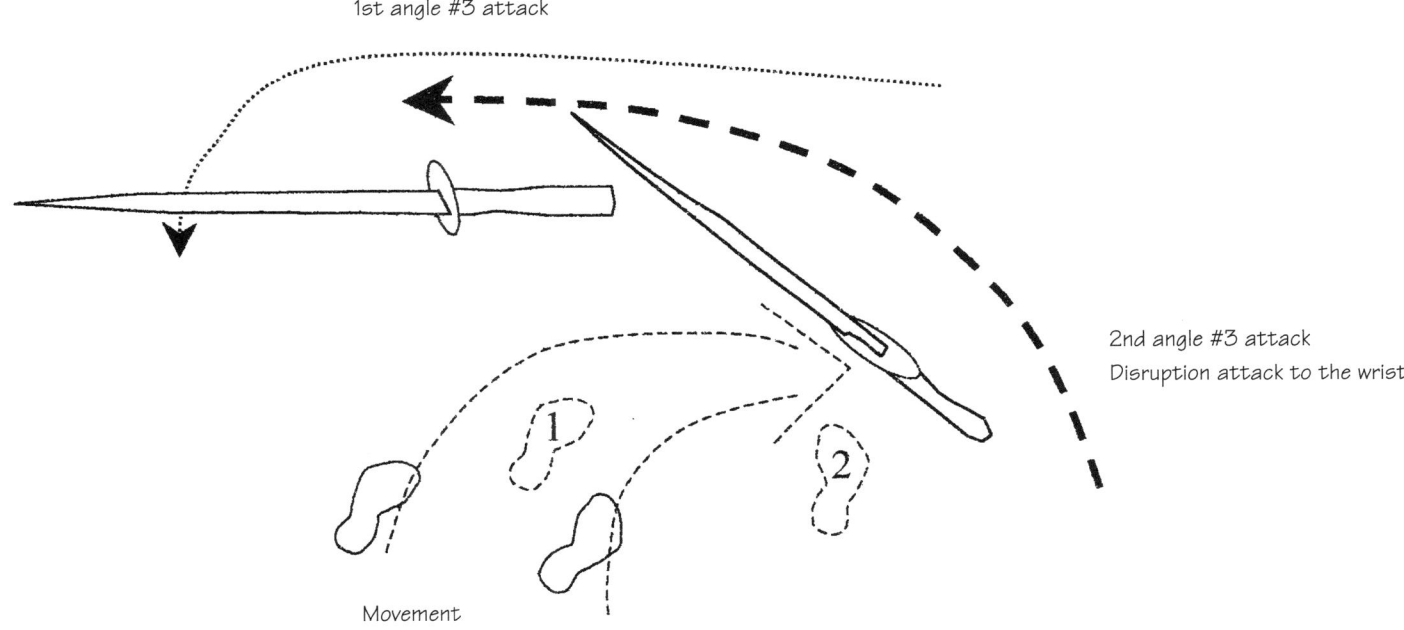

1st angle #3 attack

2nd angle #3 attack
Disruption attack to the wrist

Movement

Figure 162. Action 3: Opponent executes angle 3 of 12-angle attack pattern. His partner makes an angle 3 cut to the wrist while shifting to the right outside the box.

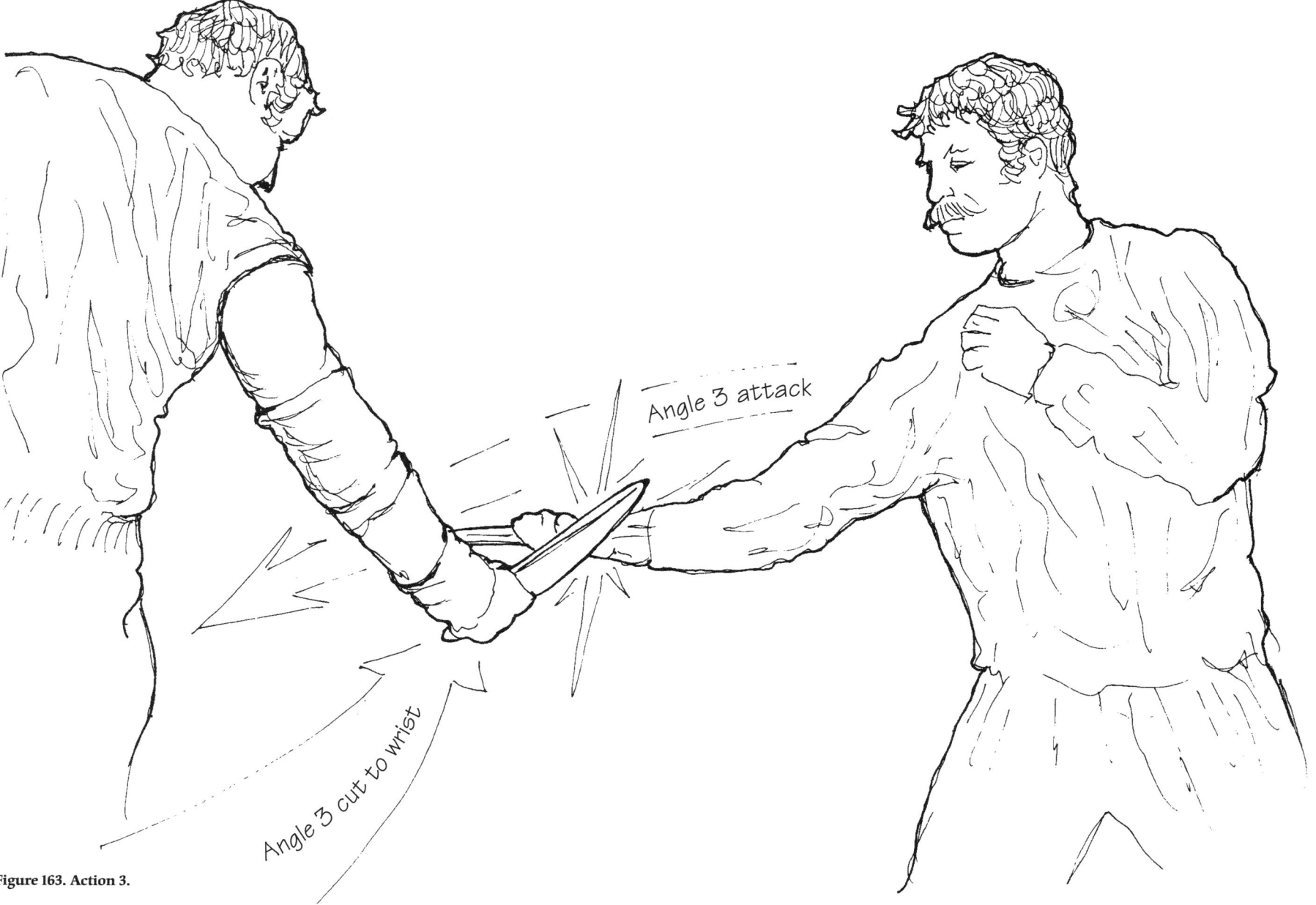

Angle 3 attack

Angle 3 cut to wrist

Figure 163. Action 3.

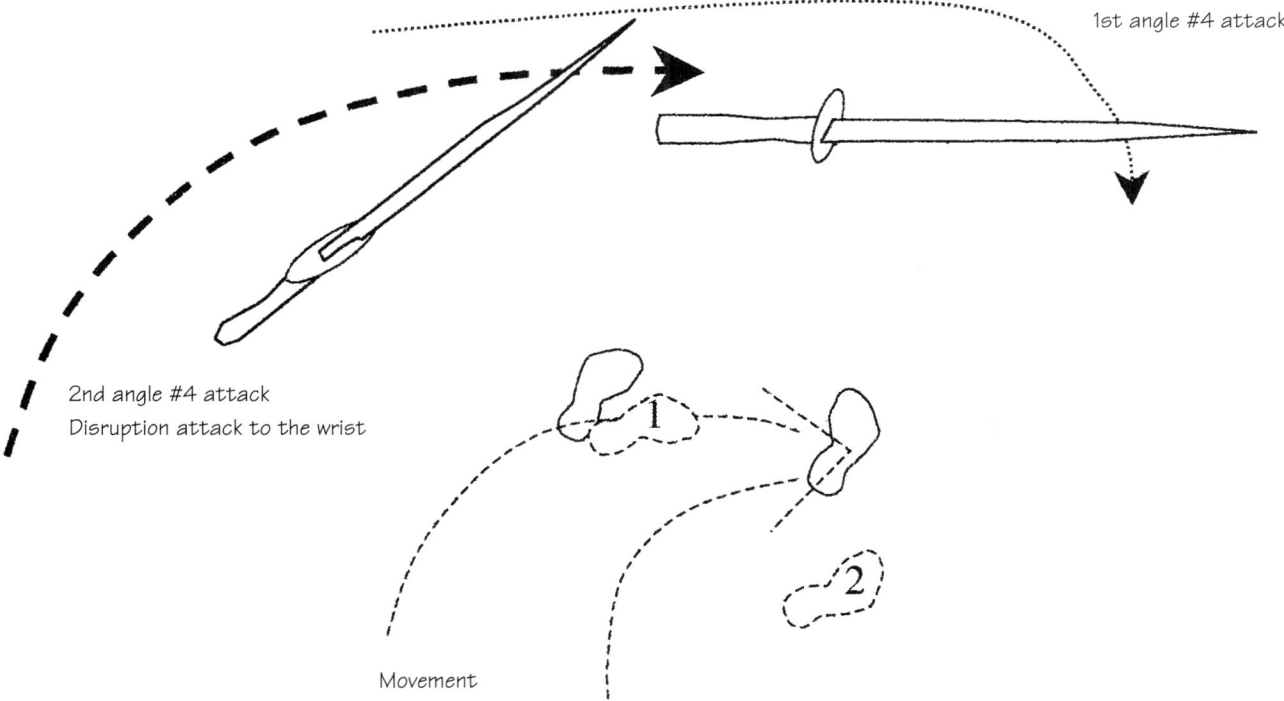

1st angle #4 attack

2nd angle #4 attack
Disruption attack to the wrist

Movement

Figure 164. Action 4: Opponent executes angle 4 of 12-angle attack pattern. His partner makes an angle 4 cut to the wrist while pivoting right on the left foot and passing the right foot to the rear. This shifting is accomplished while the fighter is as much inside the box as possible.

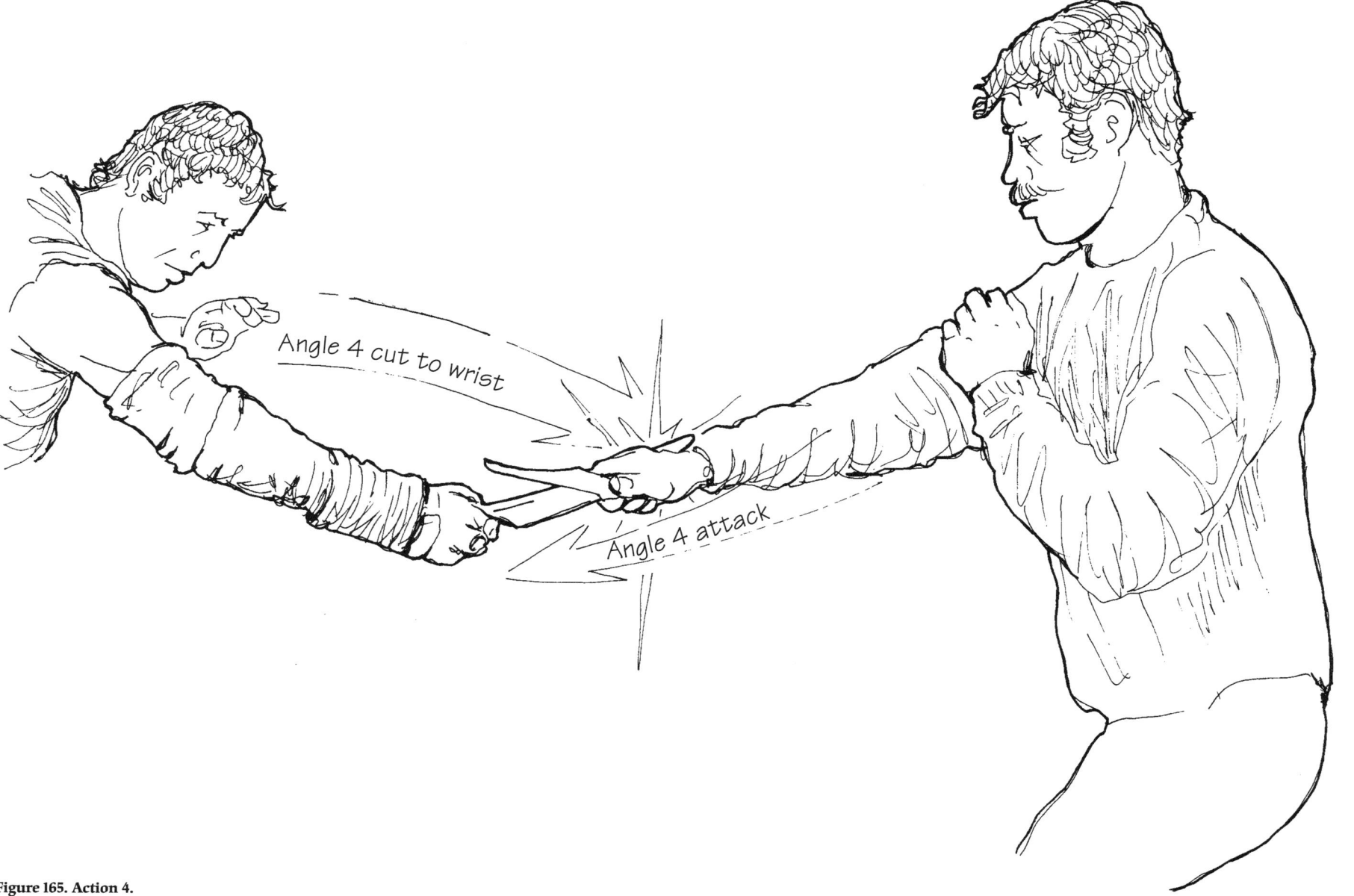

Figure 165. Action 4.

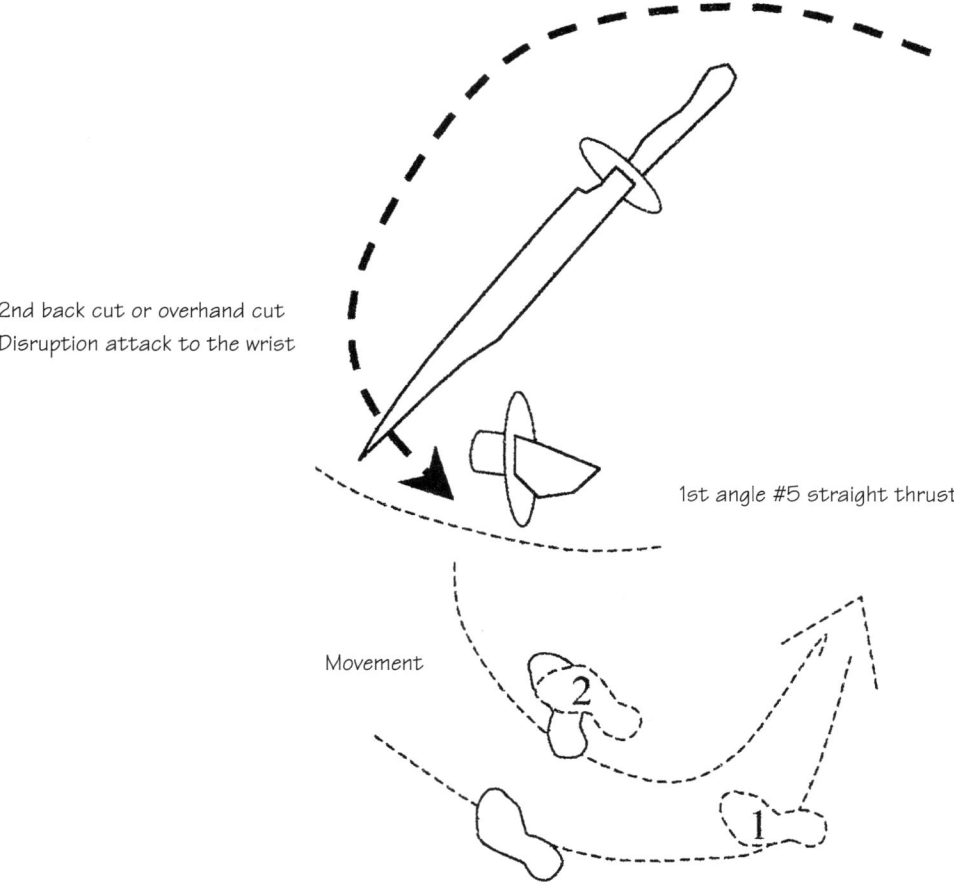

2nd back cut or overhand cut
Disruption attack to the wrist

1st angle #5 straight thrust

Movement

2

1

Figure 166. Action 5: Opponent executes angle 5 (straight thrust) of 12-angle attack pattern. His partner makes either a back cut or overhand cut to the wrist while pivoting right or left to avoid the thrust.

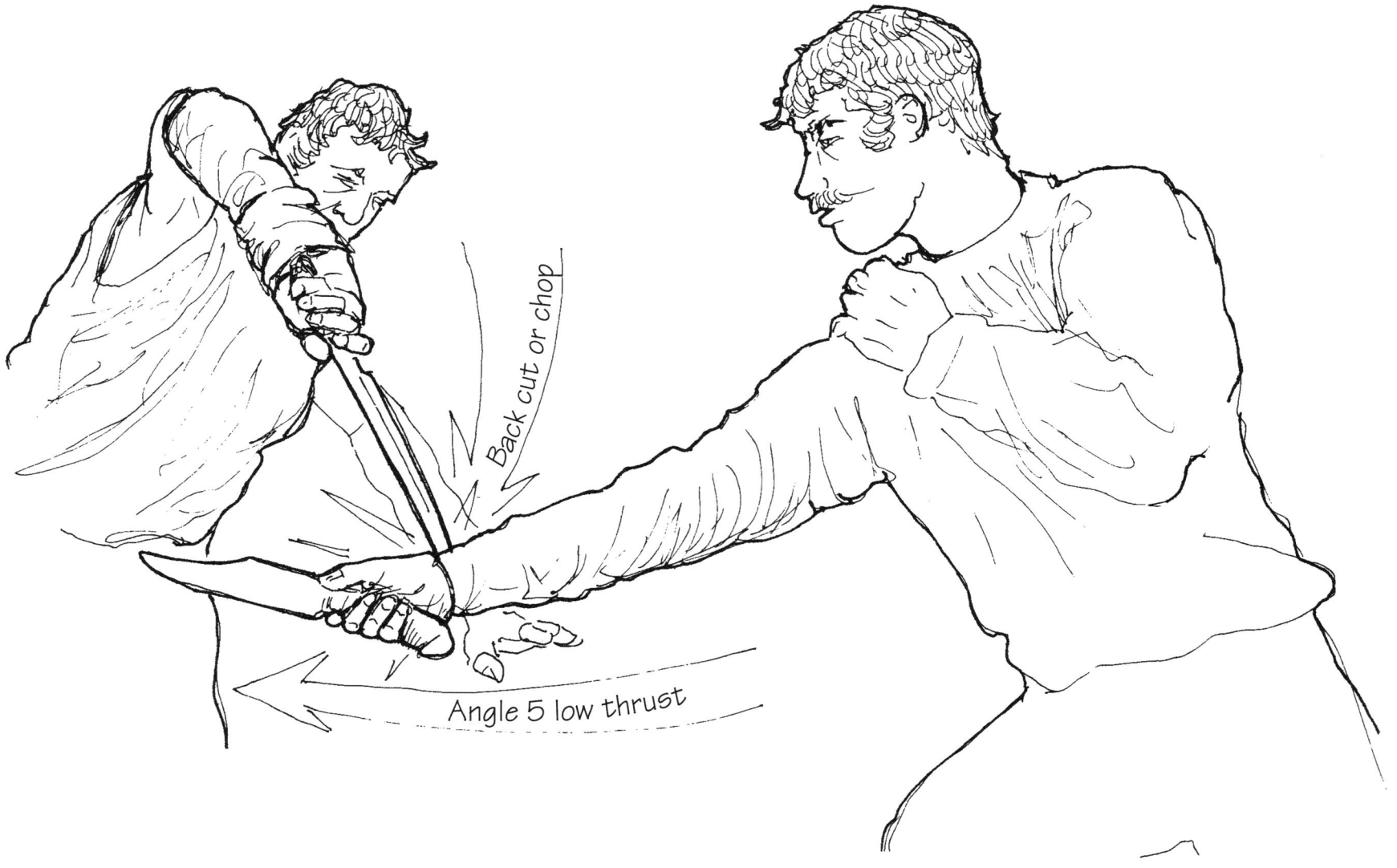

Figure 167. Action 5.

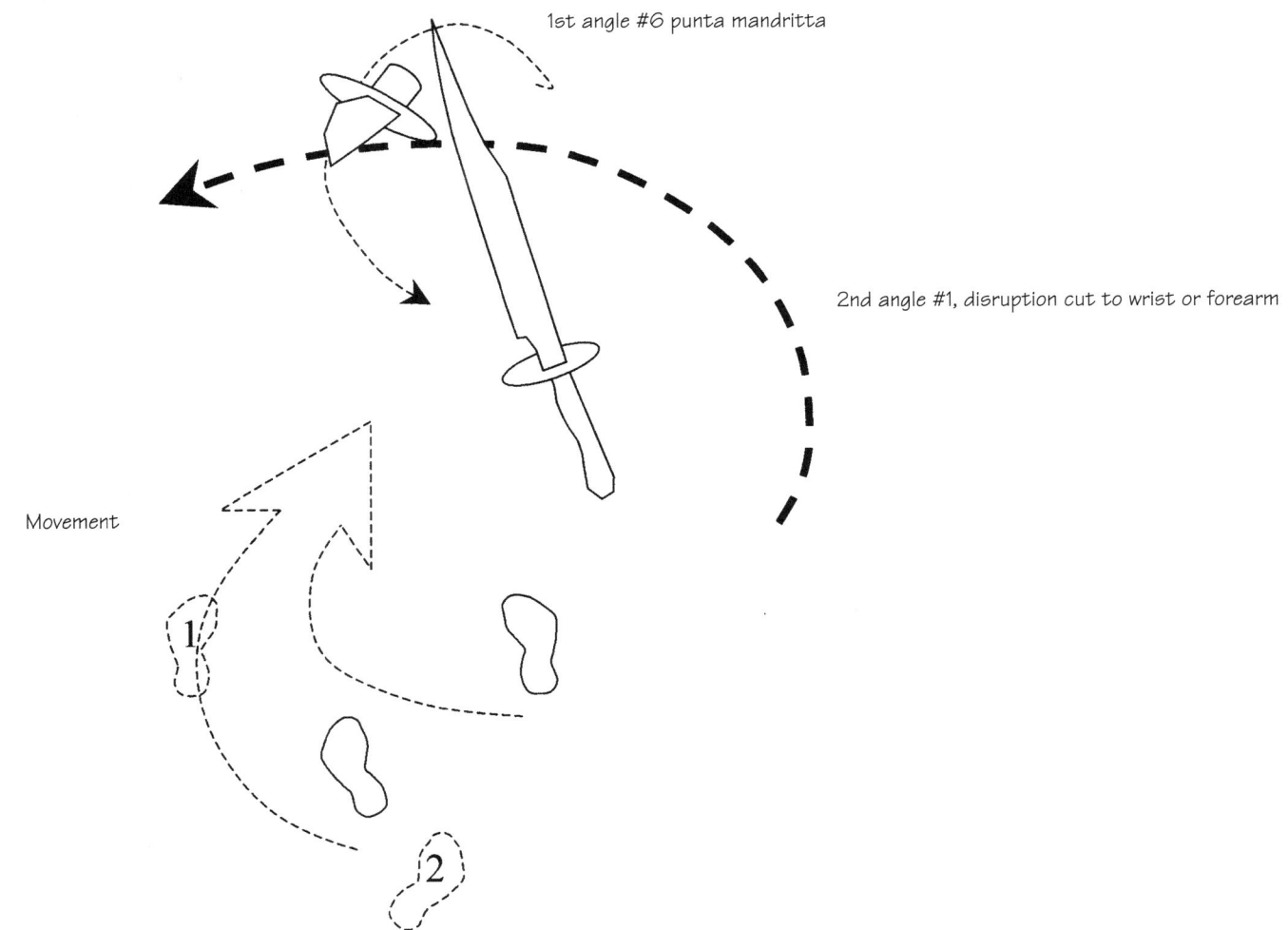

1st angle #6 punta mandritta

2nd angle #1, disruption cut to wrist or forearm

Movement

1

2

Figure 168. Action 6: Opponent executes an angle 6 (punta mandritta) of 12-angle attack pattern. His partner makes an angle 1 cut to the wrist or forearm while shifting to the left and swinging the right leg back.

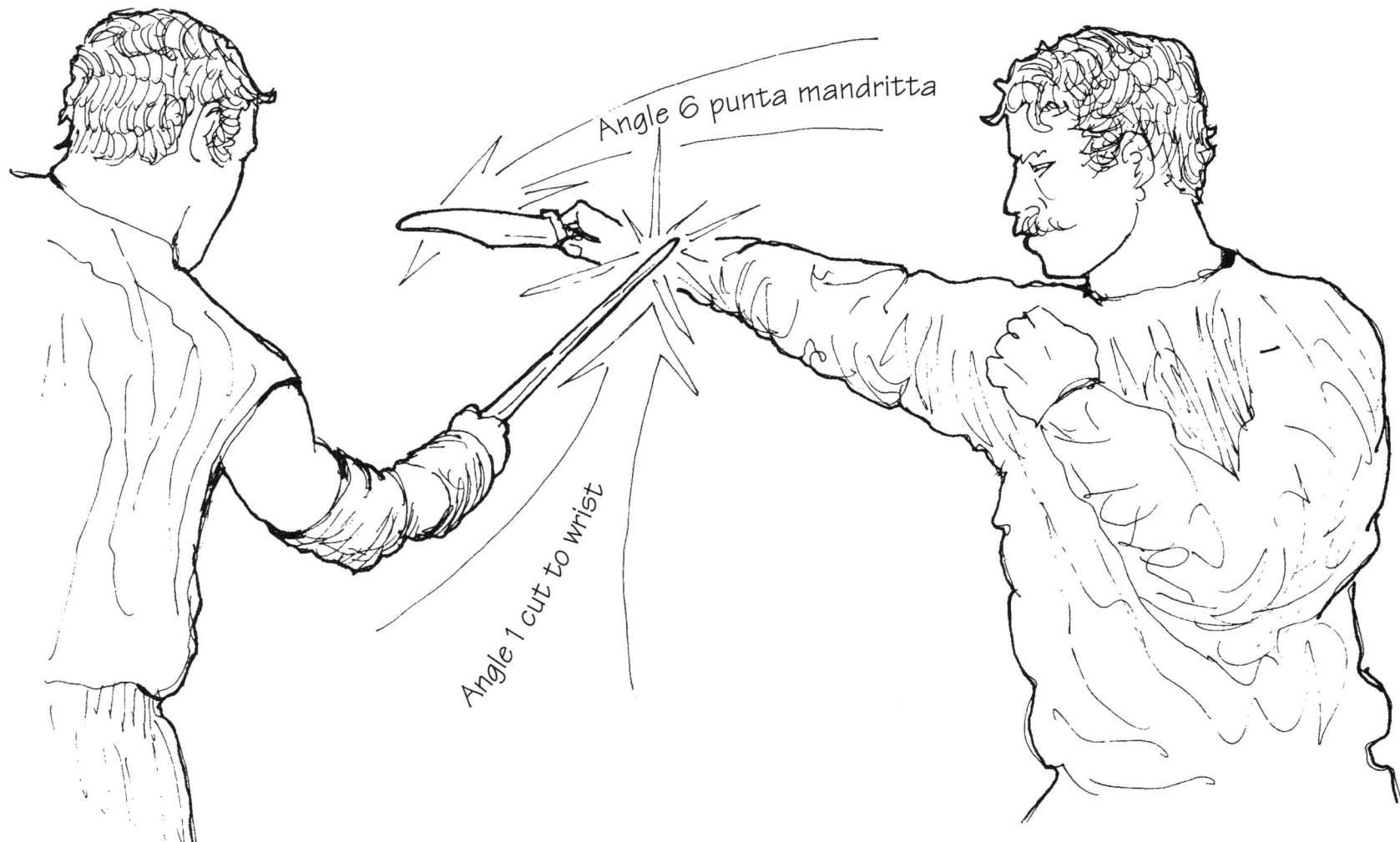

Angle 6 punta mandritta

Angle 1 cut to wrist

Figure 169. Action 6.

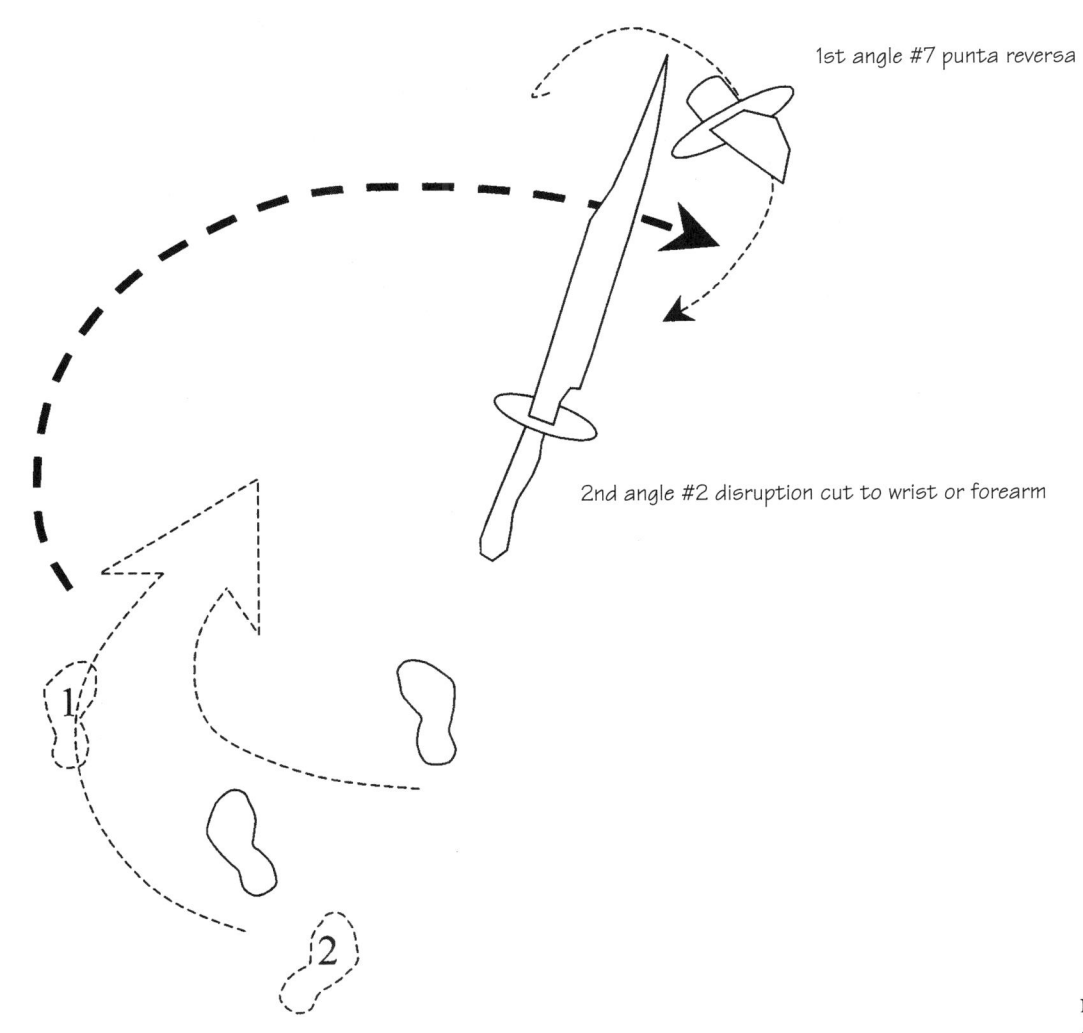

1st angle #7 punta reversa

2nd angle #2 disruption cut to wrist or forearm

Movement

Figure 170. Action 7: Opponent executes an angle 7 (punta reversa) of 12-angle attack pattern. His partner makes an angle 2 cut to the wrist or forearm while shifting to the left and swinging the right leg back.

Figure 171. Action 7.

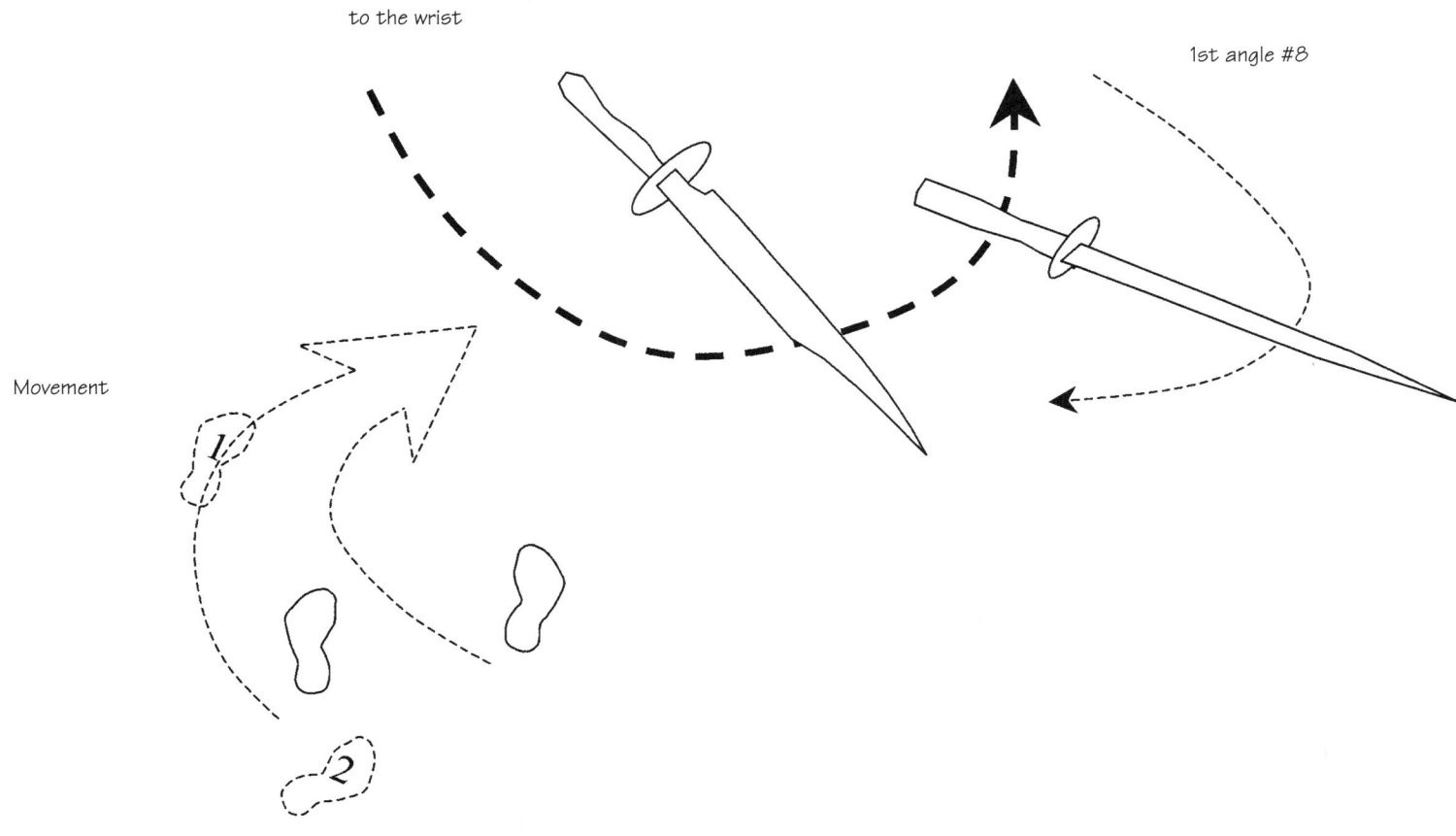

2nd angle #6 disruption attack
to the wrist

1st angle #8

Movement

1

2

Figure 172. Action 8: Opponent executes an angle 8 of 12-angle attack pattern. His partner makes an angle 6 cut to the wrist or forearm while pivoting left and sliding the right leg back.

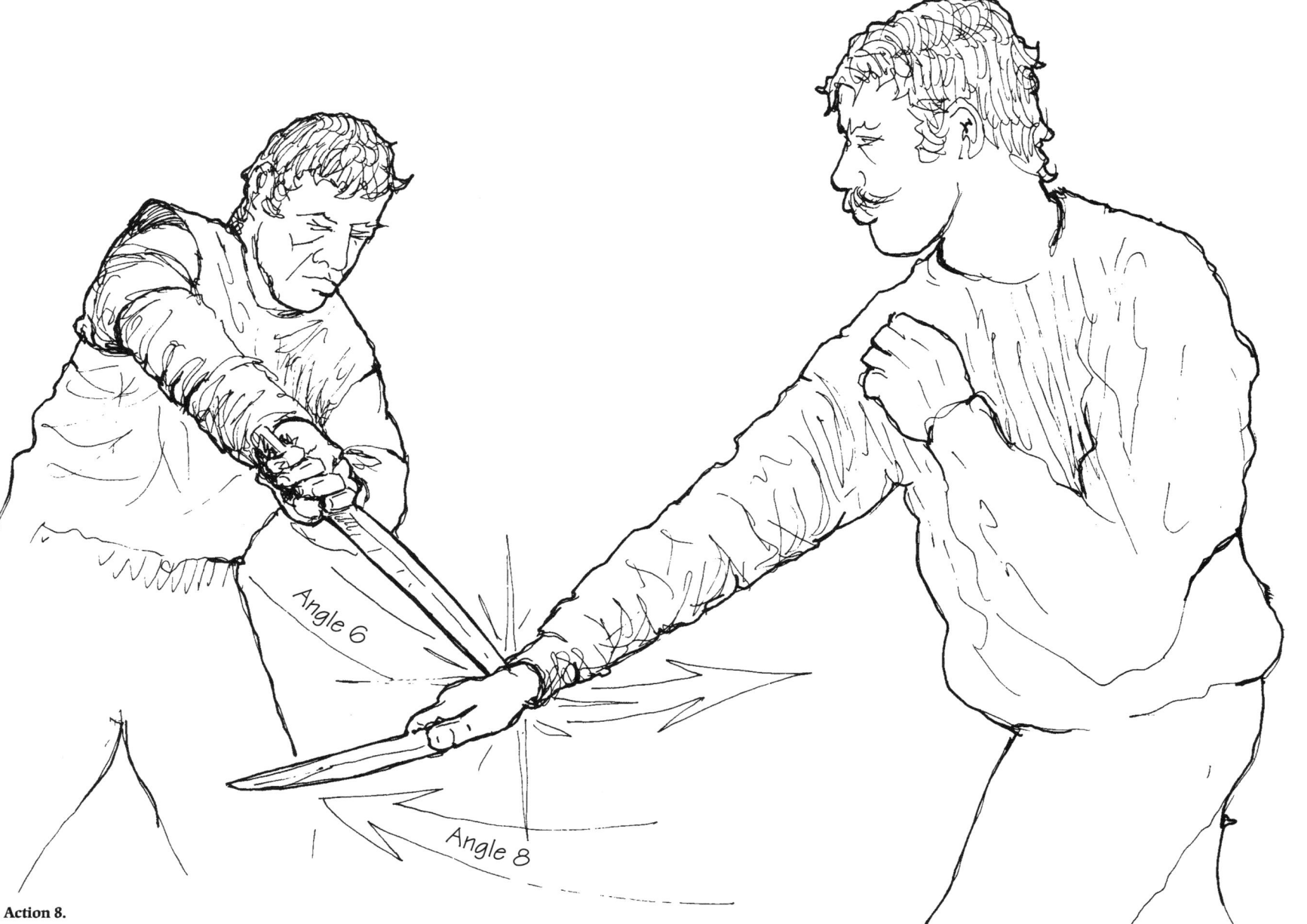

Figure 173. Action 8.

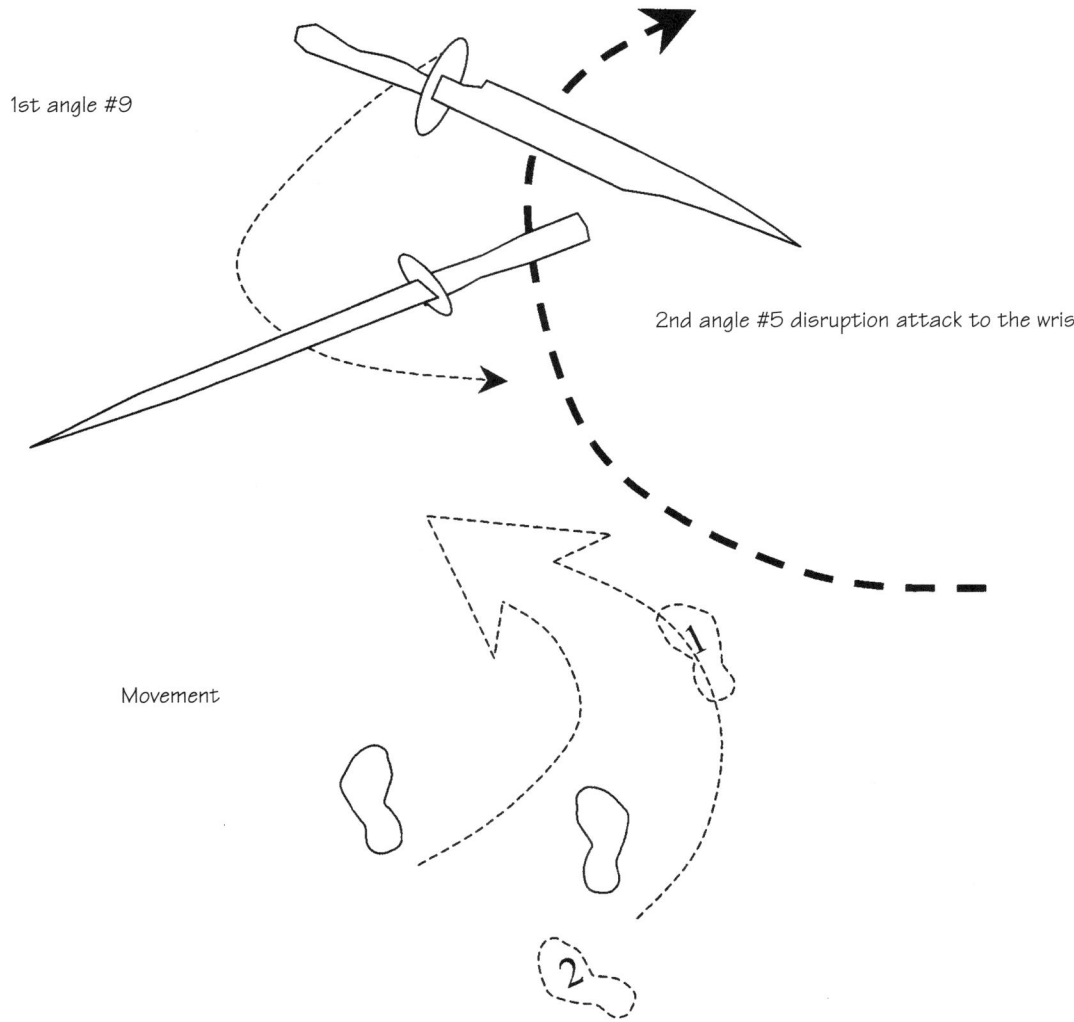

1st angle #9

2nd angle #5 disruption attack to the wrist

Movement

Figure 174. Action 9: Opponent executes an angle 9 of 12-angle attack pattern. His partner makes an angle 5 cut to the wrist or forearm while pivoting right and sliding the left leg back.

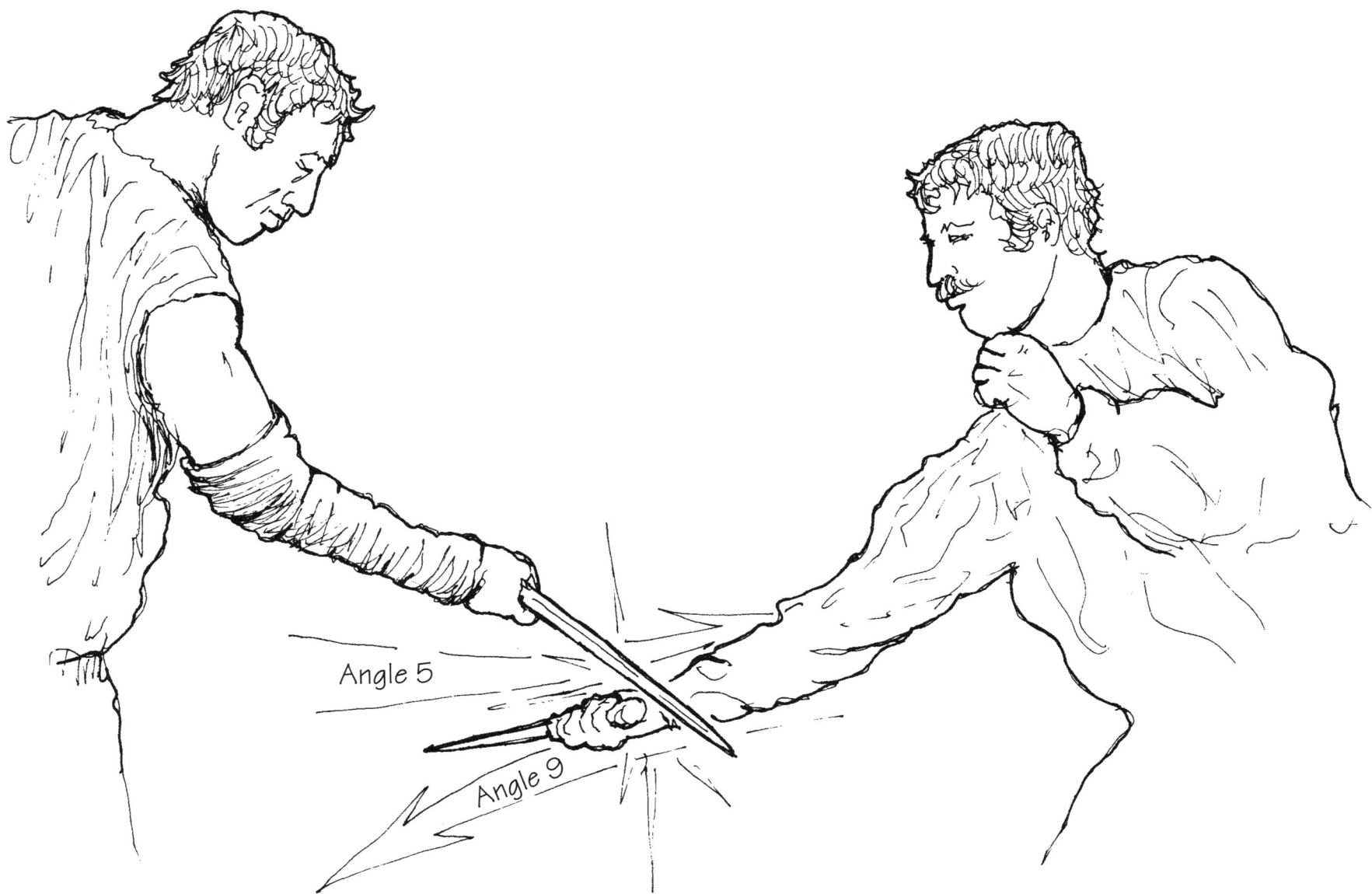

Figure 175. Action 9.

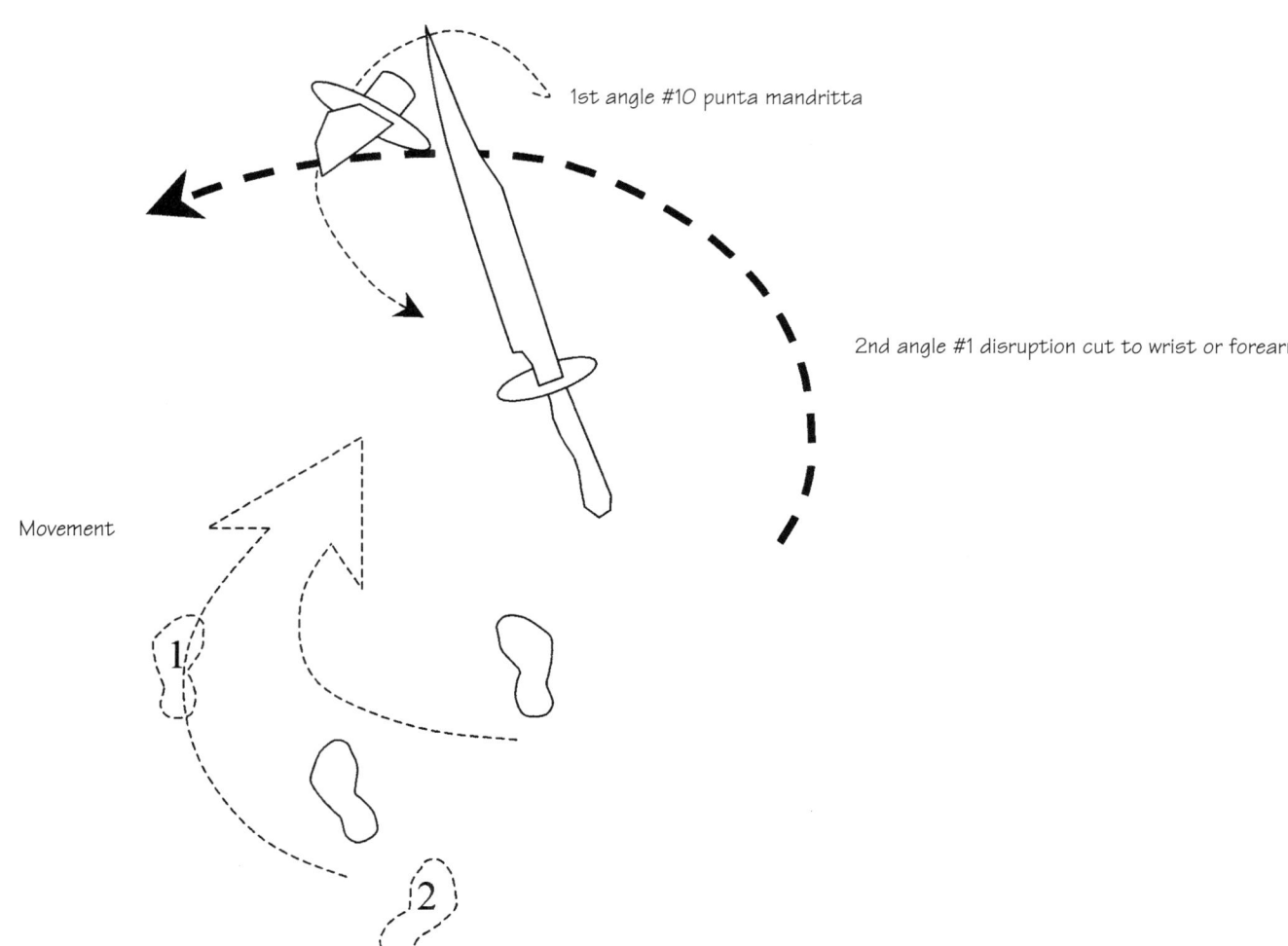

1st angle #10 punta mandritta

2nd angle #1 disruption cut to wrist or forearm

Movement

Figure 176. Action 10: Opponent executes angle 10 (punta mandritta) of 12-angle attack pattern. His partner makes an angle 1 cut to the wrist or forearm while shifting to the left and swinging the right leg back.

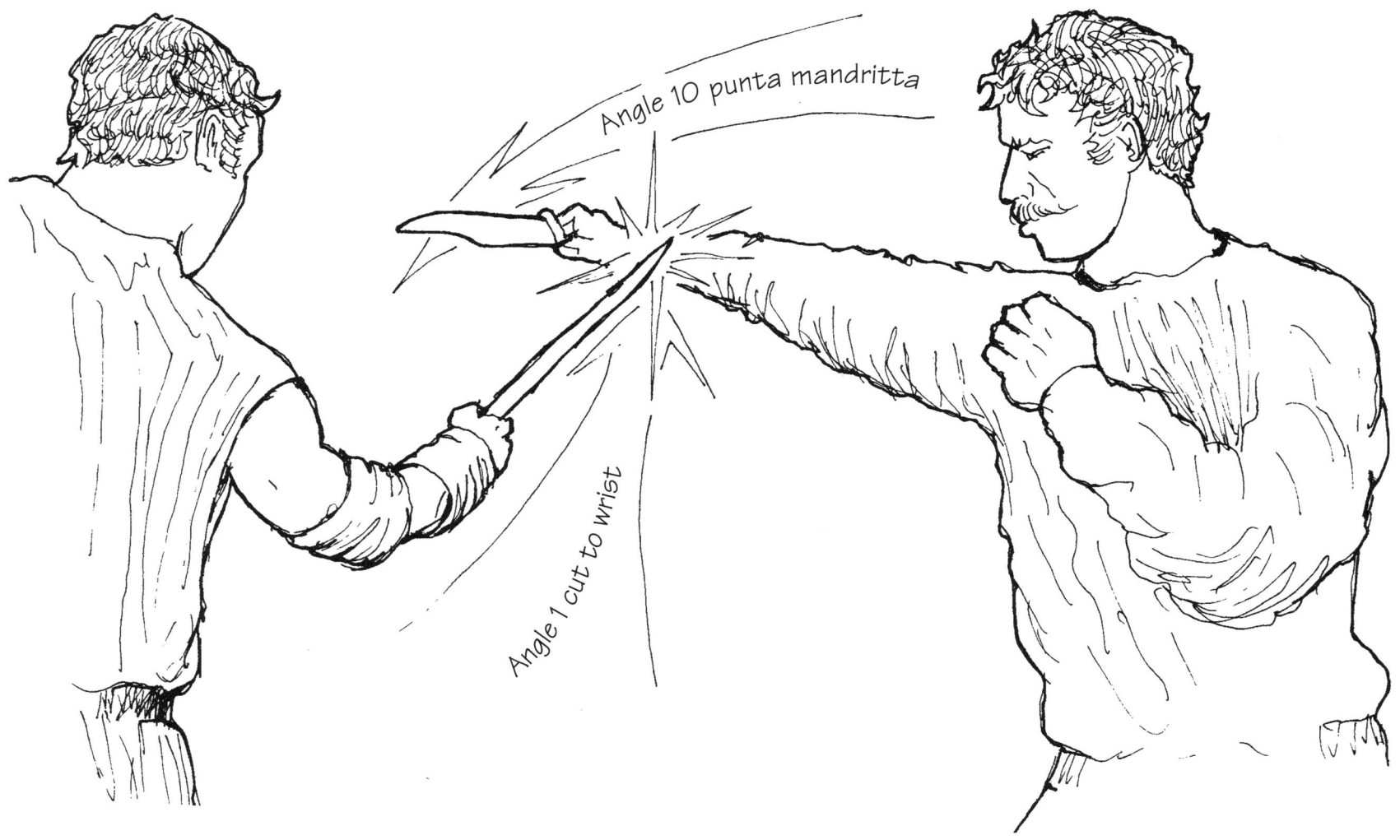

Angle 10 punta mandritta

Angle 1 cut to wrist

Figure 177. Action 10.

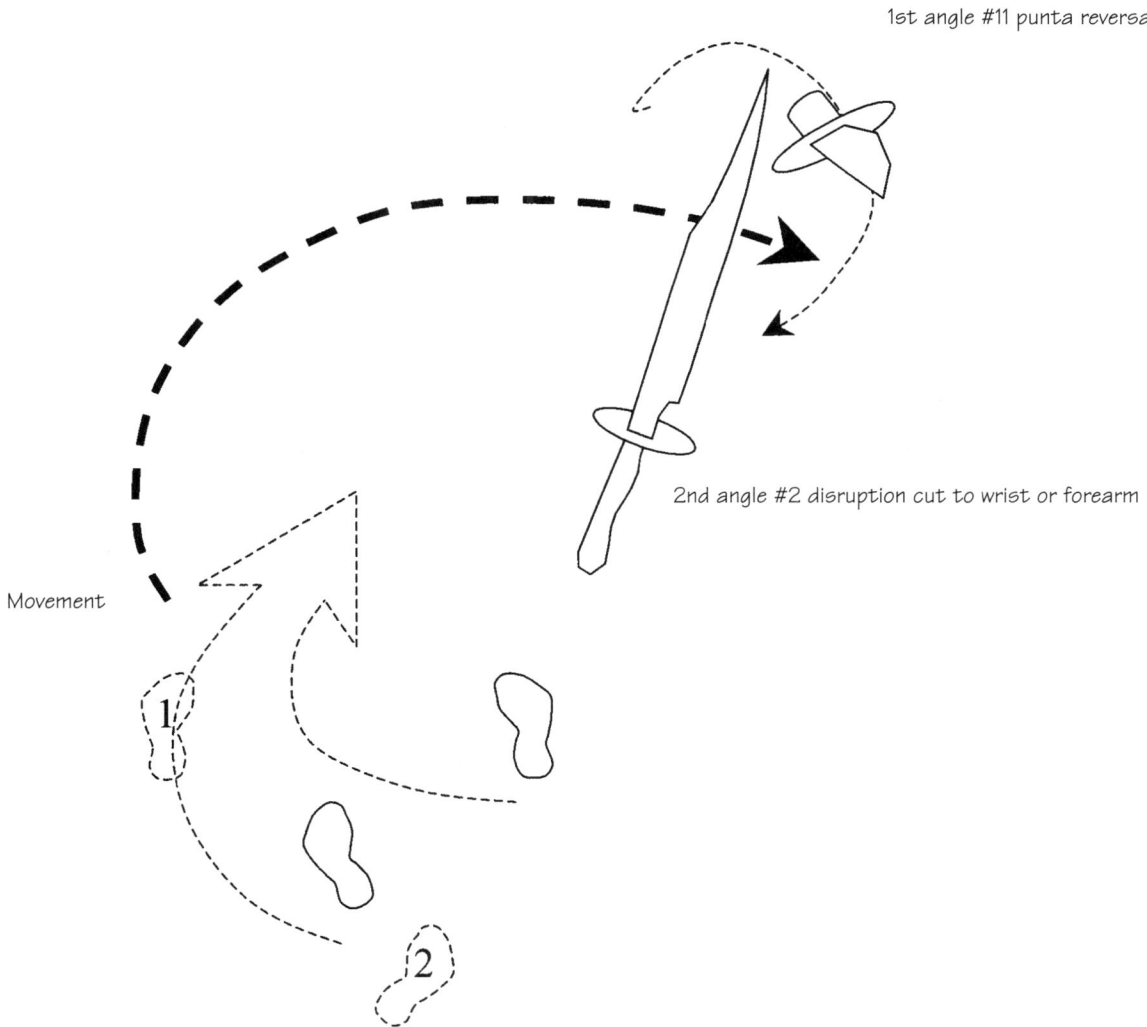

1st angle #11 punta reversa

2nd angle #2 disruption cut to wrist or forearm

Movement

1

2

Figure 178. Action 11: Opponent executes angle 11 (punta reversa) of 12-angle attack pattern. His partner makes an angle 2 cut to the wrist or forearm while shifting to the left and swinging the right leg back.

163

Figure 179. Action 11.

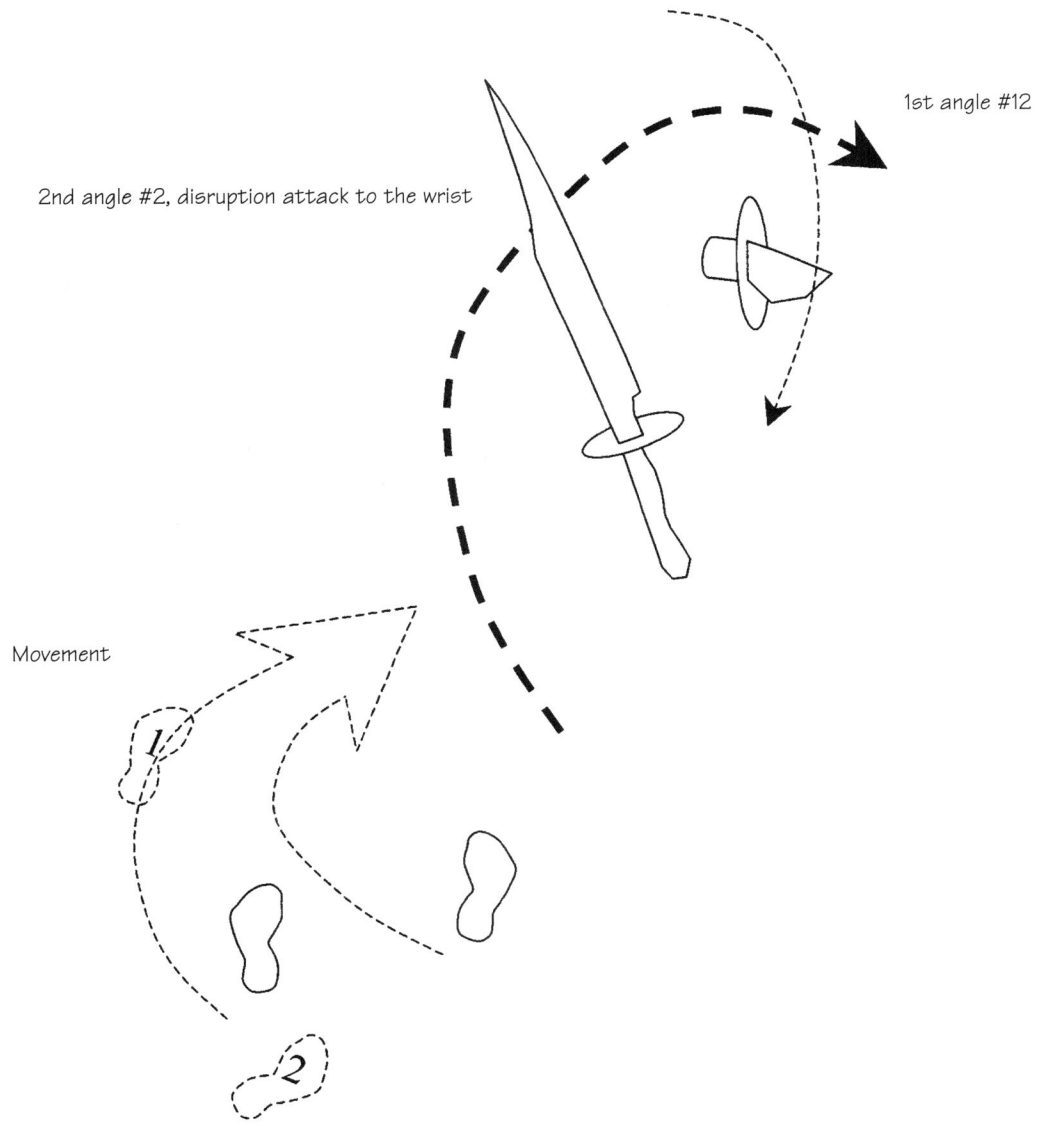

1st angle #12

2nd angle #2, disruption attack to the wrist

Movement

1

2

Figure 180. Action 12: Opponent executes angle 12 of 12-angle attack pattern. His partner makes and angle 2 cut to the wrist while pivoting left and swinging the right leg back.

Angle 12

Angle 2 cut

Figure 181. Action 12.

SECTION FOUR: THE FOREVER PRINCIPLES

This section is devoted to what, for lack of a better term, may be called the "forever principles." Simply put, these are a loose conglomeration of concepts and techniques that have prevailed as constants throughout the history of bladework. These are keys to success in the use of many different types of weapons be it knife, sword, or polearm. Individually, none of these principles is absolute, but in combination they make up a pretty good fighting system that can be used for both sport and real-life encounters. They are not unique, nor do they really deserve the classification of "system." Often we hear about individuals who have developed unique systems or special methods. Well, these do not fall into either category. They belong to no one man; these historical principles belong to everyone.

• • •

Remember earlier in the section on stances you were warned not to think of the stance as a "fixed element" but rather as the starting point from which the engagement begins. All movement for an engagement begins with some form of stance. The length and aspect of the weapon being used often dictate the nature of the stance.

We also discussed guards. While we tend to think of a stance in terms of the position of the feet, the guards relate directly to the position of the arms; as with the stance, the type of weapon greatly influences which type of guard is used.

ANATOMY OF A KNIFE FIGHT

Just as with stances, guards should be seen as only momentary positions that are passed through in the progress of attack or defense actions. The speed of the knife fight just does not allow much time for posturing. Never think of stances or guards as events in themselves, but rather link them to the concept of movement into and out of an engagement sequence where a brief pause occurs. Figure 182 shows the semi-fixed stance and guard becoming offensive and defensive techniques as the area of the engagement is entered.

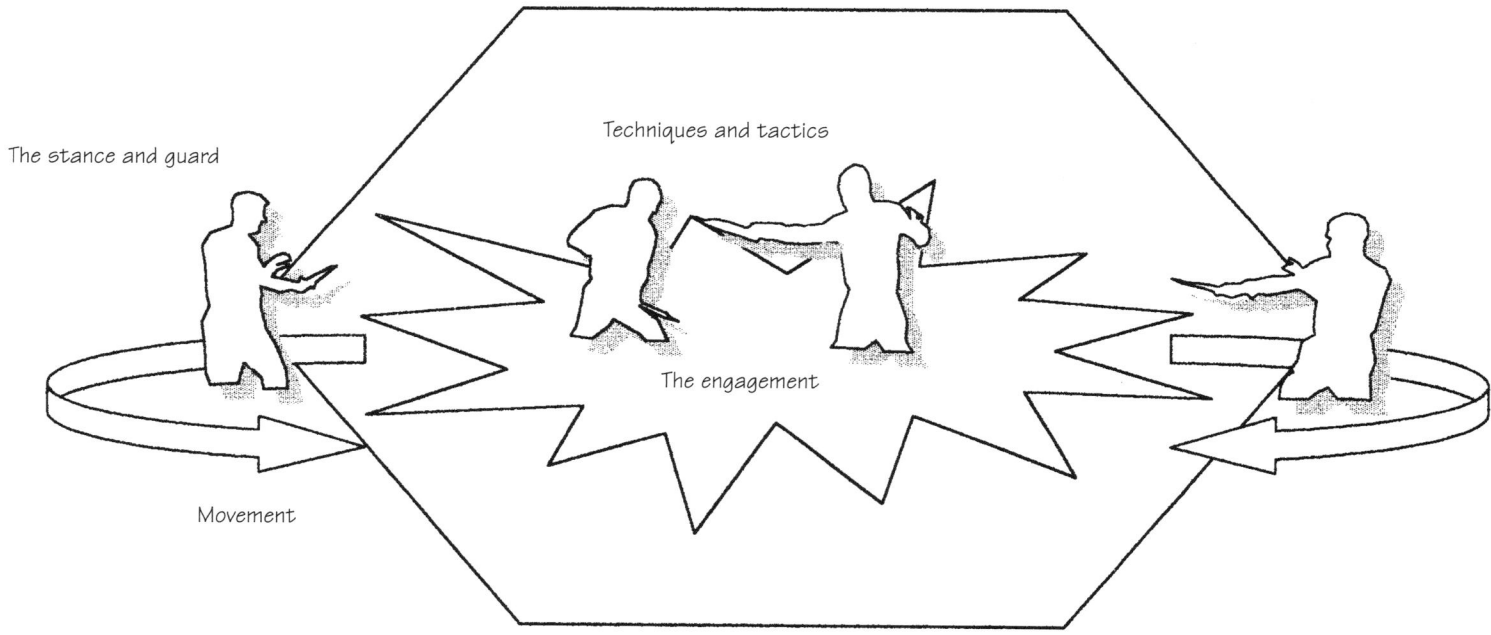

The stance and guard

Techniques and tactics

The engagement

Movement

Figure 182.

INSIDE THE AREA OF ENGAGEMENT

Inside the area of engagement things become more complex. There are many aspects that must be considered if one is to survive. Things are not fixed but in a constant state of flux or motion.

The key to working in this area is flow, not rigidity. The basic variables for the geometry of the human body are movements of the legs and torso in terms of circles, lines, and angles. For the arms and shoulders it is angles and arcs of attack and defense. Therefore what the knife fight tends to become is flow through and around angles, circles, and lines. All of which has the goal of either avoiding the attack or initiating one. Figure 183 illustrates this.

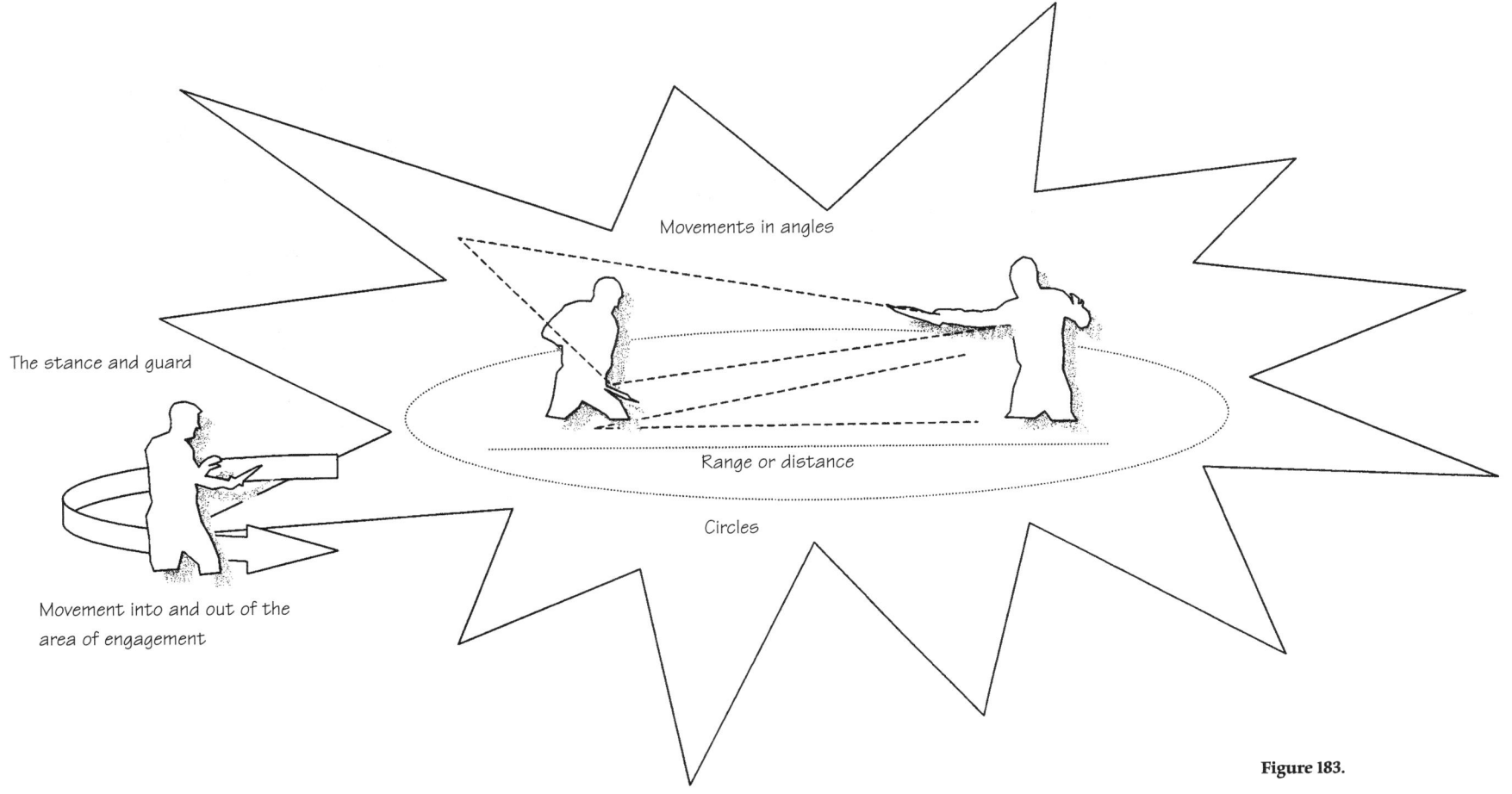

Movements in angles

The stance and guard

Range or distance

Circles

Movement into and out of the
area of engagement

Figure 183.

RANGES OF COMBAT

Before going any further, let's take a quick look at the various ranges, or modes, of a knife fight. Remember that although the type of weapon being used can often dictate what mode the fight begins in, this can rapidly change to another mode based on the tactics and techniques used by the opponents. Figure 184 shows the ranges of combat that can occur.

Medium range

Close-quarter range

Ground range

In this book the focus is on the medium, or dueling, range, and the movements discussed apply there. The bottom line for anyone desiring to learn knife fighting is to learn to work in all three ranges.

Figure 184.

MOVEMENT

Into the Engagement Area

Moving to the fight is just as important as what is done inside the engagement area. The key here is how your opponent moves into the area and coming into range with you. Does he rush in or does he take his time to approach? If he is careful not to rush his approach, you may want to do the same. If he charges in, it might be wise to wait and let the engagement area come to you.

Inside the Engagement Area

As we saw in Figure 184, movement inside the engagement area involves the variable of distance/line (range) and angles that depart left, right, up, and down from this point. There are basically three types of steps that facilitate movement within the engagement area. These are advancing step, passing step, and the lateral step.

Advancing Step

The advancing step is a cautious type of movement, since you are not sure the direction or speed your opponent will move. His skill as a fighter is unknown, and you want to make very sure that you know exactly when you are in range to attack or, more important, be attacked.

The advancing step is often used when you are first approaching. In knife fighting, distance can be very deceptive because of the short weapon and whether the opponent carries his guard with the weapon extended or with arms in chamber (more on this later). The advancing step is often seen in Japanese swordsmanship, or kendo, where the opponents seem to glide toward each other with very small movements.

The intent of the advancing step is to always maintain the guard and, more important, the center of gravity or balance. The advancing step is performed by taking a step with the lead foot and then bringing the rear foot forward until you are in the original stance. The feet are normally slid lightly on the ground or just above the ground so that you can return to a firm footing as quickly as possible. Advancing is often used within the first 3 to 5 feet before coming into range.

The advantage of the advancing step is that you can quickly move laterally forward or backward.

Figure 185 illustrates the motion of the advancing step.

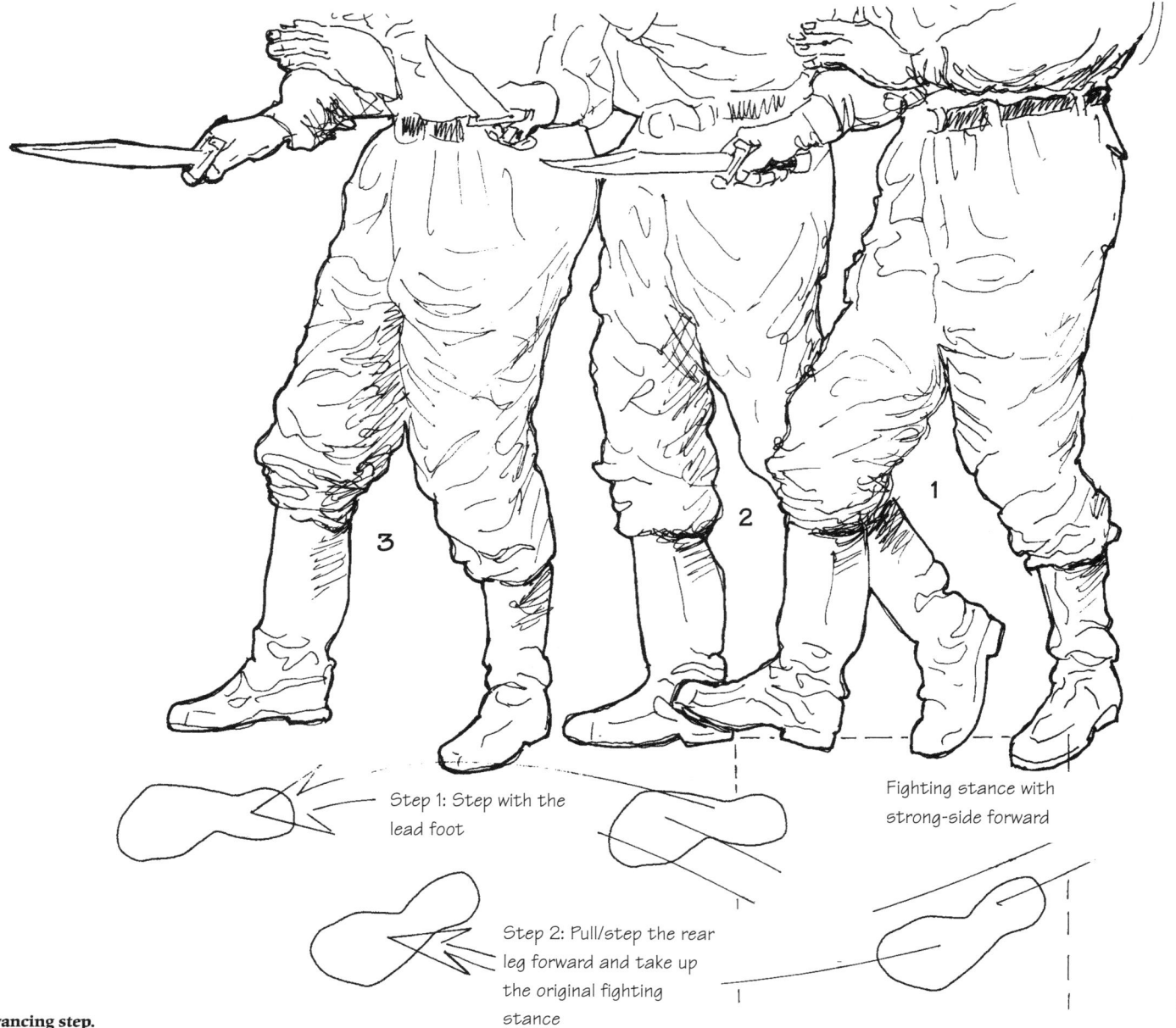

Step 1: Step with the lead foot

Fighting stance with strong-side forward

Step 2: Pull/step the rear leg forward and take up the original fighting stance

Figure 185. Advancing step.

Passing Step

The passing step is a more deliberate movement that can best be described as walking. This method may be used both offensively to attack or defensively to rapidly get one's body out of a specific target area. The passing step may be either a natural, balanced walk or wide, deep movement, which is often seen associated with a thrust or parry.

A fighter often uses a passing step to get into the engagement area and then reverts to an advancing step to get into fighting range. During a fight, the passing step is often used as a defensive measure to avoid an attack and then to launch into a counter. As with the advancing step, the intent of the passing step is to always maintain the guard and, most important, the center of gravity or balance.

The passing step is performed by taking a step with the back the lead foot (or vice versa), with one leg completely passing the other. The advantage of the passing step is that you can cover large distances very quickly, getting you into or out of attacking range. The disadvantage of this movement is that you can quickly end up in a very wide stance from which it is very difficult to recover to launch a counterattack or move. Figure 186 depicts a typical passing step.

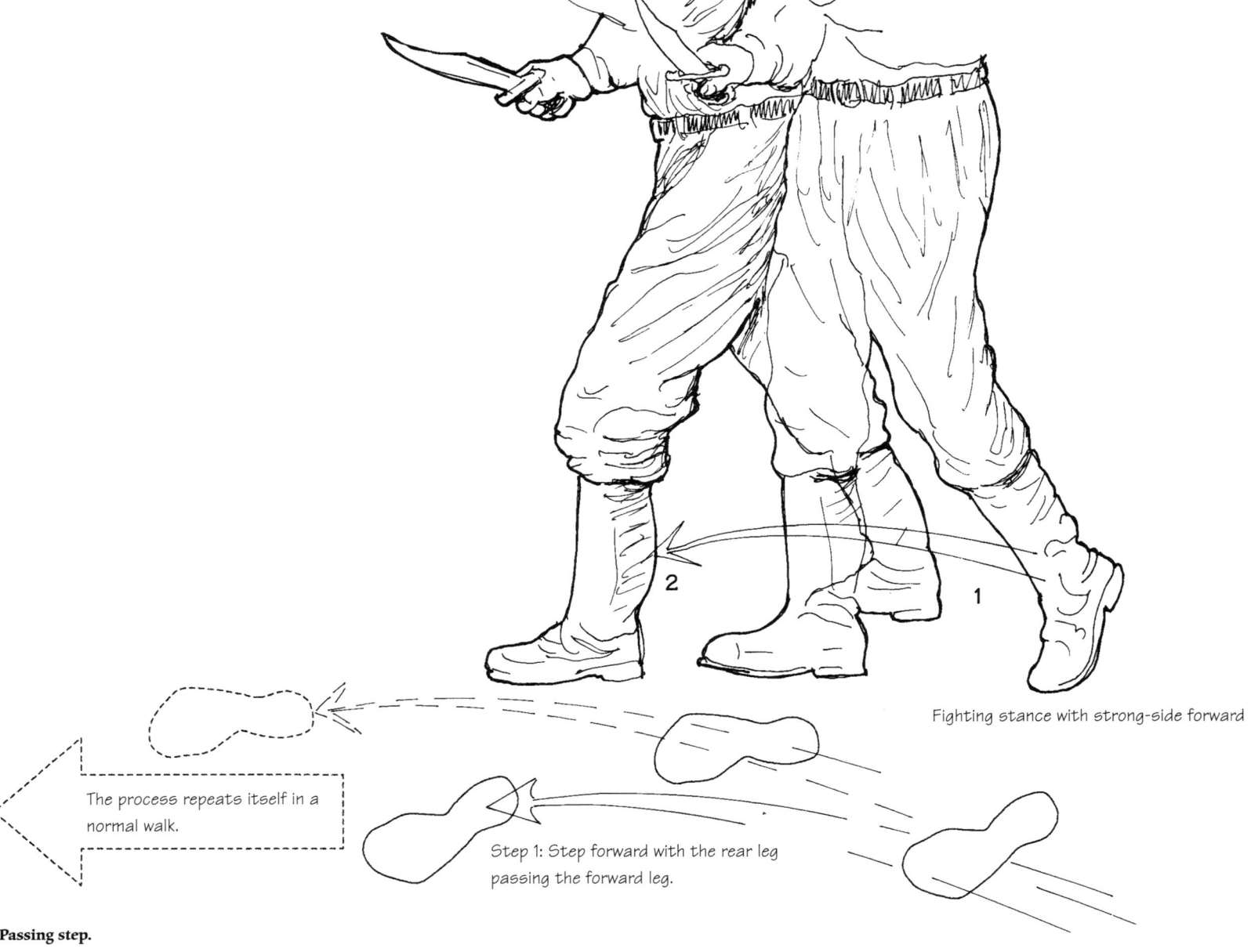

Fighting stance with strong-side forward

The process repeats itself in a normal walk.

Step 1: Step forward with the rear leg passing the forward leg.

Figure 186. Passing step.

Lateral Step

This is a side-to-side step that can be performed by shifting one foot or another to the side or angling forward or backward depending on whether you attack or defend. A lateral step normally follows a circular motion, with the angling used to launch an attack at an opening that appears during the movement. The movement is performed to the left by executing a sidestep with the trailing leg and then immediately pulling the lead leg up and forward into the original strong-side-forward stance. The lateral step creates an angle to the opponent's position and possible openings for an attack. Figure 187 depicts the lateral steps with footprints and against an opponent.

NOTE: A common failure in executing a lateral movement is stepping out too wide, thereby leaving the back leg in a stance too deep to effectively execute an offensive or defensive move.

Figure 188 depicts lateral movement to the left. Again, the intent of this motion is to sidestep to the

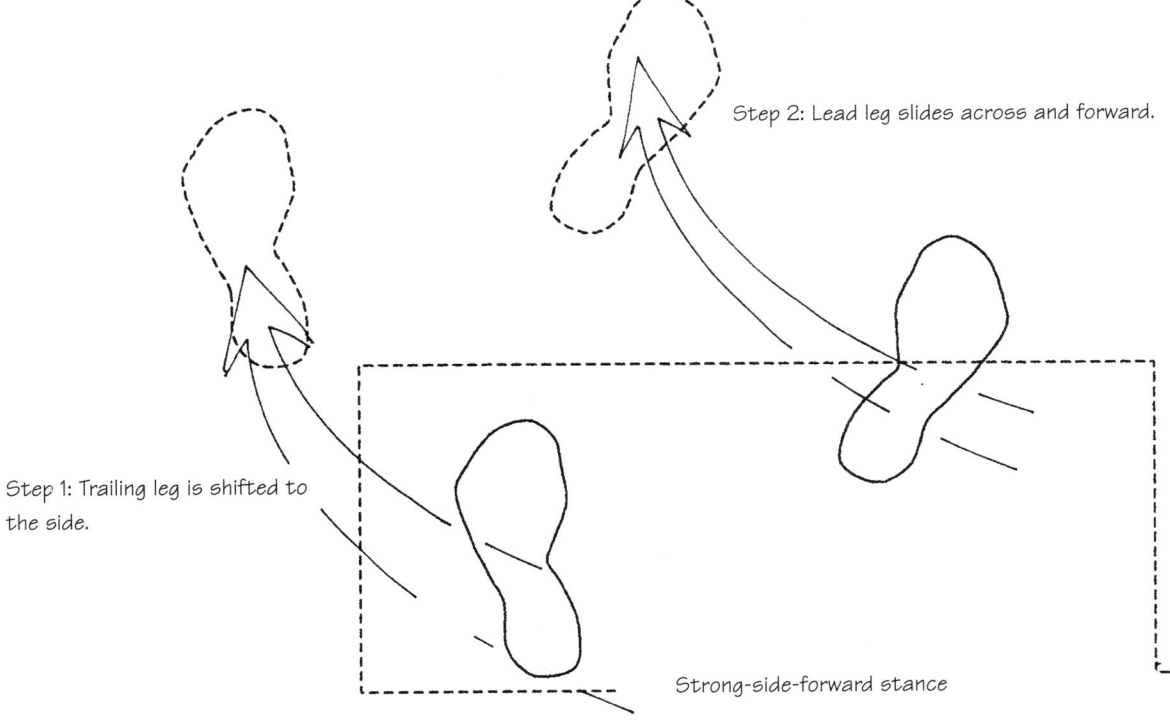

Step 2: Lead leg slides across and forward.

Step 1: Trailing leg is shifted to the side.

Strong-side-forward stance

Figure 187. Lateral step to the left.

left with the left foot and then immediately slide the right leg forward, back into a strong-side-forward stance. Remember, this is a simultaneous flowing motion from which a thrust or cut can be delivered. It can also be used to avoid an attack and set up for an immediate counter.

A lateral movement to the right requires sidestepping with the lead leg forward and to the right,

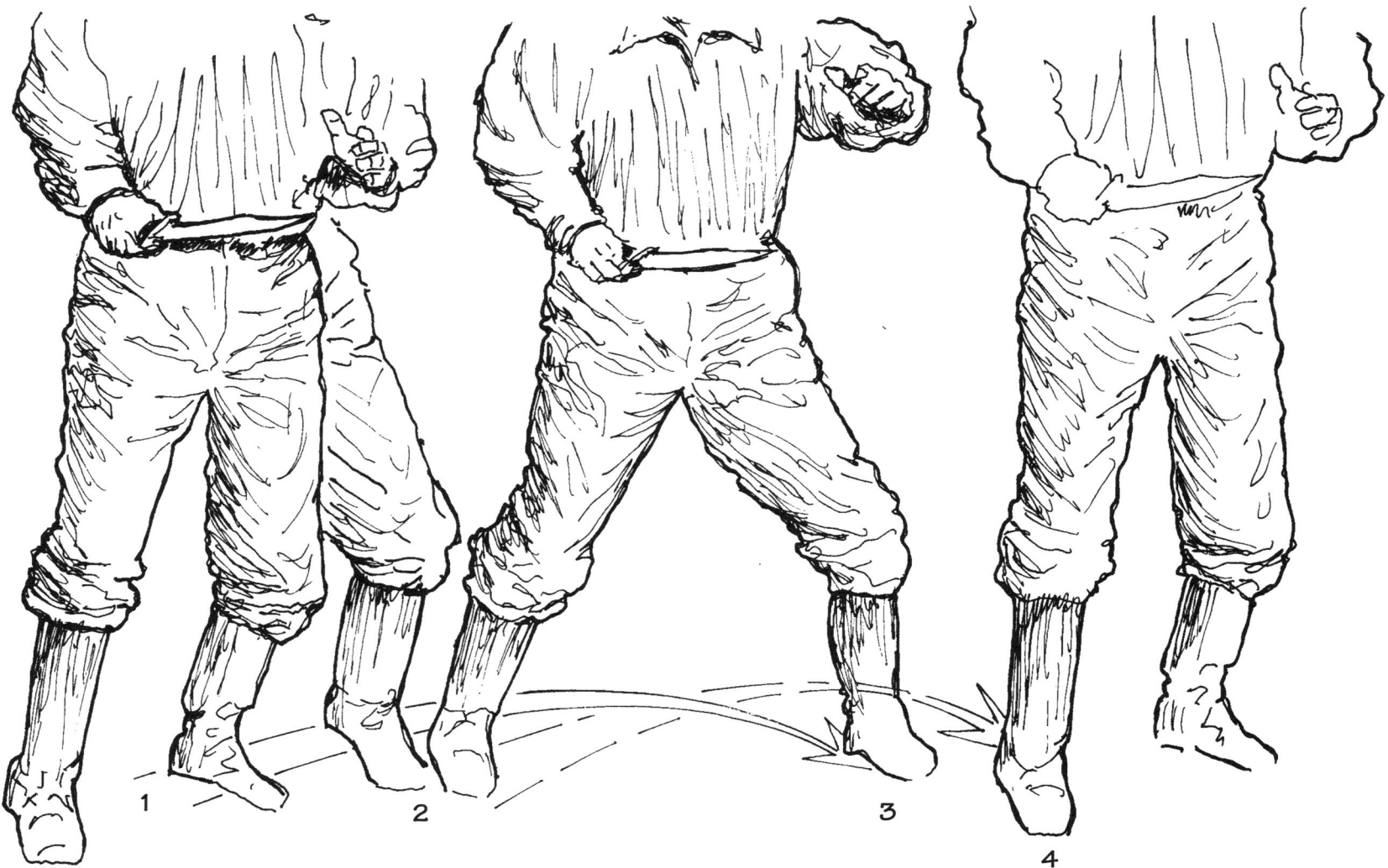

Figure 188. Lateral movement to the left.

and then quickly bringing the rear trail leg up to a strong-side-forward stance. As with the left movement, an attack can be launched after the movement is completed.

Figure 190 depicts lateral movement to the right. Again the motion is to sidestep to the right with

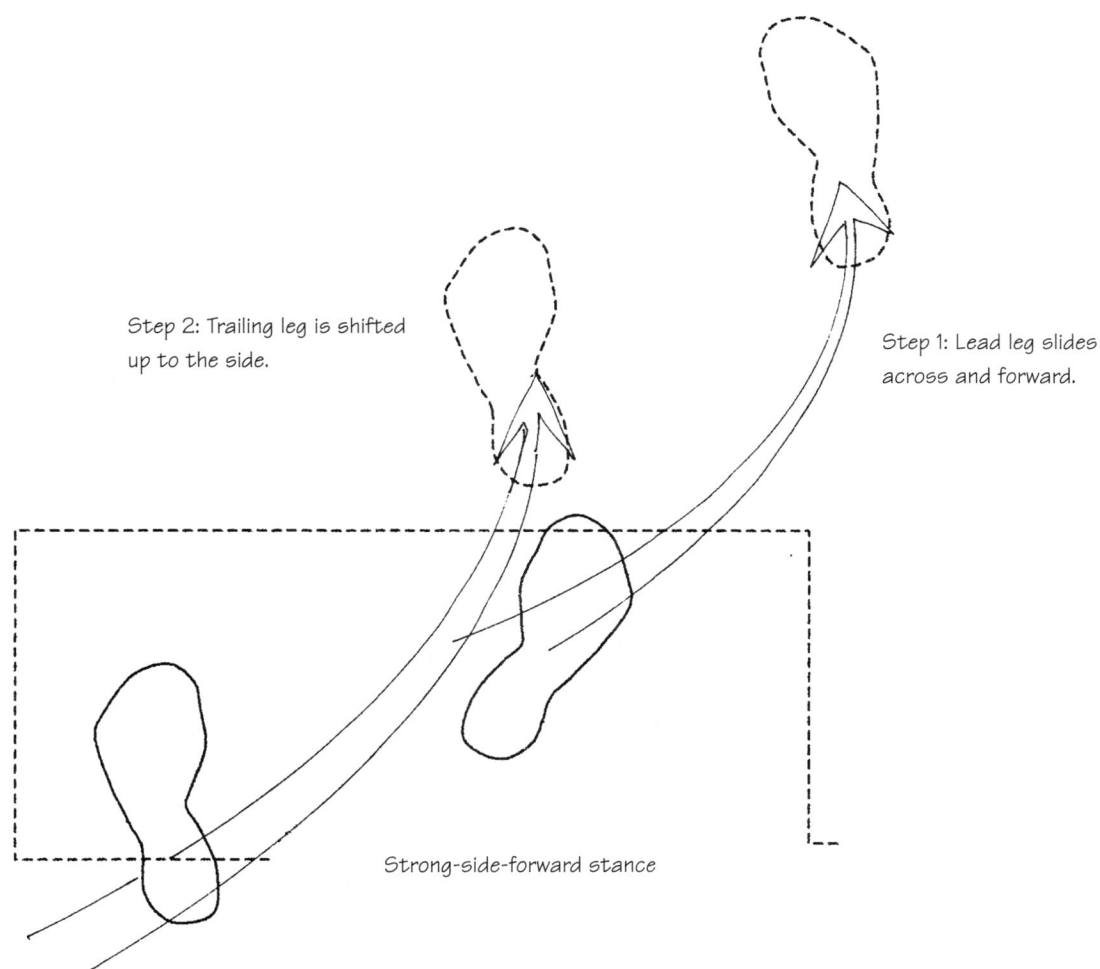

Step 2: Trailing leg is shifted
up to the side.

Step 1: Lead leg slides
across and forward.

Strong-side-forward stance

Figure 189. Lateral step to the right.

the right foot and then immediately bring the right leg forward, back into the strong-side-forward stance. NOTE: This movement takes the fighter off the original line along which his opponent is facing him.

One of the more controversial lateral-movement techniques is the crossover step. This technique

Figure 190. Lateral step to the right.

is often criticized for making a person extremely vulnerable to a leg sweep. Perhaps this is true, but probably no more so than any other form of lateral movement. In reality, the crossover step can be very effective in avoiding a leg sweep.

The movement may be executed either left or right. A move to the left is accomplished by stepping across with the lead foot from a strong-side-forward stance. Movement to the right is initiated by stepping across with the rear leg of the strong-side-forward stance. Renaissance blade masters frequently used this approach in executing offensive and defensive actions. This is not a tight movement but rather a balanced angular form of the passing step discussed earlier.

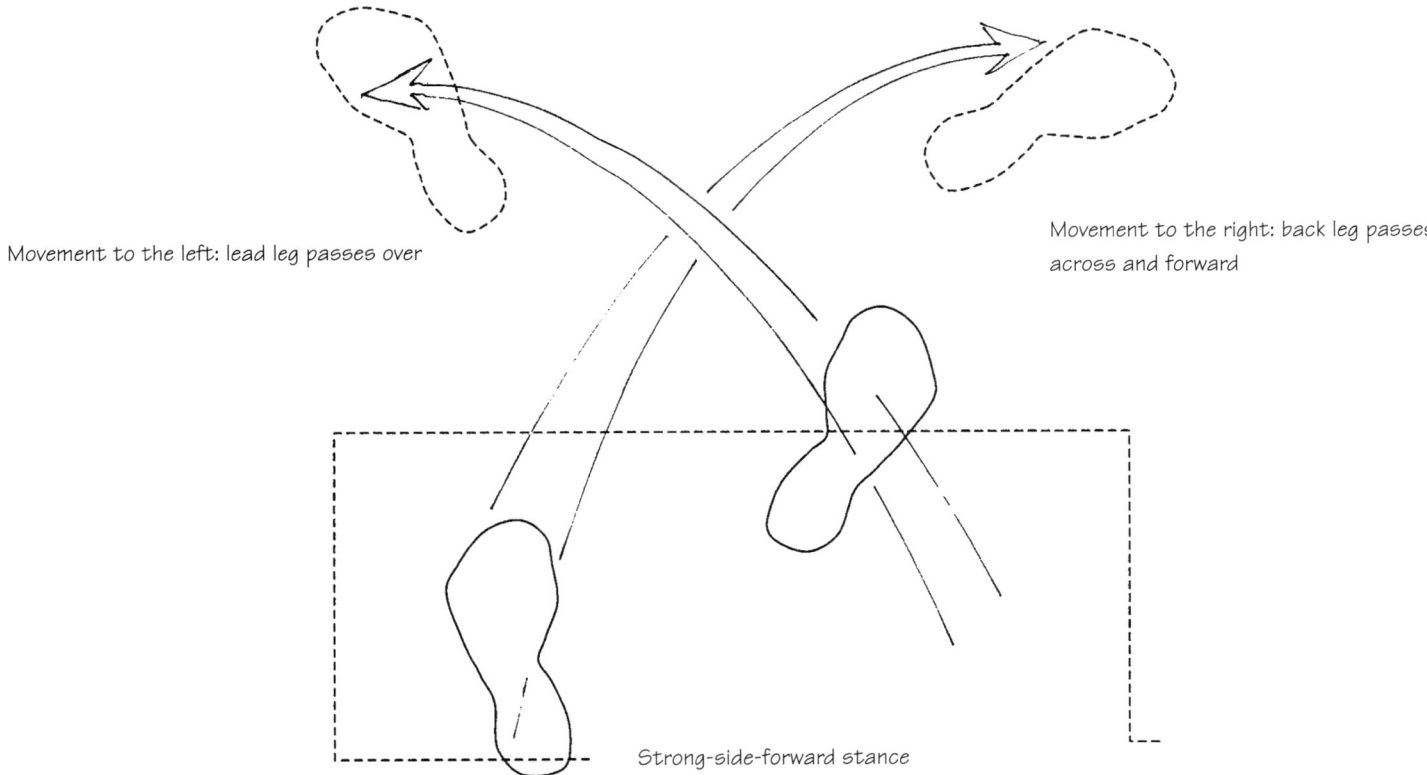

Movement to the left: lead leg passes over

Movement to the right: back leg passes across and forward

Strong-side-forward stance

Figure 191. The crossover step as a lateral movement.

Figure 192. How the crossover step may be used in conjunction with a low-line parry.

Figure 193. Another view of the crossover step to the left.

Distance

When using advancing and passing steps, you are working with the forever principle of distance. Essentially, for our purposes, distance is the range to the area nearest the opponent that one can hit or be hit by. Figure 194 depicts this principle.

When you are fighting with a big knife (in contrast to a sword or saber), determining distance can be difficult because of the shorter length of the weapon. The opponent's use of the technique of raising and lowering the point or chambering the arm adds to this illusion and can be both an advantage and a disadvantage. During an engagement the fighter must constantly evaluate this. When the arms of the opponent are extended and slightly flexed, it is relatively easy to determine distance by noting how close the opponent's point is.

NOTE: The term *range* is often use to define the principle of distance discussed above.

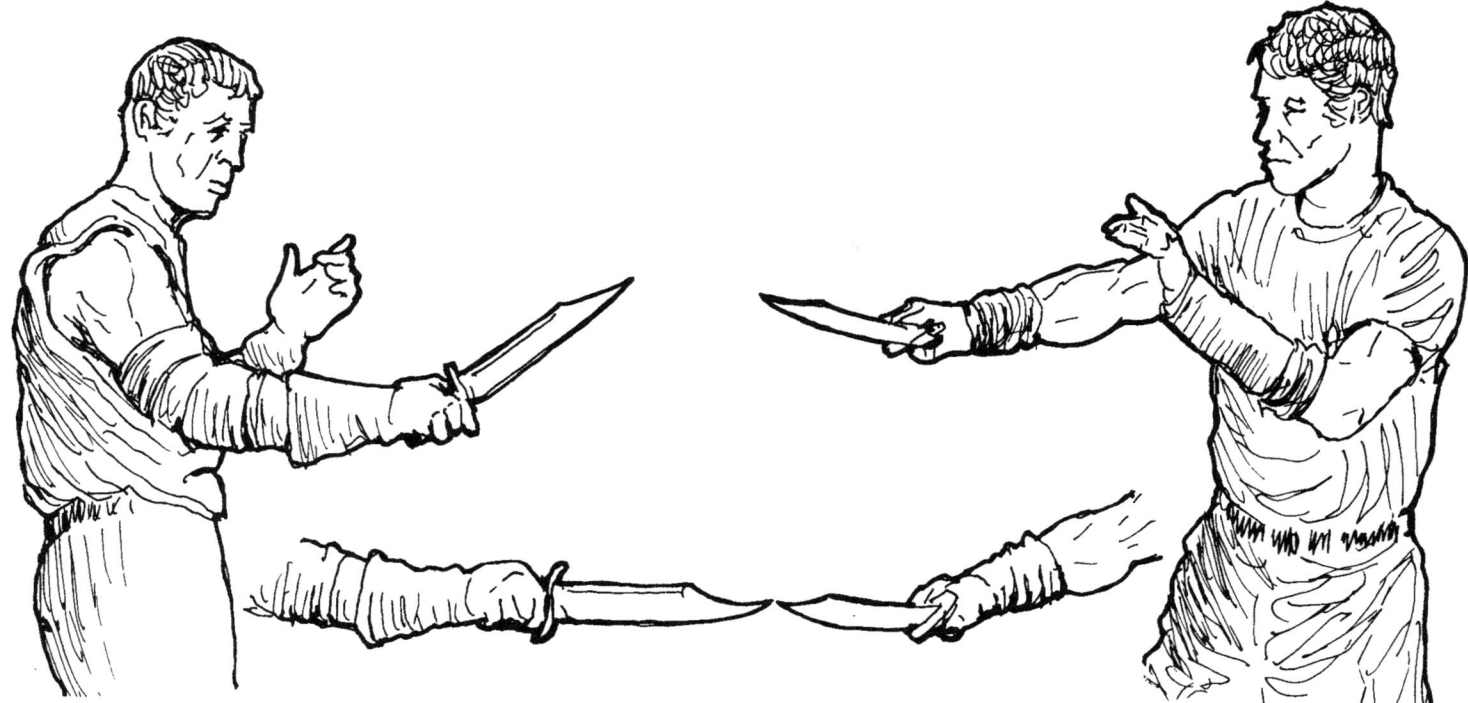

Figure 194. Being out of distance means one cannot be hit easily; within distance means one can be hit easily.

Angles (Angling)

When lateral movement and crossover steps are used, you are dealing with the forever principle of angles, or angling. Earlier we discussed the concept of inside and outside the box, when the frame of reference was the opponent and the actions he could take against you.

Some of the Renaissance masters applied movement to this principle by using a concept called *moving in and out of quarter*. Here, the fighter was centered in a large square (that was divided into four quarters) and faced his opponent. If his offensive or defensive movements took him out of the center and into any one of the quarters, he was considered moving in quarter. This approach was used to teach students to maneuver both inside and outside the box to achieve an angle or opening to deliver an attack or a counterattack. In Renaissance rapier fighting, quartatta, or incartata, referred to this principle where a rear leg is stepped around and to the side while simultaneously delivering a punta mandritta or reversa type of thrust discussed earlier. Figure 195 depicts this concept with an angling move in quarter to the left.

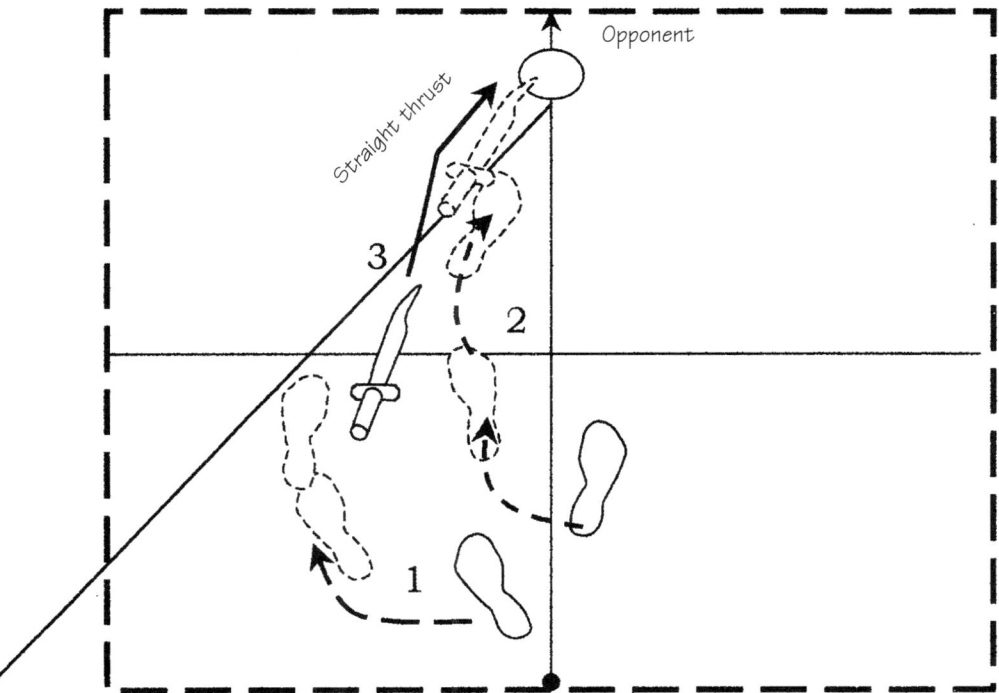

Figure 195. Note the angle created to acquire an attack opening.

185

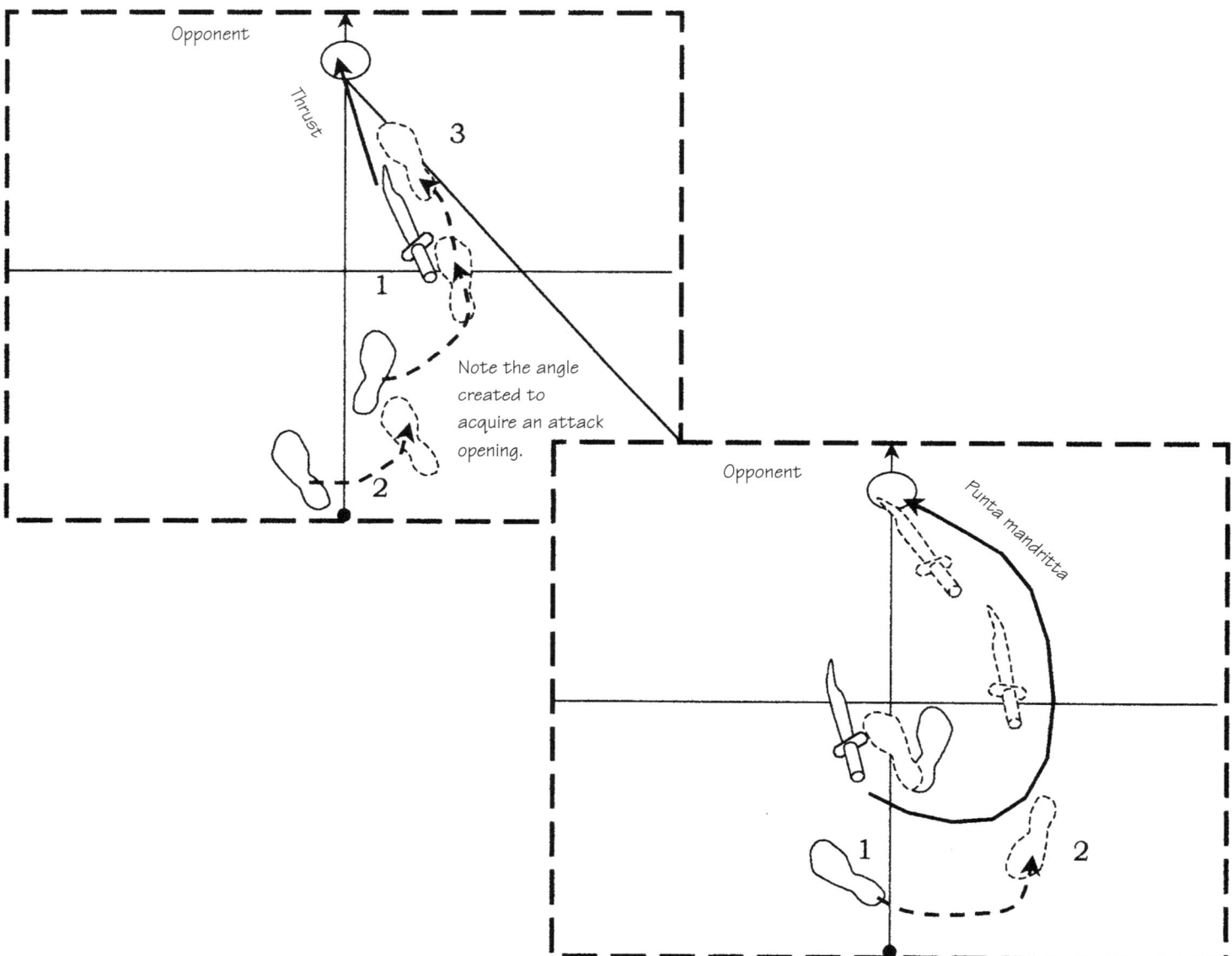

Opponent

Thrust

3

1

Note the angle created to acquire an attack opening.

2

Opponent

Punta mandritta

1

2

Figure 196. A view of angling in the opposite direction, again moving in quarter.

Figure 197. A view of the angling quartatta that is used with the punta mandritta and reversa.

Figure 198. An example of the angling principle of moving in quarter. The fighter depicted here is centered on all four quarters. If he remains centered as his opponent delivers a straight thrust, he will be hit.

Figure 199. In this example, the fighter moves to another quarter to avoid the thrust and to deliver a counterthrust of his own.

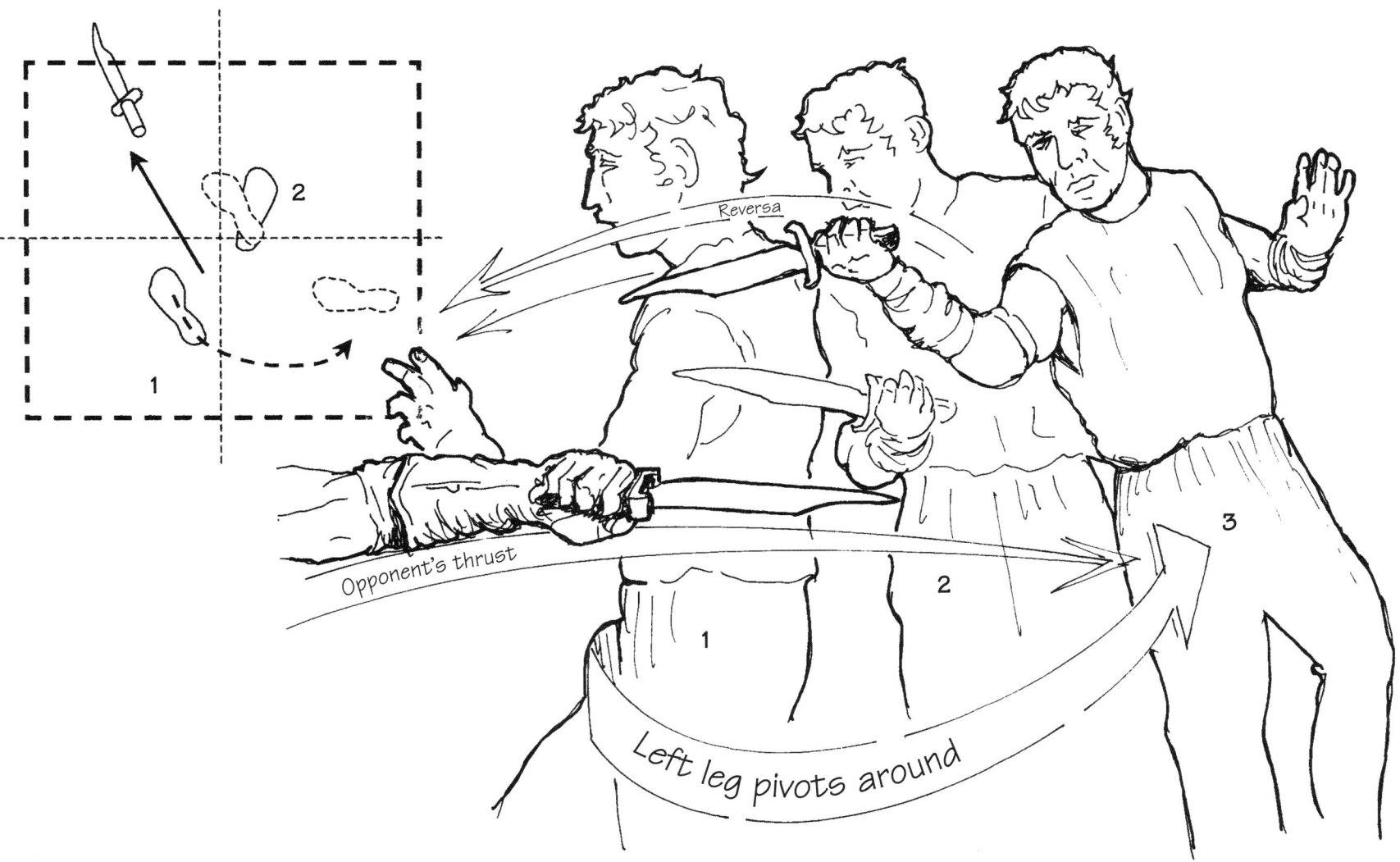

1

2

Reversa

Opponent's thrust

1

2

3

Left leg pivots around

Figure 200. Here is an example of the principle of being in and out of quarter. The fighter in this picture is in quarter. If he remains in quarter as his opponent delivers a straight thrust, he will be hit.

Another method of effecting angles to acquire target openings can be seen in the Spanish school of swordsmanship *la destreza* (1500). Although almost exclusively used for rapier and dagger fighting, *la destreza*'s application to Bowie and big-knife fighting is similar to that used with the quarter method we just reviewed. Maestro Ramon Martinez in his outstanding paper "The Demystification of the Spanish School" describes this method this way:

> The stance, attack, and defense are all within a circular concept. All fighting
> takes place within an imaginary circle on the ground. According to Girard
> Thibault in his treatise *Académie de l'Espée* (1628), the circle's diameter is deter-
> mined by the length of the swordsman standing straight with his heels together
> and his arm and index finger extended over his head. The distance from the
> ground to the tip of his extended index finger is the diameter of the circle.
> According to Carranza and Navaez, the *Diestro*, as the swordsmen are called,
> assume an upright, semiprofiled posture with the heels slightly apart. The arm is
> held straight forward at shoulder level, holding the sword with its blade parallel
> to the ground and menacing the adversary.

Figure 201. A period drawing showing the Spanish system and circle in use.

The Spanish Circle

The Spanish system of swordsmanship was designed for the rapier and dagger, therefore it is not completely adaptable to the Bowie and big-knife fighting methods. However, it does give one an example of how movement in a circular pattern can achieve the angles for attack and defense.

Figure 202 depicts the Renaissance master Gérard Thibault's view of the circle and associated footwork to achieve the angles for attack and defense. While the Spanish swordsman had the length of the rapier to help "see" the angles and openings, the knife fighter must visualize these as projecting from the point of his blade.

At first glance Thibault's diagram appears complex. However, when it is drawn out on the floor, and the circle is walked and the blade positioned along various angles, it does clarify the concept.

Movement around the circle is easily adapted using the footwork previously discussed. It should be noted that the more upright stances are best suited to the circle, whereas the lower, deeper stances are best suited to the quarter method.

Figures 203–205 depict some of the applications of the Spanish circle.

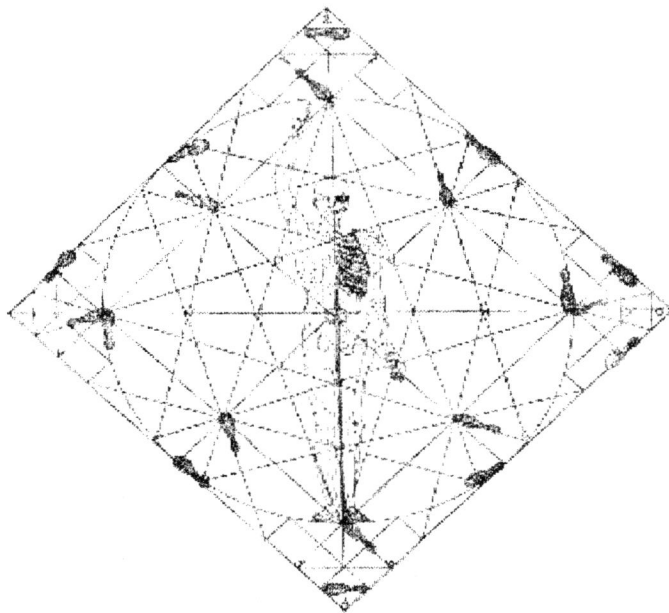

Figure 202. Gérard Thibault's diagram of the Spanish circle.

Figure 203. A period illustration showing the walk on the circle.

Figure 204 is a concept drawing of how the knife fighter might visualize the angles achieved by circular movement used in the Spanish system of swordsmanship. Again, while the rapier fighter uses the physical length of the blade to sense, or feel, the opponent's blade, the knife fighter, with the shorter blade, must visualize the angles and line.

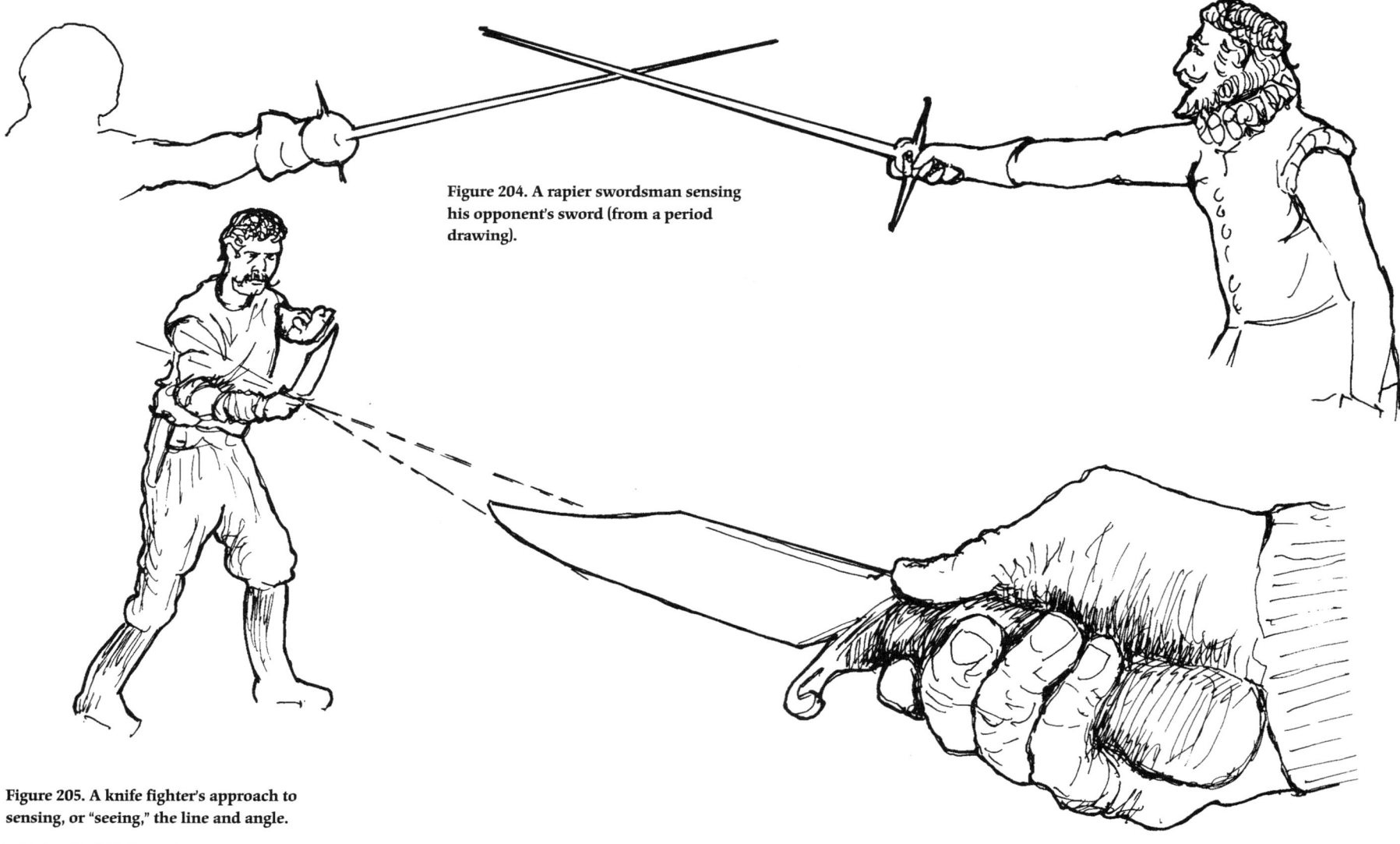

Figure 204. A rapier swordsman sensing his opponent's sword (from a period drawing).

Figure 205. A knife fighter's approach to sensing, or "seeing," the line and angle.

Applications of the Spanish Circle: Example 1

The following diagrams show some of the many aspects that can be applied using this system. For clarity, only the weapons are shown.

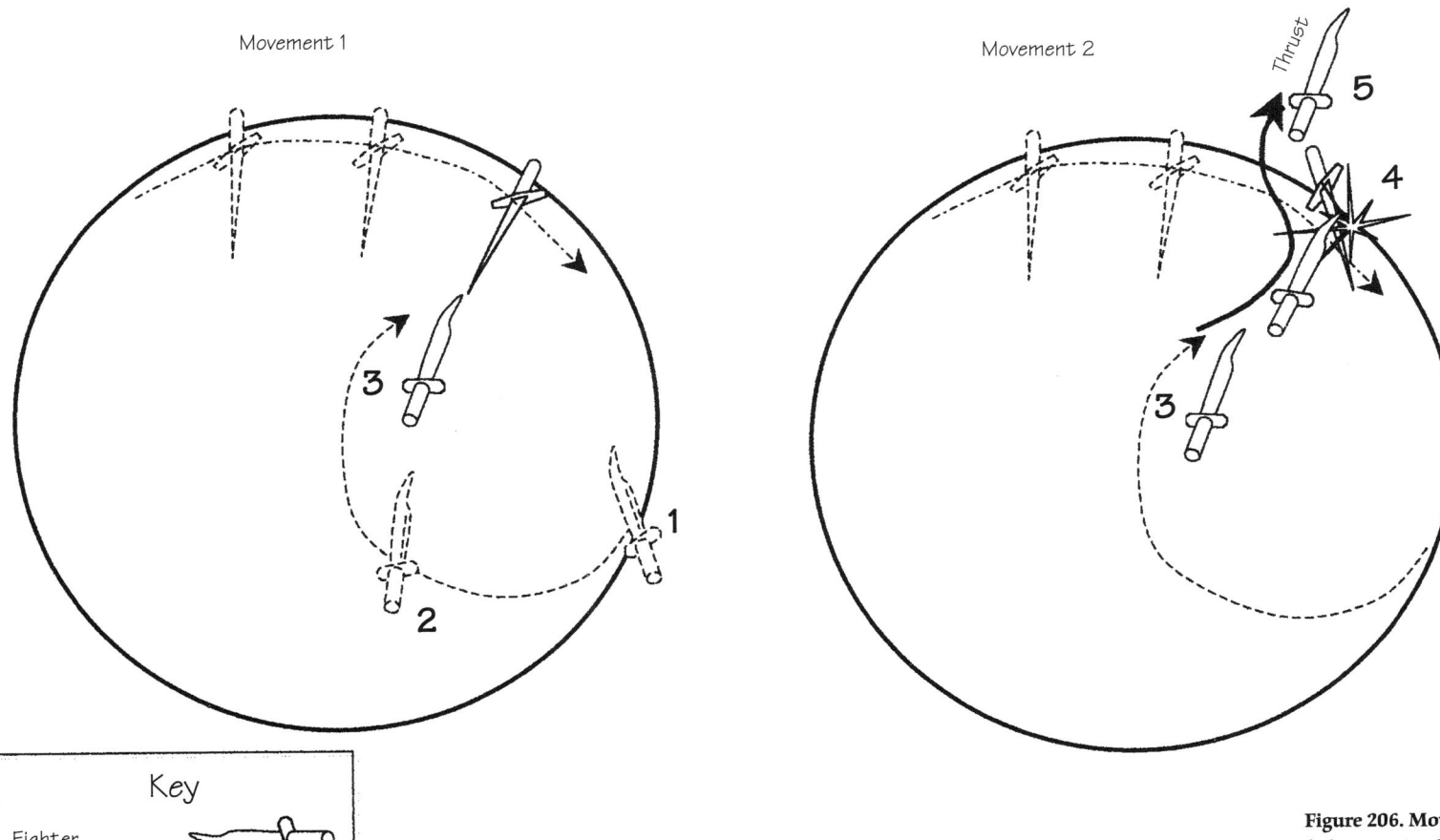

Movement 1

Movement 2

Thrust

Key

Fighter

Opponent

Foot movement

Weapon movement

Figure 206. Movement 1 begins with the fighter's using lateral movement to gradually decrease the diameter of the circle. His opponent moves along a circular line to the right. Movement 2: Once in distance, the fighter half-steps to the left and forcefully taps the opponent's blade to the right, achieving the angle, and then steps in with a thrust to the midsection over his guard.

Applications of the Spanish Circle: Example 2

Movement 1

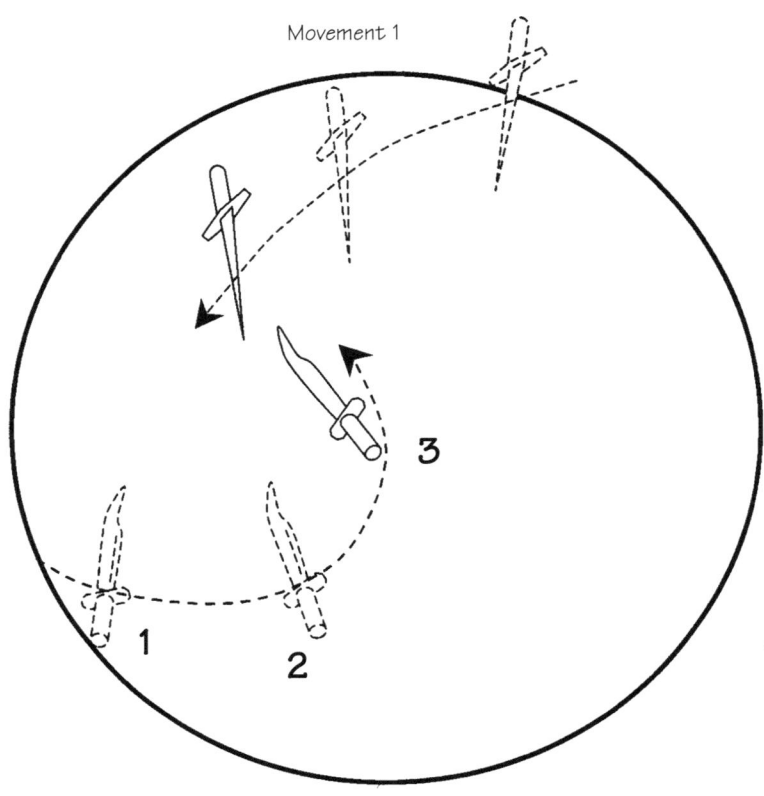

Movement 2

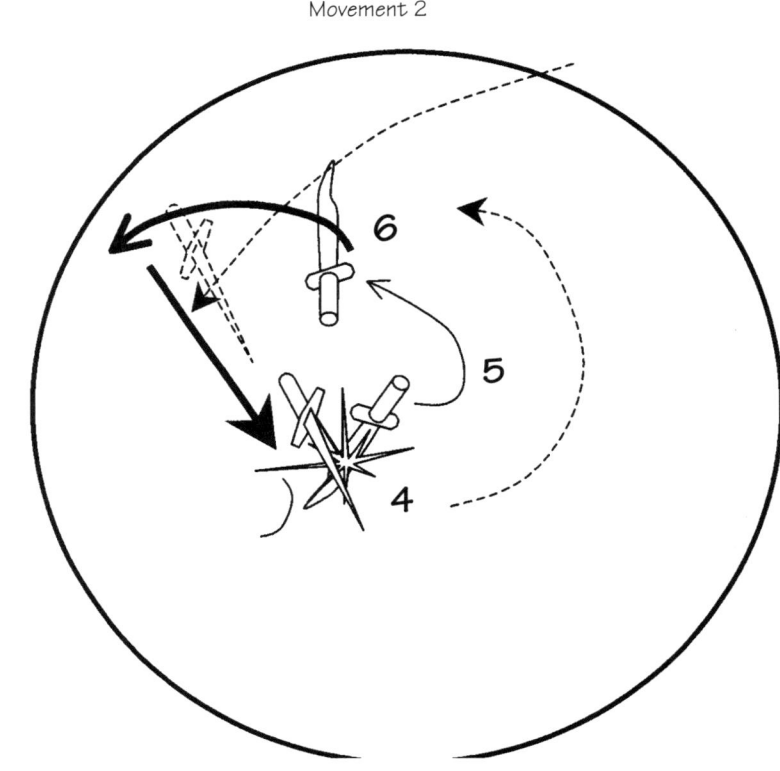

Figure 207. Movement 1: The opponent cuts rapidly across the circle diagonally. The fighter has just begun a lateral move to the right. Movement 2: The opponent executes a straight thrust; the fighter drops his point and parries the thrust to the left, simultaneously following the circle with his left leg by stepping back and around to the left. The fighter disengages from the parry and delivers an overhead cut to the opponent's neck.

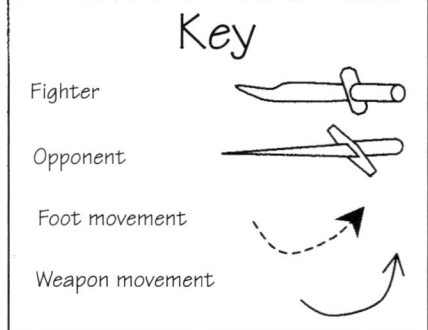

Key

Fighter

Opponent

Foot movement

Weapon movement

TRAINING NOTE: Here are four training drills that will enhance proficiency in moving laterally within the circle, in and out of quarter, and distance.

1. *Walking the circle.* Working with a training partner, begin with both partners' assuming a fighting stance. Extend the weapon arms so that the tips of the blade are about an inch apart. This determines the diameter of the circle to be walked. Using the sidestepping motion, the individual moves first to left and then back to the right. Again maintain the 1-inch separation between weapons. One complete circle to the left and then back to the right is one repetition. After completing five repetitions pull the arms back into a chamber and walk the circle again. The difficulty in maintaining distance with arms in chamber will soon become apparent. Remember, the goal of this exercise is to achieve a smooth flow of movement, which will later serve as the basis for rapid, smooth attacks or defense.

2. *Walking the line.* The next exercise is to enhance the fighter's ability to judge distance and range to a target area. Again working with a partner, assume a fighting stance with arms extended and the point of the blades approximately 1 inch apart. One partner advances while the other moves backward, both attempting to maintain the distance between the points. When both partners have moved forward and backward one time, it is considered one repetition. This exercise should be repeated five times, using both the advancing and passing steps that were discussed earlier.

3. *Adding the angles.* As an additional enhancement, both the above drills may be practiced by periodically adding a half-step left (or right) and then a forward move at certain points during the exercise. This facilitates learning to react to attacks and seeking openings.

4. *Linking all the exercises.* All three of the above drills may be linked to provide one total exercise. Begin first by walking the circle; then after five repetitions begin to walk the line. Follow this by repeating the process and adding the angles.

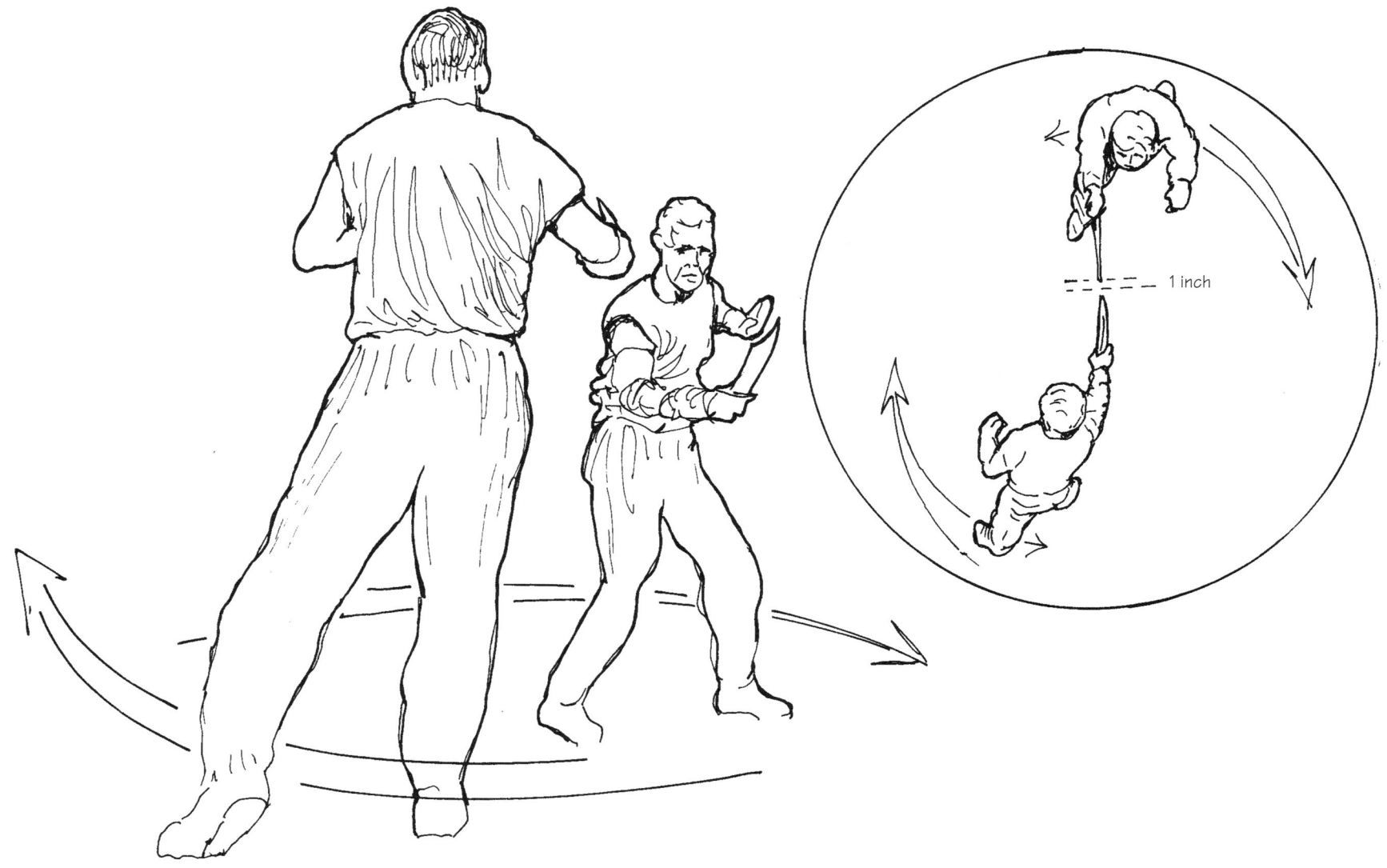

Figure 208. This diagram depicts the exercise drills for walking the circle.

Movement 1

Maintain distance

Movement 2

2

Start

1

Withdrawing partner

2

Start

1

Withdrawing partner

Figure 209. This diagram illustrates the drills for walking the line. Both the passing and advancing steps may be used for this.

Seeing

Moving in and out of quarter using the circle creates angles along which attacks or defensive moves can be affected. The point to remember here is that regardless of the application used, you must "look" in order to "see" the openings and react.

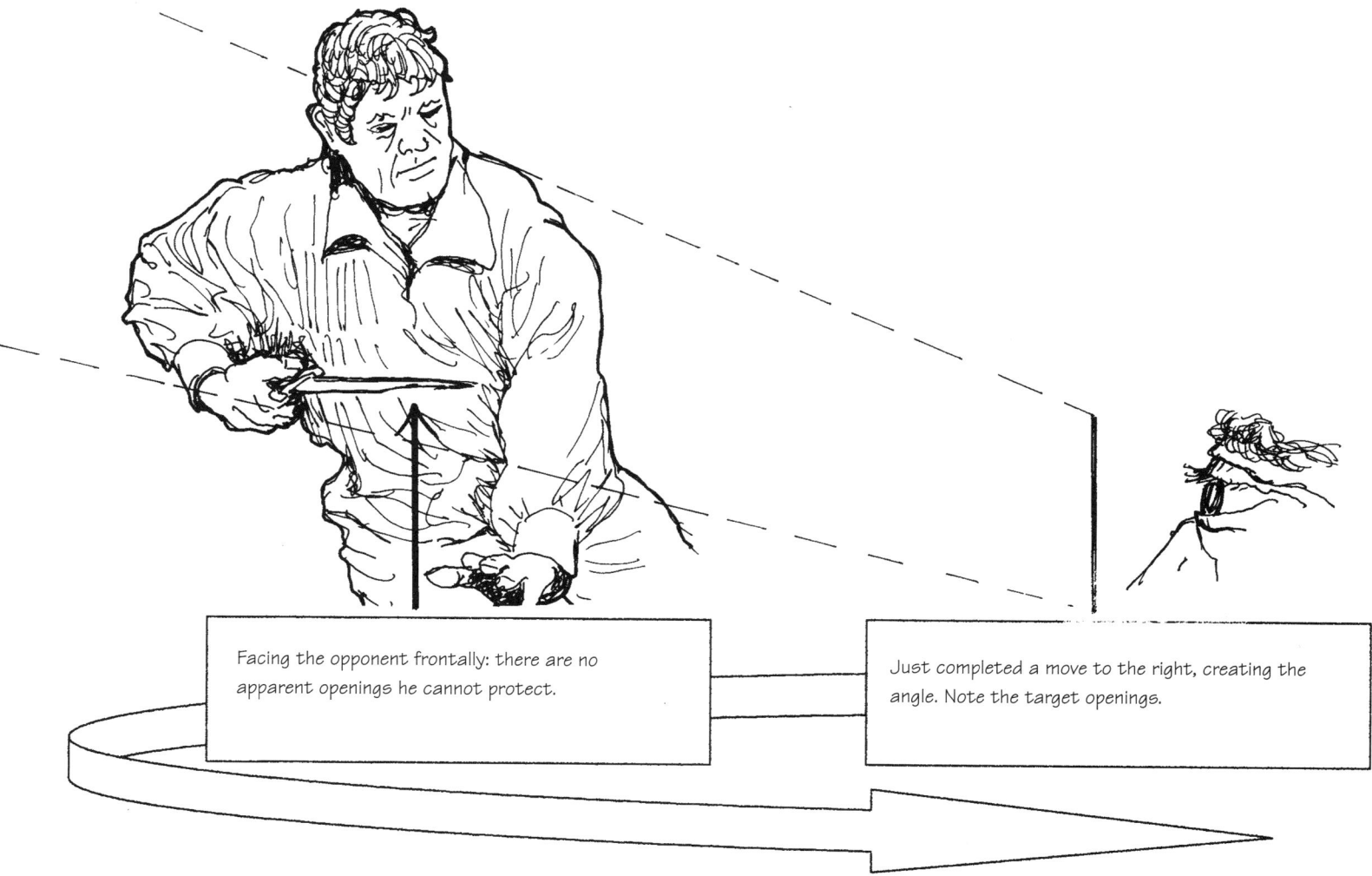

Facing the opponent frontally: there are no apparent openings he cannot protect.

Just completed a move to the right, creating the angle. Note the target openings.

Figure 210.

Height or Elevation

A final aspect of movement involves changing the position of the upper body vertically. This is accomplished by moving forward or backward, side to side, and involves a combination of bending and squatting to avoid an attack or to reposition in order to attack. A move to avoid a thrust or cut is commonly referred to as a *duck*. This aspect may be incorporated as part of the movement to achieve the angles for attack discussed previously. Figures 211 and 212 illustrate some of the possibilities.

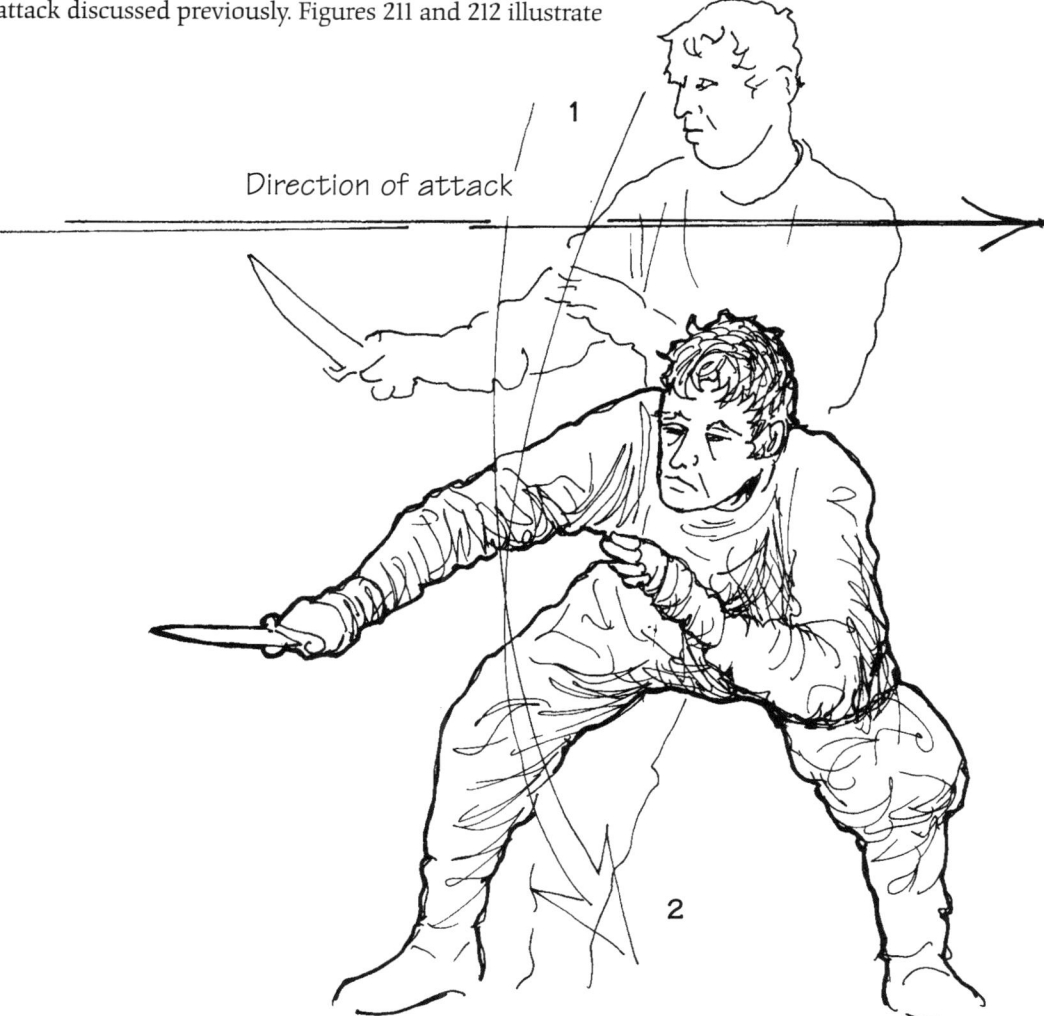

Direction of attack

Figure 211.

Two techniques for applying height or elevation to movement.

Move down and away.

Move down, away, and then back underneath.

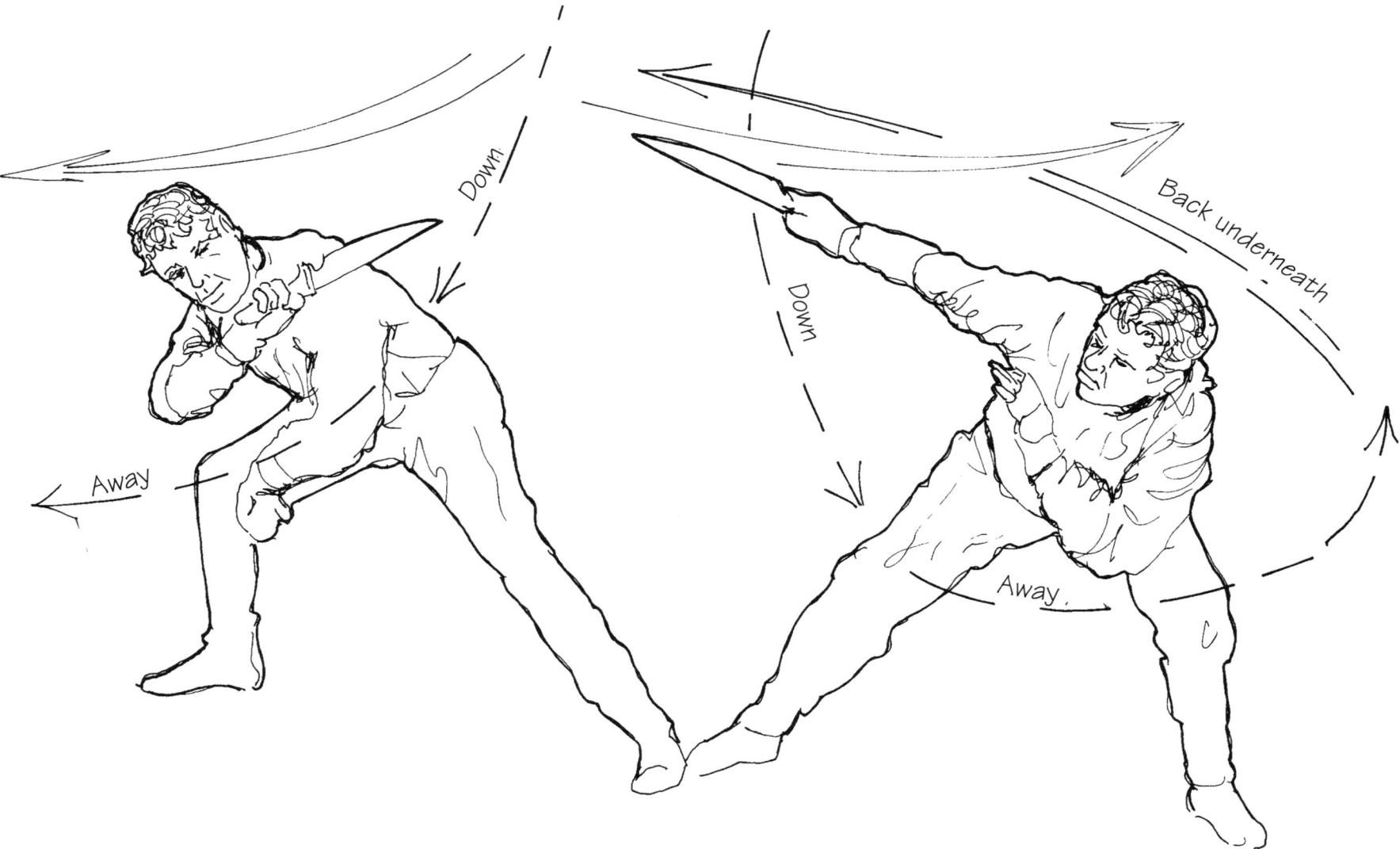

Figure 212.

SECTION FIVE: A PORTFOLIO OF TECHNIQUES, DRILLS, AND TRAINING NOTES

We are now at the point where the essential fundamentals have been covered. From this point on I will present a variety of techniques, drills, and training notes that are not easily grouped under the individual classifications discussed. Rather, this information applies to all of them in general.

The intent here is to put the concepts of bladework, movement, and targeting together in a format that will serve as a foundation for more advanced level of work. None of this material should be viewed as "the solution," but rather to stimulate thought about other possible fighting applications for the Bowie.

We have also arrived at what should be considered the "living" section of this manual. In other words, this is just the tip of the Bowie and big-knife fighting iceberg. There are many more aspects on medium, close, and ground fighting associated with this weapon that this small volume cannot begin to cover. (If you want to pursue this further, check the School of Two Swords Web site at <www.twos-words.com>, under the technique of the month.)

SIDE PARRY

The side parry is one of the simplest and most effective defensive techniques you can use. The one illustrated in Figure 213 is accomplished by movement outside the box and to the fighter's left. The technique is used here to counter a straight thrust from an opponent.

Figure 213. Step 1: As the straight thrust comes driving in, the defender raises his blade to intercept and deflect the opponent's blade to the outside. As contact is made, the right arm is chambered back.

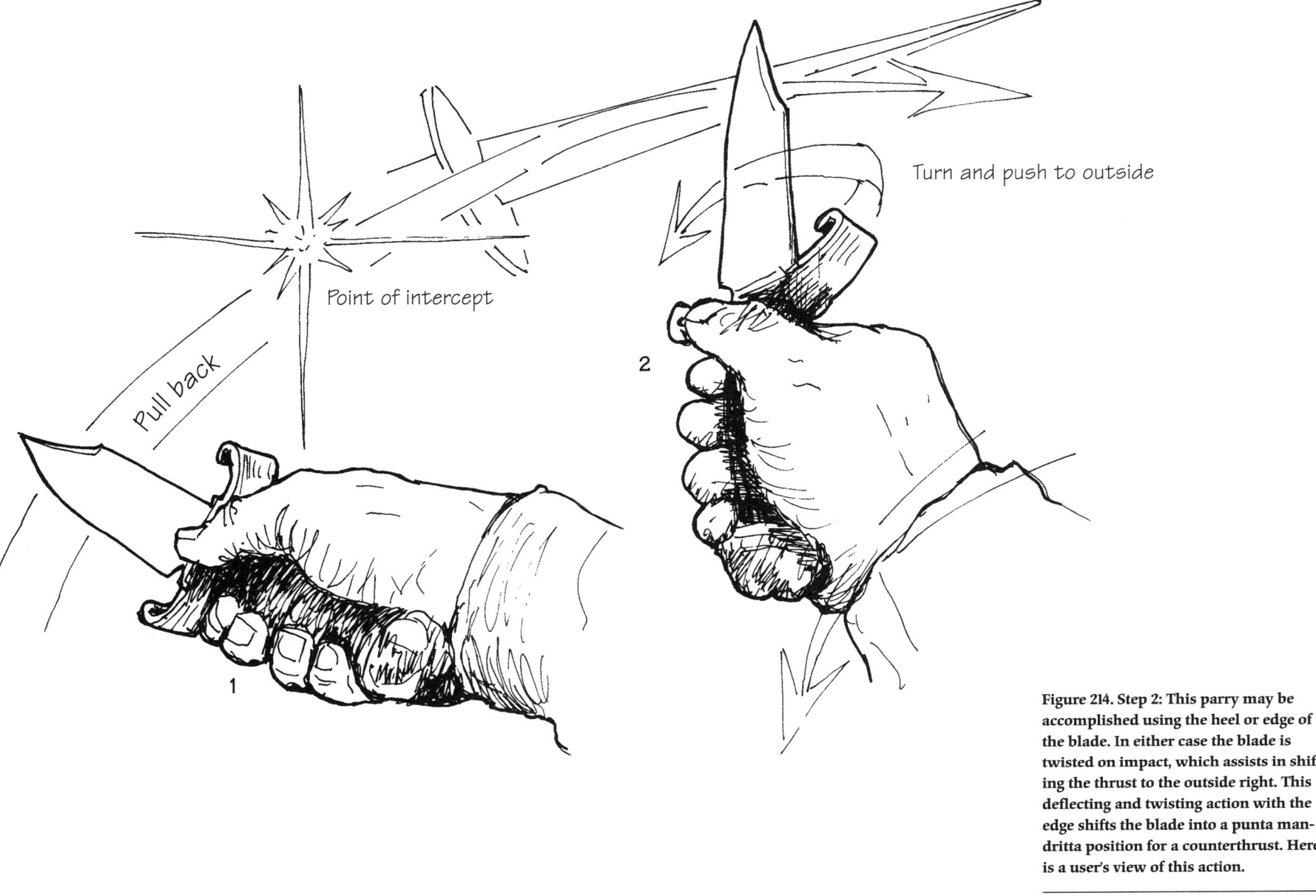

Point of intercept

Pull back

Turn and push to outside

1

2

Figure 214. Step 2: This parry may be accomplished using the heel or edge of the blade. In either case the blade is twisted on impact, which assists in shifting the thrust to the outside right. This deflecting and twisting action with the edge shifts the blade into a punta mandritta position for a counterthrust. Here is a user's view of this action.

Flow Diagram

Key

The fighter's blade

Opponent's blade

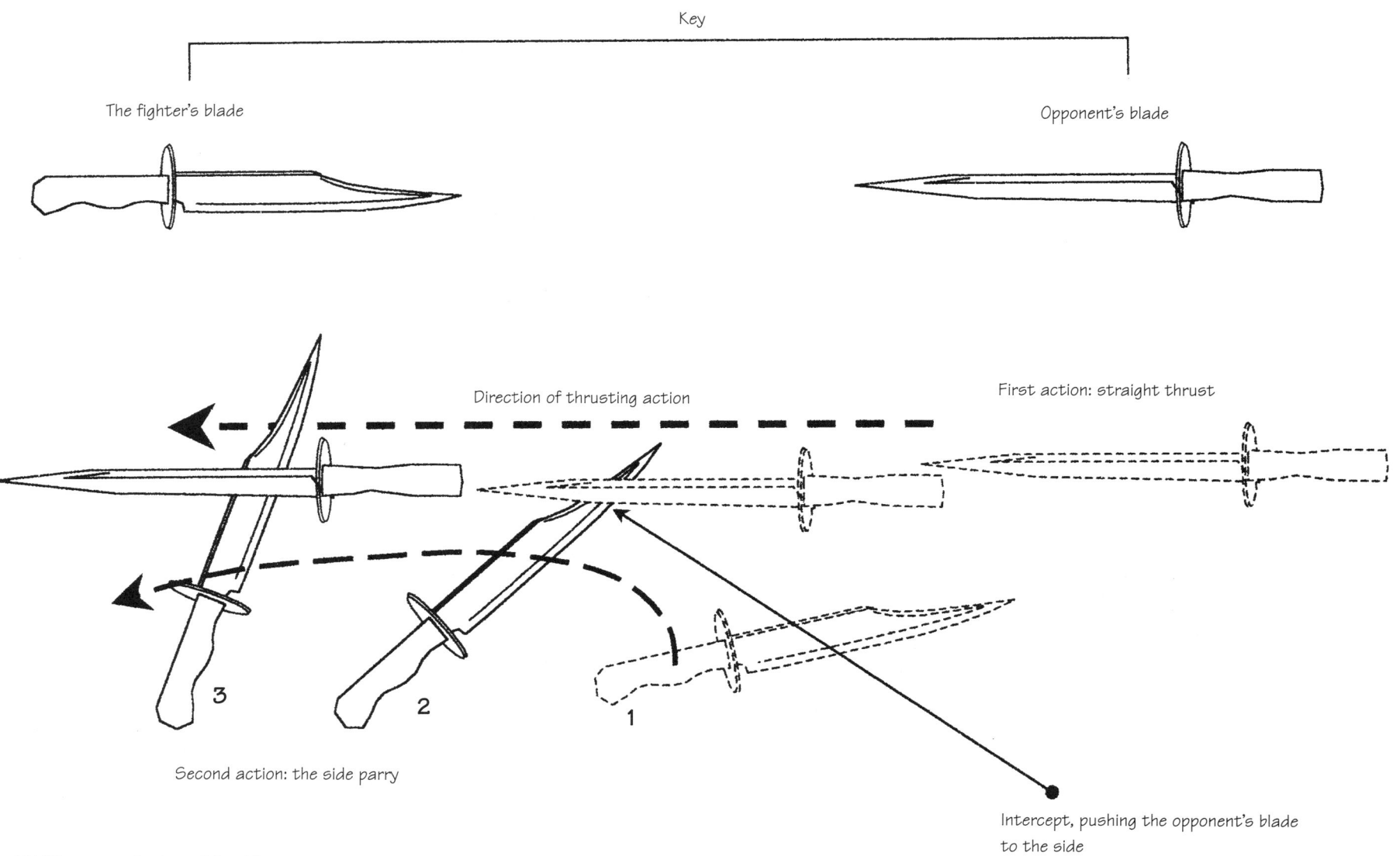

Direction of thrusting action

First action: straight thrust

3

2

1

Second action: the side parry

Intercept, pushing the opponent's blade to the side

Figure 215. Weapons-only view of the side parry.

Flow Diagram

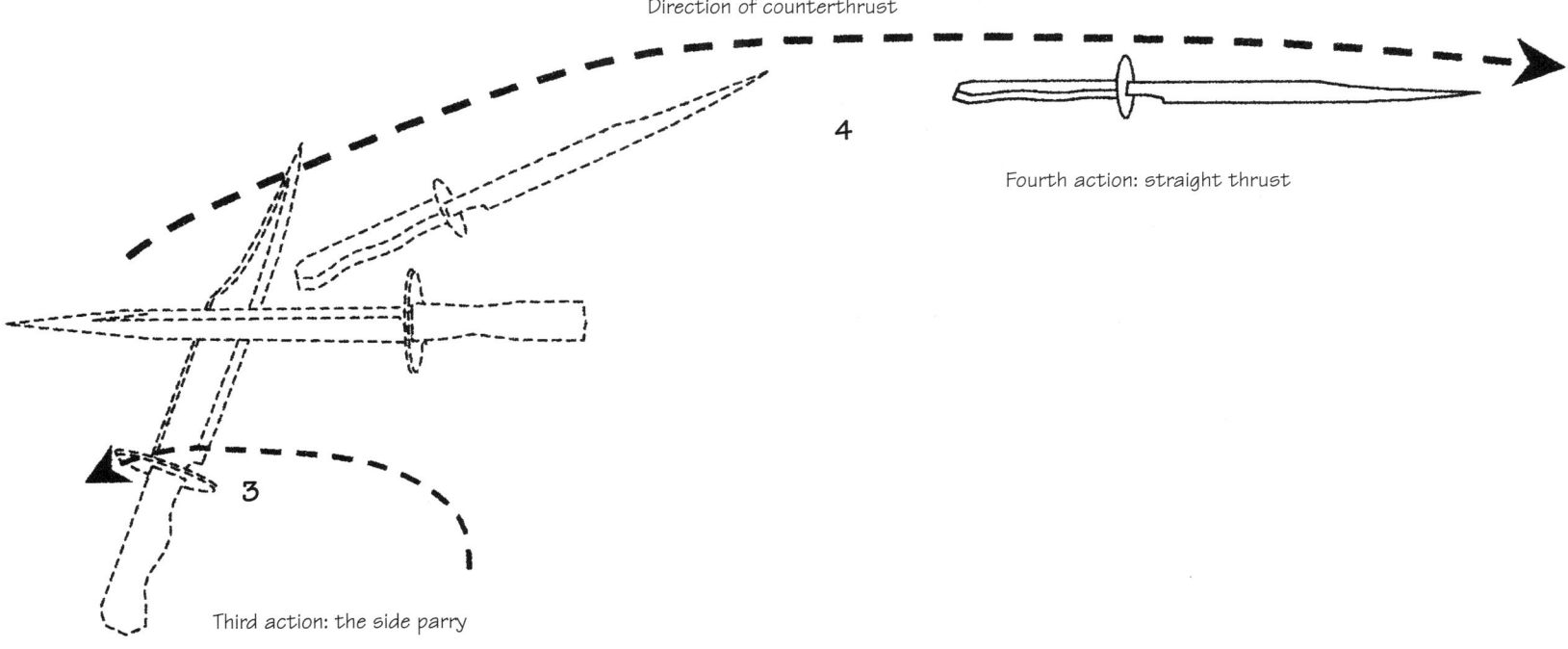

Direction of counterthrust

4

Fourth action: straight thrust

3

Third action: the side parry

Figure 216. Weapons-only view of the side parry with counterthrust.

TRAINING NOTE ON SIDE PARRY AND THRUST DRILL: This two-man drill will improve the muscle memory and control for both the side parry and thrust. Begin with both partners facing each other in a good fighting stance. The range should be close to where both partners are within striking distance. Here is the sequence:

- Partner A executes a straight thrust to Partner B's midsection. Simultaneously, Partner B executes a side parry, pushing Partner A's blade to the outside. Almost immediately Partner B executes a straight thrust to Partner A's midsection. Partner A executes the side parry and repeats the thrust he initiated earlier. Repeat this sequence, gradually increasing the speed. Both partners attempt to maintain a smooth rhythm and positive control throughout the drill.
- Once the drill is mastered, with both partners stationary, the drill can be enhanced by adding the circular movements (left/right) discussed earlier in the section on movement.
- It is important to note that this is a foundation drill that will pave the way for more advanced Bowie knife work with passing and trapping techniques.
- This drill should be practiced at least three times a week in three sets of 25 repetitions each. A repetition is complete when both partners have executed a side parry.

SAFETY WARNING: Both partners should wear eye, throat, chest, hand, and groin protection at a minimum. Do NOT practice this exercise with live steel; use wooden or aluminum training weapons.

The figures on the following pages depict this drill.

Figure 217. To "see" the flow of this drill sequence, first stare for a moment at Step 2 and then shift your eyes to the right to Step 3. Immediately shift your eyes back to Step 2. Keep repeating this and you'll "see" the drill flow.

TRAINING NOTE ON SOLO SETS AND COMBAT SCENARIOS: The solo set is nothing more than a series of techniques linked in a pattern based on a series of possible attacks/counterattacks an opponent may attempt. When a solo set is practiced with a partner executing these prearranged attacks, it is termed a *combat scenario*. At a minimum, most sets/scenarios should be composed of at least three techniques.

For teaching purposes, the solo set shown here is from the aspect of the flow and position. For flow we use a diagram that shows only the weapon. The idea here is to give the student insight into the motion of the techniques as they flow into each other. The position aspect is shown in step-by-step anatomical body motions that define the location of the torso, arms, etc., when performing the technique.

When teaching bladework, you should first explain and demonstrate the flow to the student and allow him to practice until he is reasonably comfortable with the set. Next, explain and demonstrate the solo set with a partner who also follows a prearranged set of actions.

NOTE: In some martial arts circles there is a tendency for the instructor to make immediate corrections to any error that occurs during the execution of the solo set. Often this involves stopping the student in midmotion and making finite adjustments or having him repeat the action till he gets it right. This approach is not recommended for this training. Such approaches reinforce a tendency to stop or hesitate when the technique is applied in full-speed sparring. Rather, teach the flow first and then go back and make the minor corrections to form and execution. Again, master *the flow first*.

SOLO SET 1
(SIDE PARRY, PUNTA MANDRITTA, CURL TO MIDLINE BACK CUT
OR SIDE PARRY TO HIGH-LINE BACK CUT)

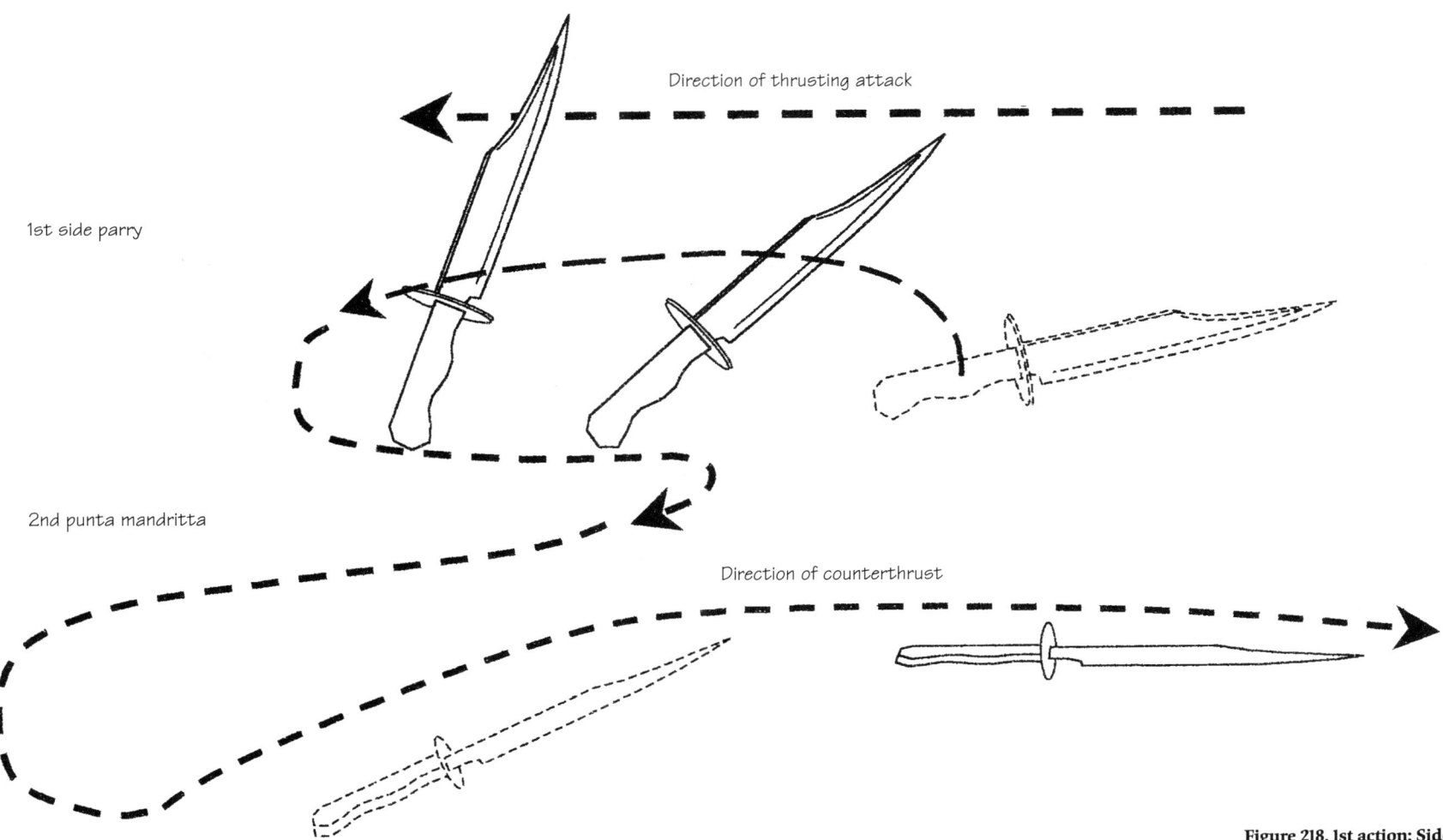

Direction of thrusting attack

1st side parry

2nd punta mandritta

Direction of counterthrust

Figure 218. 1st action: Side-parry a direct thrust to the torso and immediately execute a punta mandritta to the opponent's throat.

Position Diagram

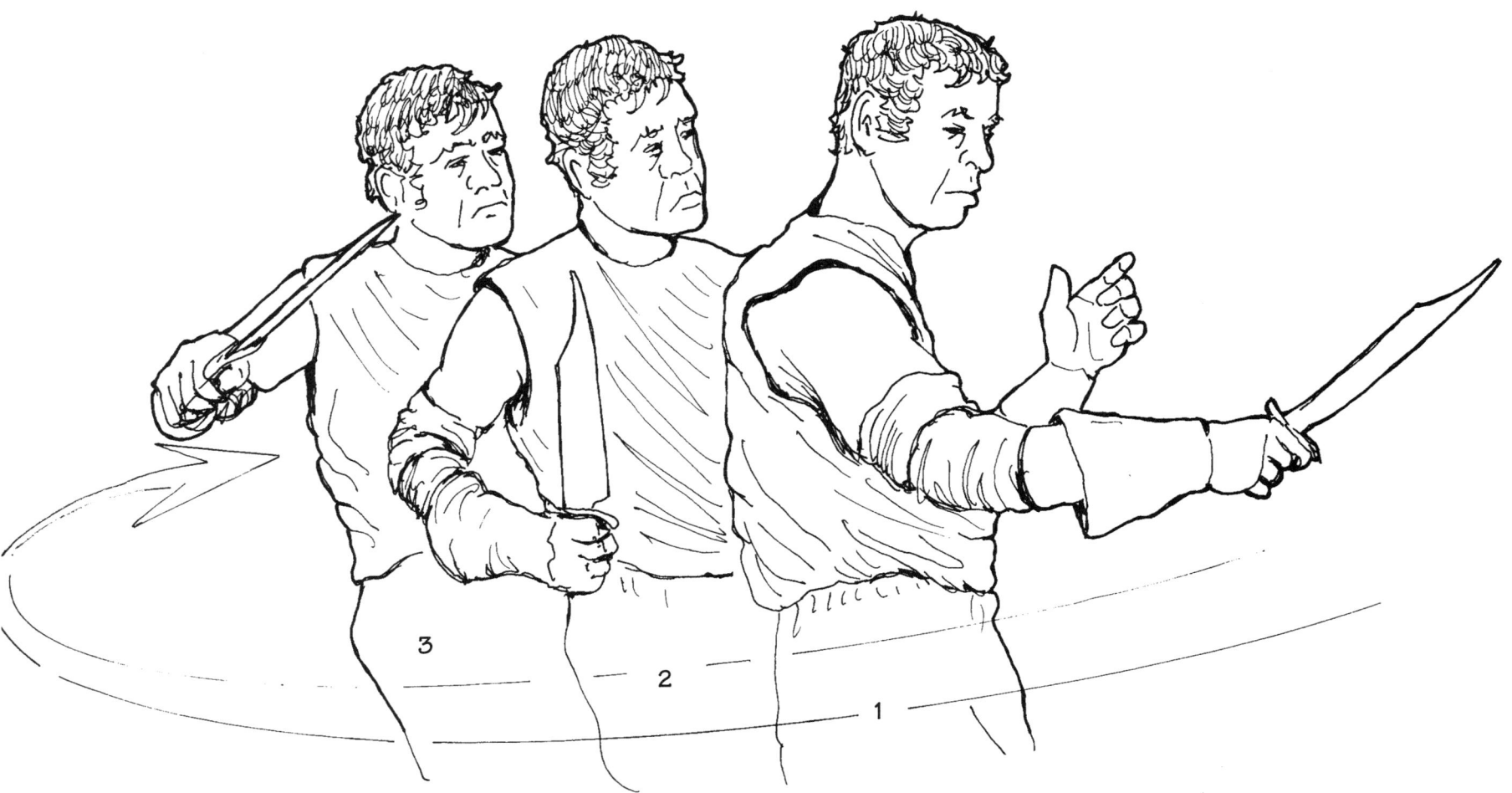

Figure 219. 1st action: Side-parry a direct thrust to the torso and immediately execute a punta mandritta to the opponent's throat.

Position Diagram

4

5

Figure 220. 1st action (continued): Side-parry a direct thrust to the torso and immediately execute a punta mandritta.

Flow Diagram

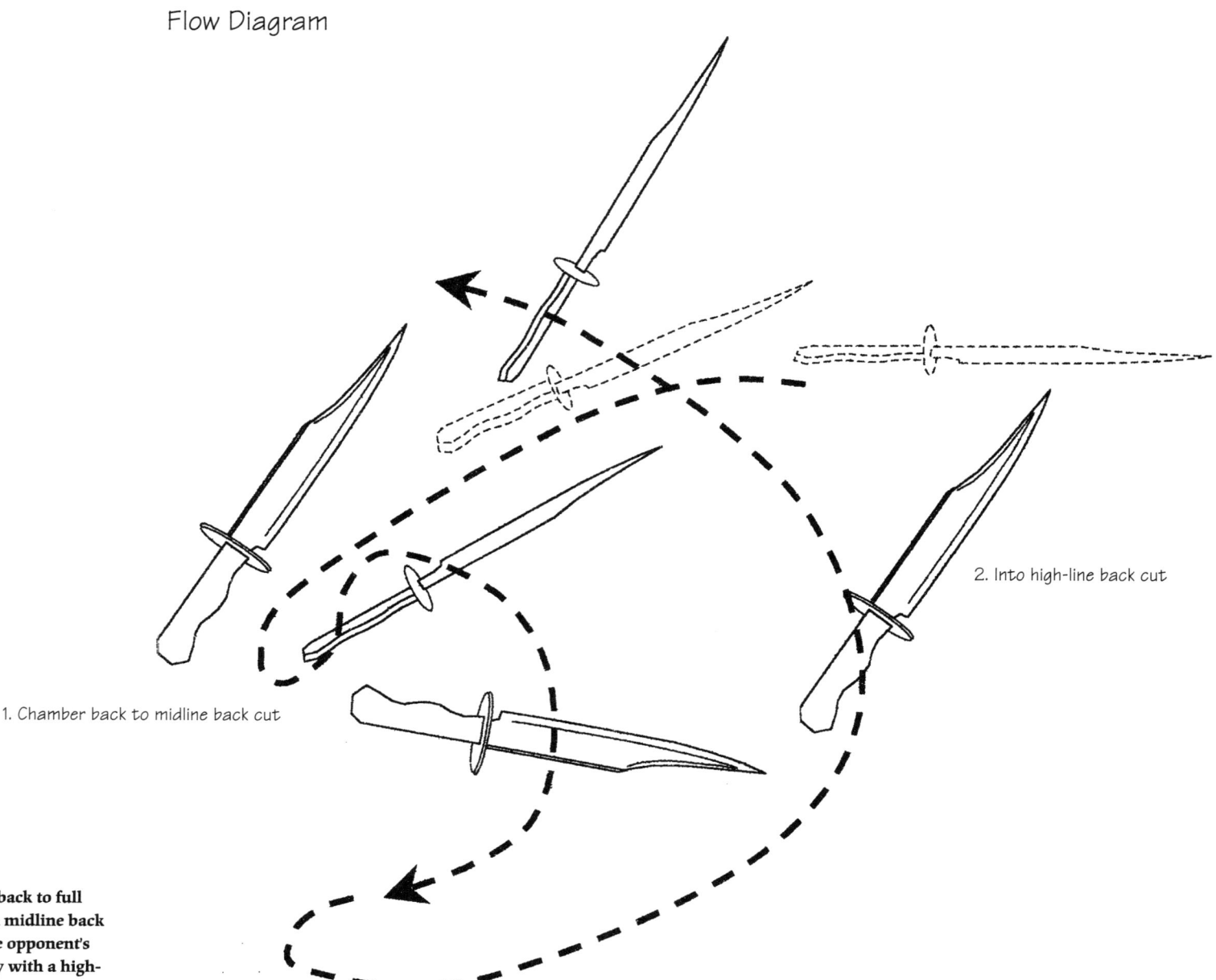

2. Into high-line back cut

1. Chamber back to midline back cut

Figure 221. 2nd action: Pull back to full arm chamber and execute a midline back cut or side parry against the opponent's arm; follow up immediately with a high-line back cut.

Position Diagram

6

7

Figure 222. 2nd action: Chamber back
and roll the blade to the right for another
side parry or midline back cut to the
opponent's hand/arm.

Position Diagram

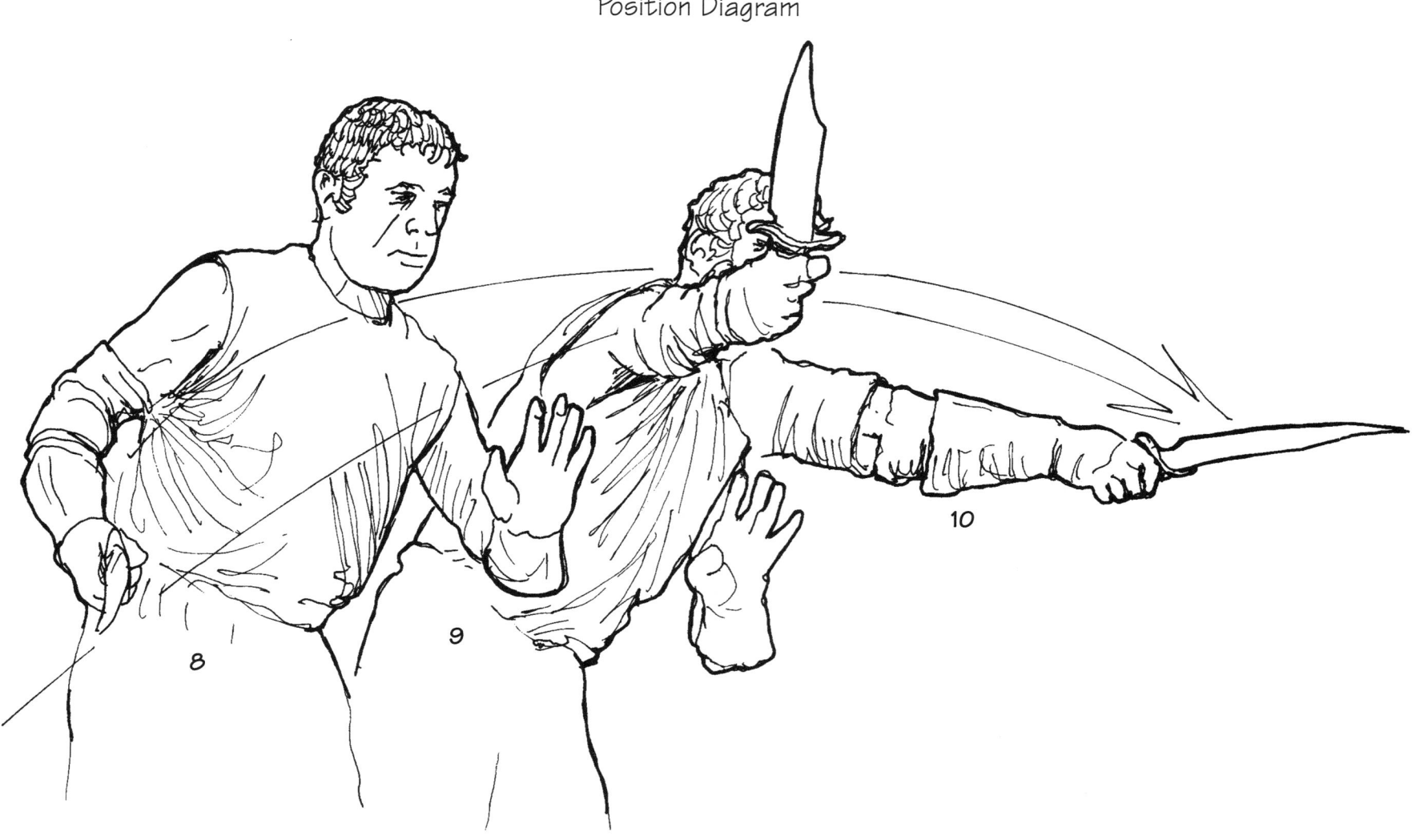

8

9

10

Figure 223. 2nd action (continued): Follow up immediately with a high-line back cut to the opponent's neck.

SOLO SET 2 (INSIDE PARRY TO THE LEFT, ATTACK WITH ANGLE 3, CROSS-BODY CHAMBER TO PUNTA REVERSA)

Flow Diagram

1st action: Drop the point, roll the right to the right, parrying the opponent's thrust to the outside. Follow through by a pull over and out of the parry into an angle 3 attack.

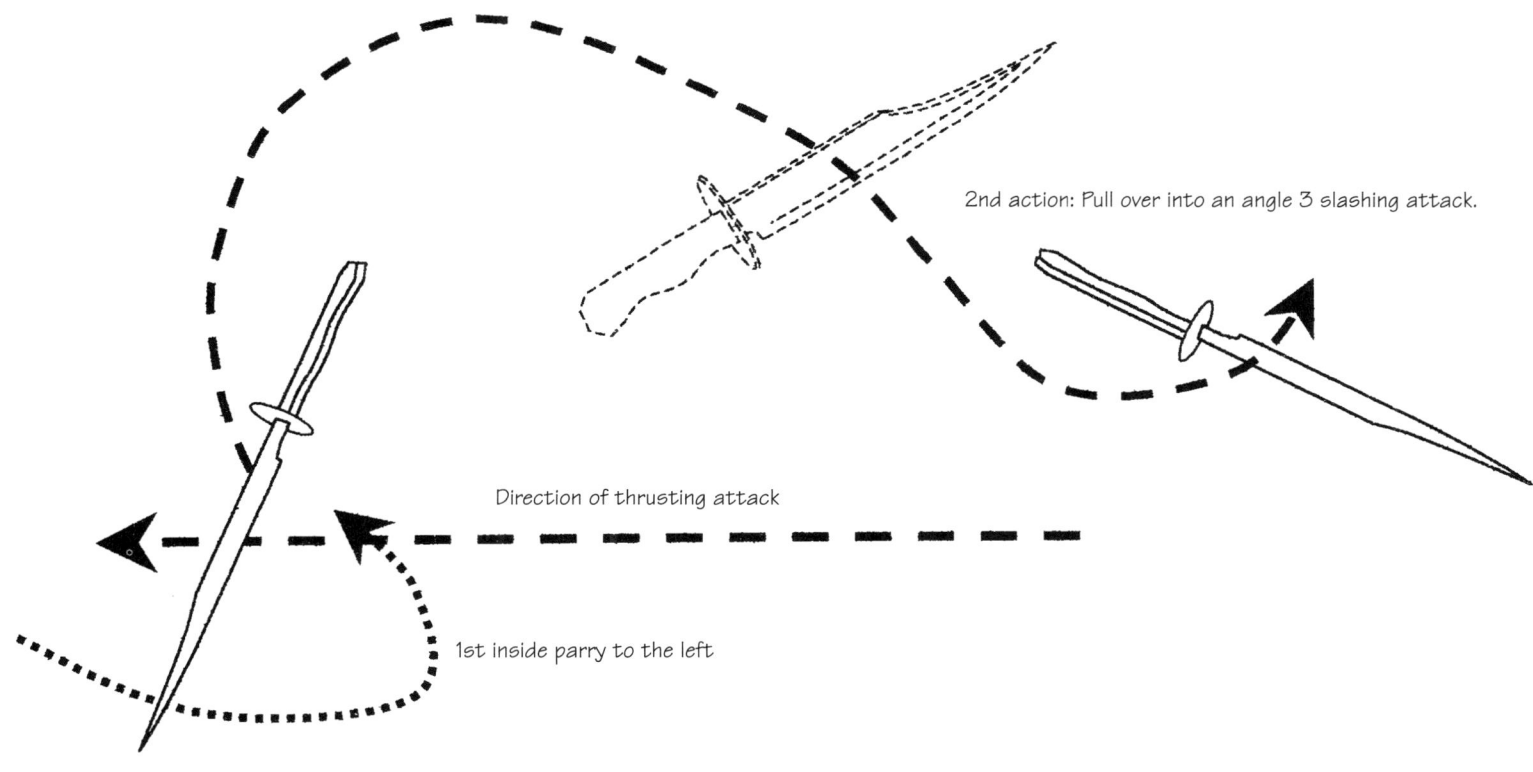

2nd action: Pull over into an angle 3 slashing attack.

Direction of thrusting attack

1st inside parry to the left

Figure 224.

Position Diagram

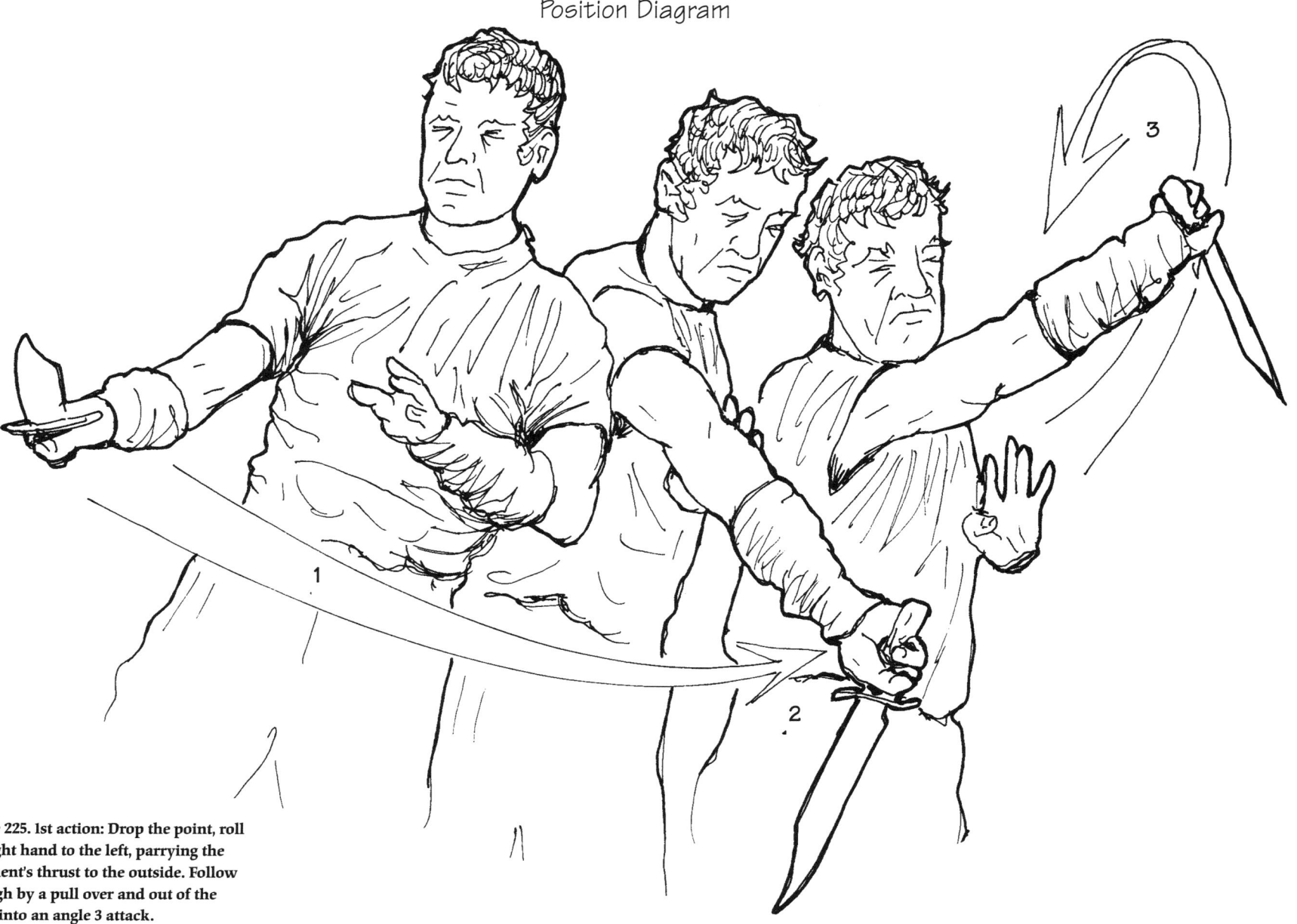

Figure 225. 1st action: Drop the point, roll the right hand to the left, parrying the opponent's thrust to the outside. Follow through by a pull over and out of the parry into an angle 3 attack.

Flow Diagram

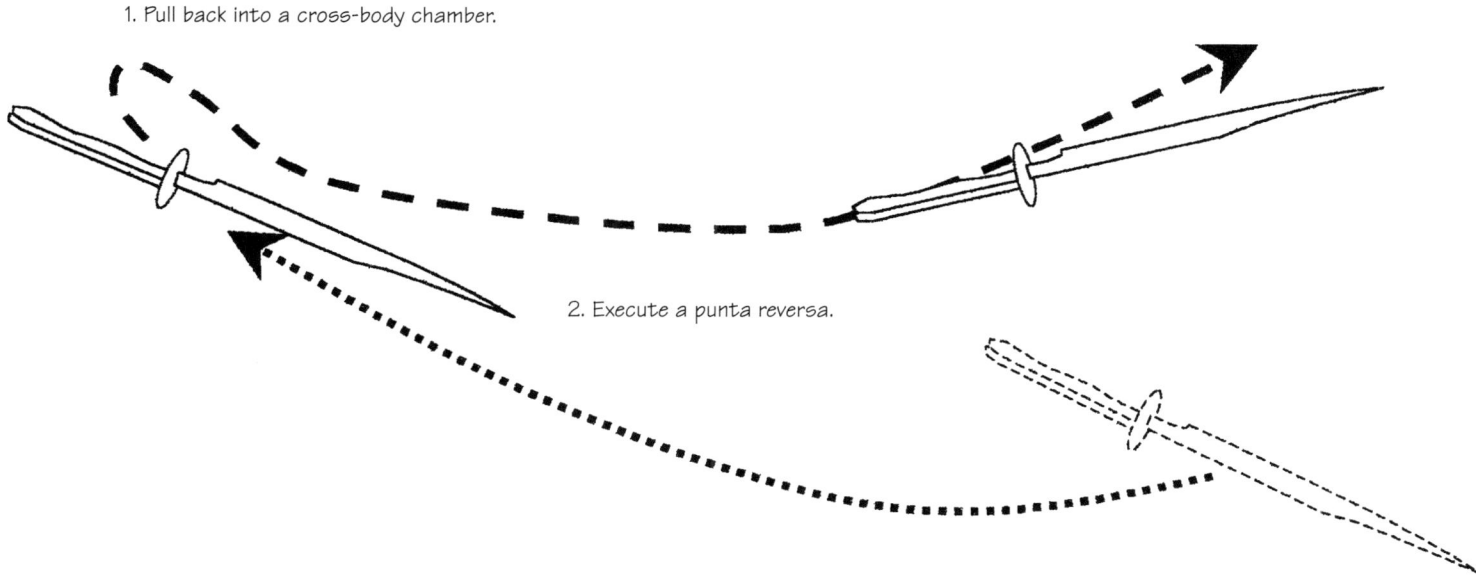

1. Pull back into a cross-body chamber.

2. Execute a punta reversa.

Figure 226. 2nd action: Immediately do a cross-body chamber across the chest and then push forcefully out into a punta reversa thrust.

Position Diagram

Figure 227. 2nd action: Immediately do a cross-body-chamber across the chest and then push forcefully out into a punta reversa thrust.

SELECTED BIBLIOGRAPHY

Sometimes that which we seek is not documented or titled as we expect. In the case of this book, the roadmaps and guideposts came from some of the most unlikely sources. I suppose that is all that needs to be said about my research sources. Take them for what you will. Remember, I'm more interested in training than going to the library.

Albaugh, W.A. *Confederate Edged Weapons*. New York: Harper & Brothers, 1960.

Amberger, C.J. "The Secret History of the Sword." *Hammerterz Forum*, 1995.

Anglo, S. *The Martial Arts of Renaissance Europe*. New Haven, Conn.: Yale University Press, 2000.

Baldick, R. *The Duel: A History of Dueling*. New York: Barnes & Noble, 1965.

Barker, M.A. *Sons of a Trackless Forest*. Franklin, Tenn.: Baker's Tree Publishing.

Biddle, A.J. *Do or Die*. Boulder, Colo.: Paladin Press, 1998.

Blade Magazine. "James Bowie's Knife." 1993.

Bryant, J. "A Knife Like Bowie's." Alamo de Parras Web site, 1996.

Burton, R.F. *The Book of the Sword*. Chatto & Windus, 1884. Reprint, New York: Dover Publications, 1987.

Cassidy, W.L. *The Complete Book of Knife Fighting*. Boulder, Colo.: Paladin Press, 1975.

Corbesier, A.J. *Squad Instruction for the Broadsword*. Philadelphia: J.B. Lippincott & Co., 1869.

Davis, W.C. *Three Roads to the Alamo*. New York: Harper & Collins, 1998.

The Dueling Oaks in New Orleans City Park. Ring Surf Net Ring, 1999.

Durham, K. *The Border Reivers*. Oxford: Osprey Publications, 1995.

Edmondson, J.R. *Mr. Bowie with a Knife: A History of the Sandbar Fight*. Houston: Write Press, 1999.

Fairbairn, Maj. W.E. *Get Tough: How to Win in Hand-to-Hand Fighting*. New York–London: D.

    Appleton–Century Co., 1942. (Reprinted Boulder, Colo.: Paladin Press, 1979).

Godfrey, J. *Treatise Connecting Small and Backsword*. T. Gardner, 1747.

Hacker, R. "Jim Bowie's Legacy." *Combat Knives* Magazine, 1997.

Hochheim, W.H. *Knife Fighting Encyclopedia, Vol. 1*. Denton, Tex.: Lauric Press, 1997.

————. *Military Knife Combat, Knife Fighting Encyclopedia, Volume II*. Lauric Press, 1998.

Hope, W. *The Complete Fencing Master*. Dorman Newman, 1692.

Hutton, A. *Cold Steel*. London: William Clowes & Sons Ltd., 1889.

"Jim Bowie and the Bowie Knife." Arkansas State Heritage Web site, 1997.

Johnston, J.R. *Accouterments III: Kentucky Rifles and Pistols, Tomahawks, Axes, Knives, Powder Horns,*

    Hunting Bags and Accouterments from 1750–1850. Golden Age Arms Co., 1997.

Kane, H.T. *Gentlemen, Swords, and Pistols*. New York: William Morrow & Co., 1951.

Kautz, P. *Connecting the Sword and the Bowie*.

Keating, J. *Bowie Basics* (video). Comtech Inc., 1996.

————. "Bowie Knives: My Two Cents." *Fighting Knives* Magazine, 1996.

————. *Crossada* (video). Comtec Inc., 1996.

————. *Double Knife Sets* (video). Comtech Inc., 1996.

————. *The Deadly Backcut* (video). Comtec Inc., 1996.

————. "The Ultimate Fighting Bowies." *Tactical Knives* Magazine, 1996.

Landry, S.O. *Dueling in Old New Orleans*. New Orleans: Harmonson Publishers, 1950.

Loriega, J. *Sevillian Steel*. Boulder, Colo.: Paladin Press, 1999.

M.D.R. *Manual del Baratero*. Imprenta de D. Alberto Goya, 1849.

Marozzo, A. *Opera Nova*. Published in two parts: 1536 and 1568.

Martinez, R. "The Demystification of the Spanish School." New York: Martinez Academy of Arms, 2000.

Peterson, H.L. *Arms and Armor in Colonial America*. Bramhall House, 1956.

Petter, N. *Worstel-Konst*. Romeyn de Hooge, 1674.

Styers, J. *Cold Steel*. Boulder, Colo.: Paladin Press, 1974.

Swetnam, J. *The Schoole of the Noble & Worthy Science of Defence*. Nicholas Oaks, 1617.

Taylor, J. "Alamo Hero's Bowie Discovered in Massachusetts." *Blade* Magazine, 1988.

Thorpe, R.W. *Bowie Knife*. Albuquerque: University of New Mexico Press, 1949.

Turner C., and T. Soper. *Elizabethan Swordplay*. Carbondale: Southern Illinois University Press, 1990.

Weingartner, S. "Weapons (The Gladius)." *Military History* Web site, 2000.

Wellman, P.I. *The Iron Mistress*. New York: Doubleday & Co., 1951.

Williamson, B. *The Bowie Knife's Origins*. Geocities Web site, 1999.

Williamson, W. "The Rich Legacy of Samuel Bell." *Blade* Magazine, 1987.

ABOUT THE AUTHOR

Dwight McLemore is a retired combat arms officer with the U.S. Army and is an accomplished bladesman and instructor. He is renowned for his vast knowledge of Bowie and big-knife fighting and has more than 18 years' experience in self-defense and martial arts. The owner of the School of Two Swords, McLemore is rated expert level with the American Knife Congress, is certified in kung fu, and holds 1st dan in kendo.